Portraits of Pride II

Portraits of Pride II

Chinese-American Legacies—First 160 Years in America

美華之光

Chinese Historical Society
of Southern California

Publisher
L. P. Leung: Project Director and principal founder of the Portraits of Pride Series
Chinese Historical Society of Southern California (CHSSC)
415 Bernard Street
Los Angeles, CA 90012-1703
Website: www.chssc.org
E-mail: popchssc@yahoo.com

Manuscript
L. P. Leung: Editor-in-Chief
Randall Bloch: Lead Editor

Artwork
Marian Chew: Book design and production
Jason Jem: Design consultant and select portrait photography
Fenton Fong Eng: Cover design

Printed in China by C&C Offset Printing Company

Copyright © 2011.

ISBN 978-0-930377-01-4

Library of Congress Cataloging-in-Publication Data
Portraits of pride II : Chinese-American legacies, first 160 years in America.
      p. cm.
  L.P. Leung, project director.
  Includes bibliographical references and index.
  ISBN 978-0-930377-01-4
  1. Chinese Americans--California--Biography. 2. Chinese Americans--Biography.
  3. Scholars--United States--Biography. 4. Scientists--United States--Biography.
  5. Artists--United States--Biography. 6. Entertainers--United States--Biography.
  7. Musicians--United States--Biography. 8. Nobel prize winners--United States--Biography.
  9. Celebrities--United States--Biography. 10. California--Biography. I. Leung, L. P.
  F870.C5P67 2011
  979.4'04951--dc22
                        2010046015

Prologue

Railroad magnate Charles Crocker recalled the courage and integrity of the Chinese railroad worker, declaring "Without Chinese labor we would be thrown back in all branches of industries, farming, mining, reclaiming lands and everything else." (*The Asian American Almanac*: "Who are the Chinese?" p. 47.)

Skillful, Daring and Hardworking Railroad Workers

Chinese immigrants worked on the most difficult and dangerous western section of the Transcontinental Railroad when few others would take on the risk. It is estimated 2,000 died on the job. Their work was a pivotal part of the most important infrastructure project in the United States at that time. At the Promontory Point ceremony when the east coast and the west coast were connected in 1869, the work of Chinese immigrants was not mentioned and no Chinese immigrant was present.

The east/west railroad connection made many people exceedingly rich with money and land grants. Among them were the Big Four railroad magnates: Charles Crocker, Mark Hopkins, Collis Huntington and Leland Stanford.

Agricultural and Land-claiming Experts

The Chinese brought their agricultural expertise from their homeland to convert the turtle swamps of the Sacramento-San Joaquin River Delta into the richest farmland in California. Since Chinese immigrants were forbidden to own land, they helped many white landowners prosper, and their own contributions and horticultural skills have gone mostly unrecorded.

With the completion of the Transcontinental Railroad, California farm products were able to ship to the eastern seaboard year-round.

Pioneers in the Commercial Fishing Industry

The first fishing Chinese families settled in the Monterey area in the 1850s, crossing the ocean in two boats sailing from China's Guangdong Province. The stories of the Chinese who pioneered commercial fishing, and who made enormous contributions to the economy of the Pacific West in the late 1800s and early 1900s, is largely unknown and untold. In time, Chinese immigrants established fishing camps from the Oregon border to Baja California and along the Sacramento Delta. Their catches were dried and shipped to China, Chinese communities, and local markets.

Men and Women of Science and Engineering

According to U. S. Census reports, in 2000 less than 1% of the U.S. population was Chinese-American.

During the 1930-50s, some of the best Chinese scientific brainpower came to America, doing high security research for the United States. Many were involved in the top secret Manhattan project. The McCarthy era communism scare forced most of them to return to China where their know-how brought China up to speed in the nuclear and missile fields. The Christopher Cox Commission Report of the 105th Congress failed to mention this gift of U.S. high technology brainpower to China.

The second generation of engineering students came from Hong Kong and Taiwan. They were very important contributors to our nation's defense and space exploration.

Departments of science and engineering in our nation's top universities have an overwhelming proportion of Chinese Americans in the ranks of their professors and researchers.

Outstanding, World-changing Individual Achievements

Some of these are widely known "Superstars," while many "Unsung Heroes" are known only in their own fields.

Dr. An Wang, founder of Fortune 500 company Wang Laboratories, wrote in his book *Lessons*, "I founded Wang Laboratories to show Chinese could excel at things other than laundries and restaurants." Was he being too boastful?

Following are some of the individual, world-changing achievement stories in this book:

- Dr. Charles Kao's developments in fiber optics which transformed global communications and enabled the Internet.
- Dr. M.C. Chang who is considered the "Father of In Vitro Fertilization," and co-inventor of the first oral birth control pill.
- Dr. David Wong's research to create the most prescribed antidepressant drug, Prozac, and others.
- Dr. H.S. Tsien's summation of the "Jet Propulsion Bible" and his pioneer concept of Dyna-Soar that combined aerodynamics and space research.
- Dr. Flossie Wong-Staal's research work to discover the HIV virus and the mapping of its genetic structure.
- James Wong Howe's award-winning cinematography when minorities were not welcome in the craft unions.
- Yo-Yo Ma, the traveling UN "Ambassador with a Cello."
- Iris Chang, writer/historian, bringing forth to the world the "forgotten holocaust" of the Japanese military's atrocities in China during WW II.

In a project of this magnitude, any errors or omissions will strictly be the responsibility of the volunteer Project Director and Editor. Selections of portraits in this book are based on the merits of the achievements and their impact on the United States and the world.

To acquire one or more copies of *Portraits of Pride II: Chinese-American Legacies–First One Hundred Sixty Years in America*, please contact the Chinese Historical Society of Southern California at 415 Bernard St., Los Angeles, CA 90012-1703. Voice: 323-222-1918; email: popchssc@yahoo.com; web: www.chssc.org.

L.P. Leung
Project Director and Editor-in-Chief

FREE LIBRARY-BOOK PROGRAM

Mission Statement of the
Chinese Historical Society of Southern California:
*"To increase awareness of Chinese American heritage
through public programs, education and research."*

This second Portraits of Pride book is our effort to research and record the Chinese American legacy over the last 160 years. Our free to libraries distribution program will ensure that Portraits of Pride will be on the shelves of our nation's libraries and that this legacy will not be forgotten.

The Portraits of Pride project is proud of its past and future financial sponsors in allowing the book to be distributed free to libraries and learning institutions. To date, over 7,000 copies of Portraits of Pride I have been donated to public, school, and college libraries across the United States.

Through the generous contributions of our supporters, we plan to distribute 20,000 copies of this book, *Portraits of Pride II:Chinese-American Legacies–First One Hundred Sixty Years in America*, to libraries throughout America.

Your interest and support of our programs are greatly appreciated. Donations of any amount are welcome.

Thank you.

Chinese Historical Society of Southern California
Portraits of Pride–Free Library Book Program
415 Bernard Street
Los Angeles, CA 90012-1703
(323) 222-1918
popchssc@yahoo.com
www.chssc.org

Contents

Acknowledgments

by L.P. Leung, Project Director

It took more than a year to research and conceptualize the theme of this book, and over two more to recruit volunteers to write the portraits, secure rights to the photographs, edit, and put the book together. And now, *Portraits of Pride II: Chinese-American Legacies–First One Hundred Sixty Years in America* is complete.

Not being a historian or a writer but a retired CPA, I sometimes questioned myself as to how I could be entrusted with such an important project. During the process, I wondered how the final version could be written to convey a positive message, even though Chinese Americans had been treated so harshly and regarded with such low esteem. Throughout this journey, I felt a sense of pride as well as excitement, passion, and an awesome responsibility. It has been a most challenging, rewarding and worthwhile task. I am very proud to have had a part in this endeavor.

There are thousands of Chinese Americans who in the last one hundred and sixty years made lasting contributions to the United States and to the world. It is our goal to re-dedicate and record their accomplishments for future generations before these contributions are totally forgotten. We are aware that this volume cannot be inclusive of all deserving individuals. For that, I offer my sincere apology. Perhaps someone will prepare an even more inclusive follow-up in the near future.

For their support throughout these three-plus years, I owe a special debt of gratitude to the following:

- Dr. Wing Mar and his wife Joyce for their faith in the project and their unfailing support at difficult times.
- Margie Lew, charter member of the Chinese Historical Society of Southern California, for her constant encouragement and support for the project. (Lew was the first editor of the Society's monthly newsletter, *News 'n Notes*, and the biannual edition of the *Gum Saan Journal*).
- Bobbi Leung, my wife, who put up with my sometimes somber mood swings and helped correct my Chinese-English.
- Edgar Wong, for his support, counsel, and lessons learned from Portraits of Pride Book I.
- Marian Chew, with the guidance of Jason Jem, for her artistic and professional layout of the finished product.
- The Chinese Historical Society of Southern California for giving this project the freedom to do its work.

I am grateful for the valuable input and participation of the families and friends of many of those we are honoring, which made the stories even more personal and special.

The core team members of Portraits of Pride Book II include several from the Book 1 project, and new members. Their experience and ideas have helped contribute greatly to the completion of this project. They are Wing and Joyce Mar, Gordon Hom, Pete Chinn, Bill Chew, Edgar Wong, Dong Kingman, Jr., Jack Ong, Jason Jem, Randy Bloch, Marian Chew and Yvonne Chang.

We thank all the volunteer writers whose names are listed with each of their portraits. We convey our appreciation to the editors of *Caltech News* for permission to reprint the article on Dr. H. S. Tsien, pioneering rocket scientist; the Royal Swedish

Academy of Sciences and Mrs. Gwen Kao for permission to use Mrs. Kao's Nobel Prize acceptance speech delivered on behalf of Dr. Charles Kao; and to the *Chinese American Forum* for permission to reprint Dr. James Wei's article sharing his experience of "Making It in America."

Special thanks to Randy Bloch who did extensive research and wrote a number of portraits, and for his efforts to secure rights to a number of photographs; to Maureen Bloch who helped proofread many of the edited portraits; to Yvonne Chang who updated the appendix of historical material and created the book's index; and to Pete Chinn who came up with an appropriate four-character Chinese name for the book.

Lastly, I want to acknowledge the magnificent and tireless fundraising efforts of Dr. Wing Mar. There is no one more dedicated to the Portraits of Pride project than him.

With pride, we dedicate this book to:

I. The Individuals and Groups in our Portraits;

II. The Founders and Charter Members of the Chinese Historical Society of Southern California—*their vision for Chinese-American history inspired the work in this book and also the first book in the Portraits of Pride series; and lastly*

III. *I dedicate this volume to the memory of my son,* Timothy Scott Leung. *His untimely passing at age 42 in March 2010 was a reminder of the importance for Chinese Americans of Tim's generation and future generations to learn about the lives of our persevering pioneers. By reading Portraits of Pride I and II, these young people will understand those pioneers' struggles and subsequent successes, and unquestionably be proud of their own Chinese-American heritage.*

Introduction

Portraits of Pride II: Chinese-American Legacies–
First One Hundred Sixty Years in America

L.P. Leung, Editor-in-Chief

Chinese Americans are an integral part of the American success story. It is with great pride and honor that this book, *Portraits of Pride-II: Chinese-American Legacies–First One Hundred Sixty Years in America* is presented by the Chinese Historical Society of Southern California. Within these pages are to be found the significant and lasting contributions of the Chinese minority since the 1840s. Groups of pioneer laborers, from railroad workers and levee builders to farmers and fishermen, played a significant role in developing the infrastructure of California and the West. In the fields of science, medicine, and to a lesser extent, fine arts, their achievements have made an enduring impact on the United States and the world.

John McDougal, the first governor of California, called Chinese immigrants "one of our most worthy of our newly adopted citizens." (Mary Coolidge, quoting McDougal in her 1909 book, *Chinese Immigration*.)

The first group of Chinese came to California prompted by the "streets of gold" stories of American steam ship owners. The second group was recruited to work on railroad jobs that other laborers found too dangerous and difficult. Chinese fishermen arrived in much smaller groups to pioneer the California fishing industry. Many moved on to work in the farmlands after railroad work ended. In most cases, Chinese found or created jobs that European immigrant workers did not want.

Upon breaking ground for the Central Pacific Railroad in Sacramento on June 8, 1863, Governor Leland Stanford praised the Chinese workers for their good work and called for more to come. While the Chinese were working on the railroads, the Civil War was being fought for the noble cause of abolishing black slavery. And yet, discrimination against the Chinese was legal. Denied of the right to vote, they were unable to challenge and overcome anti-Chinese legislation by the federal and state governments.

During the depression of the 1870s, Irish immigrant Dennis Kearney gained popularity speaking to unemployed workers in San Francisco, denouncing the railroad monopoly and blaming Chinese immigrants for white laborers' economic woes. All his orations ended with shouting, "The Chinese Must Go!" Campaigning for political office and no longer needing Chinese workers, railroad magnates Stanford and Charles Crocker supported the Chinese Exclusion Act of 1882. The Act unilaterally violated the key provision of the Burlingame Treaty of 1868 of freedom of migration between China and the U. S. Never in the history of the United States has an ethnic group legally been so humiliated and repressed. However, in spite of harsh taxation and discrimination, Chinese immigrants displayed great courage and fortitude. Their triumph of the human spirit, against all odds, will warm a compassionate heart—and the stories of their great accomplishments will inspire current and future generations.

We would be remiss in not mentioning that our successes as Chinese Americans could not have happened if there were not enough people of good will in this great country, especially in the academic institutions that lent us a hand by providing the training, opportunity and support to excel. For Chinese Americans it has been a bittersweet journey.

Part I

Portraits of Superstars and Unsung Heroes

M.C. Chang

Father of In Vitro Fertilization & Co-Inventor of the First Oral Birth Control Pill

By L.P. Leung

- Dr. Min-Chueh (M.C.) Chang's 46-year scientific career spanned the full spectrum of mammalian reproduction, from the promotion of in vitro fertilization to contraception.

- He was co-developer of the first orally administered birth control pill—a world changing event that made planned parenthood easily accessible and effective. According to some sources, more than 80% of American women and countless women around the world used the "Pill" at some time in their reproductive years.

- Dr. Chang received six Nobel Prize nominations and was elected to the National Academy of Sciences Hall of Fame in 1990.

"He can be called the father of in vitro fertilization."
~Amy Zuckerman, *Worcester Magazine, July 27, 1988*

Overview

The year was 1960 and the first orally administered birth control pill had been approved by the U.S. Food and Drug Administration. It was a revolutionary development in contraception: the progesterone hormone pill quickly became the method of choice for "invisible" birth control around the world.

Reproductive biologist, Dr. Min Chueh (M.C.) Chang, is best known for his work to develop the "Pill." Equally significant is his work in the field of mammalian reproduction: he contributed to the understanding of in vitro fertilization, capacitation, and the conditions required for mammalian eggs to be fertilized. His work in his field is wide-ranging; his findings have appeared in nearly 350 professional publications and academic presentations.

In the field of reproductive science, M.C. Chang must be regarded as one of the giants of his time. His contributions to our understanding of the early events in the process of reproduction among the mammals are truly monumental but, beyond that, the fruit of his labors over the past half-century have brought concrete benefits to human health and family welfare and have liberated women from the age-old burden of unwanted pregnancies and excessive childbearing.
~Roy O. Greep, PhD, Harvard University, Journal of Andrology, November/December, 1992.

Dr. Chang's Education and Affiliation with the World-Renowned Worcester Foundation

M.C. Chang, born and educated in China, received his bachelor's degree in behavioral psychology in 1933. In 1938, he won a national examination for a much-prized fellowship at Scotland's Edinburgh University. There he studied animal husbandry with an emphasis on artificial insemination.

In 1939, upon an invitation from Sir John Hammond and Dr. Arthur Walton, Chang landed a research assistant position at Cambridge University studying ram spermatozoa and reproductive biology. He received his doctorate degree in 1941. At Cambridge he studied artificial insemination techniques that later proved important to his career. Dr. Chang and Dr. Walton were responsible for the first calf produced by artificial insemination at the Cambridge University farm.

After World War II, Chang was torn between returning to China or seeking a research position in the United States. His mentors at Cambridge advised him to go to America and do "good work." He was interested in the successful work of endocrinologist Dr. Gregory Pincus in 1935 on *in vitro fertilization* of rabbits. No researcher, however, had been able to replicate the process, even Dr. Pincus. When in 1945 Pincus offered him a fellowship to work on *transfer of cow eggs and perfusion of ovaries*, Dr. Chang accepted.

Dr. Pincus and Dr. Hudson Hoagland—co-directors of the fledging Worcester Foundation for Experimental Biology in Shrewsbury, Massachusetts—had established a reputation for wide-ranging biological research. The Foundation's

researchers were encouraged to work at their own pace and in their own style. This laissez faire atmosphere seemed to enhance scientific initiative and productivity among the staff of international professionals. Postdoctoral researchers from around the globe were attracted to the idyllic Worcester campus for its advanced and innovative thinking.

M.C. Chang became the first principal scientist of the Foundation. He remained there for his forty-six year scientific career and mentored countless top reproductive scientists from around the world.

Marvin Richmond Photo, University of Massachusetts Medical School

fortune) and a motivated philanthropist on women's issues. Sanger and McCormick sought easier, more practical ways for women to plan and control the size of their families. They specifically sought an oral *progesterone* compound as effective in contraception as cumbersome subcutaneous injections. After meeting with Drs. Chang and Pincus, they committed research funding for the project to the Worcester Foundation.

Chang and Pincus began studying female hormones and their effects on ovulation. Chang took on the task of identifying compounds that, when ingested orally, would imitate the combined action of progesterone and *estrogen*. Experimenting with rabbits, Chang discovered that high blood levels of many *progestins* would shut down the ovaries and prevent ovulation. Eventually the team developed a compound including estrogen, and progestin extracted from Wild Mexican Yam. Human clinical tests were successfully completed in Massachusetts, Haiti and Puerto Rico.

One of Dr. Chang's early projects at Worcester was verifying the claim of Dr. Pincus's successful 1935 in vitro fertilization experiment. Chang took up the study in the 1940s and discovered why other scientists had repeatedly failed to confirm it. Working with rabbits, Dr. Chang discovered that sperm must undergo *capacitation*, i.e., a spermatozoon must go through post-ejaculation alterations within the uterus or fallopian tubes before it can fertilize an egg.

Applying his sperm capacitation techniques, Dr. Chang's lab was the site of many firsts. Among them:

+ 1959: first in vitro fertilization of a rabbit;
+ 1964: first in vitro fertilization of a hamster;
+ 1969: first in vitro fertilization of a mouse;
+ 1974: first in vitro fertilization of a rat.

Dr. Chang often said science is a matter of team collaboration. Development of a convenient, safer method of human contraception was a byproduct of his understanding of fertilization. It took Chang's relentless research, Dr. Pincus's overall direction and planning, gynecologist John Rock's clinical tests on humans, various pharmaceutical companies' work to produce chemical compounds, and countless others' efforts, to make the Pill a success.

The "Pill" and its World-Changing Effect on Planning Parenthood

In the 1950s, the advent of oral contraception began with a visit to Worcester Foundation by family planning activist Margaret Sanger, and Katherine McCormick, widow of Stanley McCormick (heir to the International Harvester

The FDA approved the Pill for human use in 1960. Despite its widespread use and indisputable effectiveness, it was controversial and generated debate on the morality and health consequences of promiscuity and premarital sex. The Pill had to overcome objections on moral and health grounds in a number of high-profile court cases before it became widely available. In some institutions, notably the Catholic Church, the role of sexuality is yet unresolved.

The Pill gave women the sexual freedom without fear of pregnancy that previously was exclusive to men, thus contributing to the sexual revolution of the twentieth century. Singer Loretta Lynn's 1975 song, "The Pill," told of a married woman using the Pill to liberate herself from her traditional roles of wife and mother. The Pill changed women's lives by allowing them to pursue both motherhood and careers.

Dr. Chang's Major Achievements in Understanding Mammalian Reproduction

Dr. Chang's long, illustrious career produced many breakthrough findings in mammalian reproduction. These include:

1. Capacitation of sperm – In a series of 1940s studies of rabbit ova fertilization, Chang was intrigued by the apparent delay period before ejaculated sperm could penetrate and fertilize an egg. After years of investigation, he found breakthrough evidence that sperm deposited in the female reproductive tract must undergo capacitation.
2. Cold shock phenomenon – Dr. Chang observed and documented that at a temperature of 13 degrees Celsius or below, sperm would disintegrate, thus destroying its fertilizing capability.
3. In vitro fertilization – The successful in vitro fertilization of a rabbit in 1959 was Dr. Chang's crowning glory. This came after a succession of failed attempts by other scientists.
4. Surrogate motherhood – Another giant step for humanity was Chang's success in creating the first rabbit *surrogate mother*. He fertilized a black rabbit's eggs with a black rabbit's sperm in vitro, and transferred them to a surrogate white rabbit, producing a black litter.
5. Single individual sperm – Dr. Chang dispelled the notion that fertilization of an egg requires a huge number of spermatozoa. In fact, it is the physiological structure of single individual sperm that effects fertilization.
6. Human applications – More than any scientist in the twentieth century, Dr. M.C. Chang developed techniques that made new reproductive technologies available to humans. Other medical scientists, using his capacitation theory, forged ahead with human applications with the first successful *test tube baby*. Louise Joy Brown was born in England in 1978.

Honors and awards conferred on Dr. Chang include:

+ 1954 – Albert Lasker Award - *Planned Parenthood – World Population.*
+ 1961 – Ortho Medal – *The American Fertility Society.*
+ 1971 – Carl G. Hartman Award - *The Society for the Study of Reproduction.*
+ 1987 – Wippman Scientific Research Award – *The Planned Parenthood Federation of America.*

Dr. Chang Reflects On His Life and Career at the Worcester Foundation

I have had a very pleasant and comfortable life during the past 40 years at Worcester Foundation.... I am a timid and peace-loving soul who hates to fight and to grumble, and so I like to have a peaceful life, doing the things I like to do. During this past 40 years I was able to do just this and thus I have fulfilled my ambitions quite well. Recently Dr. Mark Mason asked me whether I have achieved what I had planned for my life. My answer was, "I achieved more than I wished for, so I should be very happy in my old age."

Dr. Chang and His Family

M.C. Chang met his American-born wife, Isabelle Chin, at Yale University Library three years after arriving in the U.S. In addition to being his wife and mother of their three children, she was a gracious hostess to Dr. Chang's colleagues, students and visiting international scholars. She is a journalist and the author of seven books.

Mrs. Isabelle Chang wrote of Dr. Chang in the Worcester, Massachusetts, *Record*: "[Dr.] Chang always said that he wished better for his students than himself. Indeed, at the very last scientific paper he presented in Lisbon, Portugal, he flashed a picture of Dr. Yanagimachi and Dr. Michael Bedford on the screen and said, 'these two students will carry on my work.'"

Dr. Ryuzo Yanagimachi pursued his advances in cloning research at the University of Hawaii for over 35 years. The first male animal cloned from adult cells was announced in 1999.

Marvin Richmond Photo, University of Massachusetts Medical School

Dr. Chang's three children are successful professionals in their chosen fields:

+ Francis Hugh Chang is director of a California philanthropic foundation.
+ Claudia Chang is an anthropologist and archaeologist.
+ Pamela O. Chang is an architect and civil engineer.

For this portrait, daughter Pamela recalled affectionately of her father:

Although my father didn't talk much about his past, I know he grew up in a world totally different from the one I know.

When my father first went to college (in China), he was active in politics until he realized that he was in danger, literally, of losing his head. Then he switched to science. He enjoyed experimental science. Once, he tried to describe his school projects to his mother. She scoffed at him, saying that he was 'just playing around.' In later life, he often referred to his work as 'just playing around.'

My dad studied neurophysiology and psychology in college. After graduation, he and a classmate decided to try to win scholarships to study in Britain. Because they did not want to compete against each other, they drew lots to see who would try for the psychology scholarship. My dad lost. He spent the summer in the mountains cramming for an examination in animal husbandry and "singing English"—his description of language practice. The cramming paid off and he was off to Edinburgh University, Scotland.

Chance and circumstances played a tremendous role in the direction that my father's life took and he was lucky in having the help of many good friends. But he worked extraordinarily hard to make the most of the chances that came his way. Perhaps because of his gratitude for his own lucky opportunities, he was very generous in sharing work and credit with his colleagues.

In my opinion, however, his greatest good fortune was his ability to think clearly, to focus on what is important, and to ignore distraction. This, of course, made him a difficult father—he had low tolerance for stupidity and for what he perceived as lack of ambition. He believed the furtherance of knowledge to be the highest pursuit. He expected his children, with our comparative head start in life, to surpass his achievements. When we did not, he was, naturally, disappointed. Later in life, he had to be content at having fathered no great scientists, but at least, in his own words, 'decent human beings.'

The author is indebted to Mrs. Isabelle Chang and Pamela O. Chang for their contributions providing information and factual review.

C.S. Wu

World's Distinguished First Lady of Physics

By L.P. Leung

"Dr. Chien-Shiung Wu had 'richly earned the right to be called the world's foremost female experimental physicist.'"

~Robert Goheen, President, Princeton University – 1958

"C.S. Wu was one of the giants of physics. In the field of beta decay, she had no equal."
~Dr. Tsung-Dao Lee – Columbia University, Nobel Prize in Physics – 1957

"She was 'the renowned physicist who turned the discipline on its head by disproving the law of conservation of parity, showing that the laws of nature are not always symmetrical with respect to right and left.'"

~Columbia University News, February 17, 1997

"When she knocked out the principle of parity, she established the principle of parity between men and women."

~Playwright Clare Boothe Luce – 1957

To physicists around the world, Dr. Chien-Shiung (C.S.) Wu will always be known as "The Madame Curie of China." She is recognized for the "elegance and high aesthetic quality" of her experimental physics achievements as well as being the first 20th century, Chinese American woman to be a leader in that field.

Dr. Wu's father, an educator in China, was a rare proponent of gender equality in an era and society that were male-dominated. Thus, her given name, Chien-Shiung, was gender-neutral and could easily be the name of a man. She acted on his encouragement to pursue an education, earning her Bachelor of Science degree in 1934.

AIP Emilio Segre Visual Archives, Physics Today Collection

security Manhattan Project, performing atomic research. There, Columbia's scientists used diffusion techniques to separate the fissionable uranium isotope, U-235, from the more common uranium-238. Amid swirling political controversy, it is generally believed the atomic bomb shortened the war against Japan and greatly reduced American casualties.

Dr. Wu's participation in and knowledge of the top secret Manhattan Project prevented her from returning to China after World War II. She survived McCarthy era purges of non-American scientists who were suspected of communist affiliation. Consequently, Dr. Wu turned to teaching and research. She spent over 40 years at Columbia University where she published a number of important scientific papers and mentored many top students from around the world. Wu was appointed Columbia's first Pupin Professor of Physics in 1973. In 1985, Columbia University named a section of its new Physics and Engineering Research Center the "Wu Chien-Shiung Physics Laboratories" to commemorate her outstanding contributions.

Wu came to the United States in 1936. At UC Berkeley, she studied under E.O. Lawrence, a Nobel laureate and inventor of the cyclotron. She received her doctorate in physics from Berkeley in 1940.

Dr. Wu taught at Smith College and Princeton University from 1942 to 1944.

A Long and Distinguished Career at Columbia University

In 1944, Dr. Wu joined Columbia University's research staff as a senior scientist and was recruited to join the top

Dr. Wu was known throughout her career as a meticulously accurate experimental physicist who was in demand to put new theories to the test. Her crowning achievement, however, was the 1956 experiment that disproved the *law of parity* in physics.

Disproving "Parity Conservation"

Before 1956, the "self-evident" nature of *parity* made physicists unwilling even to consider the possibility of its violation. "Parity" means right-left symmetry. For example, if two systems are mirror images of each other but otherwise entirely identical, *parity conservation* states that despite the mirror image difference, all subsequent evolution of the two systems should remain identical. Simply stated, nature is not biased toward left-handed or right-handed systems and those reactions like subatomic particles always act symmetrically.

AIP Emilio Segre Visual Archives

It was her fellow physicists, Drs. T.D. Lee and C.N. Ning who jointly researched and published the historic paper *Question of Parity Conservation in Weak Interaction*, but it was Dr. Wu who devised and conducted the confirmative experiments to prove the existence of parity violation, which radically altered modern physical theory.

The Experiment

Dr. Wu and her collaborators at the National Bureau of Standards in Washington, DC, carried out this difficult but fundamental experiment using atoms of the radioactive el-ement Cobalt-60 chilled to .01 degrees above absolute zero. Between Christmas, 1956, and New Year's Day, exciting results emerged from the laboratory, convincingly showing that in at least one fundamental physical process, electrons did not behave as Dr. Wu had expected. Physicists had long assumed the opposite. They even constructed their theories so as to ensure the corresponding mathematical property, *call parity*, would remain unaltered, i.e. conserved, in all subatomic processes. The experiment thus heralded parity's fall from its exalted position alongside well-conserved physical quantities such as energy, momentum, and electrical charge.

The result was so significant that Drs. Lee and Ning were co-winners of the 1957 Nobel Prize in Physics. Dr. Wu was extremely disappointed she was not a co-winner; many physicists agree she should have shared the prize.

It is now known that parity violation exists nearly maximally in all weak processes.

Confirmation of Fermi's Theory of Beta Decay

In nuclear physics, *beta decay* is a type of radioactive decay in which a beta article is emitted. Beta decay occurs when, in a nucleus with too many neutrons, one of its protons or neutrons is transformed into the other.

In 1934, Enrico Fermi had developed a theory of beta decay that included the neutrino—presumed to be massless as well as chargeless. Subsequently, serious discrepancies emerged between Fermi's theory and confirming experiments. In 1949 and 1960, in a series of well-designed experiments, Dr. Wu and her collaborators measured the allowed and forbidden *beta spectra*, correcting many mistakes of previous experiments. She obtained the first successful measurement of low-energy electrons emitted by beta decay. The findings firmly established Fermi's theory, and disproved the alternative *Konopinski-Uhlenbeck formulation*. The Cobalt-60 experiment of Wu, et al, was a turning point in physics. The experiment itself established the violation of parity and *charge conjugation symmetry*, but also was the precursor of many tests for multiple kinds of symmetry violations.

Dr. C.S. Wu is the author of *Beta Decay*, a standard reference book for nuclear physicists.

Professional Recognition
In recognition of her brilliant career in the field of experimental physics, Dr. Wu received more than 40 honors and honorary degrees from around the world. Among them are:

+ Research Corporation Award – 1958
+ Hon. Doctorate of Science – Princeton University
  – 1st woman recipient – 1958
+ Comstock Prize – U.S. Academy of Sciences – 1964
+ Royal Society of Edinburgh – 1969
+ First female president of the American Physical
  Society – 1973
+ National Medal of Science – 1975
+ Wolf Prize in Physics – 1978
+ Pupin Medal – Columbia University (highest
  scientific honor) – 1991

As one of the few female scientists of her time, Dr. Wu

was keenly aware, and openly critical, of male chauvinism in the sciences. Aside from her outstanding research, she paved the way for women students to pursue fields of scientific study. Her contributions, both in physics and in social advancement of women, were invaluable.

References

1. Columbia University News, February 17, 1997.
2. Dicke, William. Chien-Shiung Wu, 84, Top Experimental Physicist. New York Times, February 18, 1997.
3. UK Resource Center for Women in Science, Engineering and Technology.

David T. Wong

Internationally Recognized Biochemist and Neuropharmacologist

By Wing Mar

- Dr. David T. Wong received the Pharmaceutical Manufacturers Association Discoverers Award in 1993 for his role in developing Prozac (Fluoxetine).

- The development of Prozac revolutionized psychiatry's approach to depression.

- He was a member of research teams that developed drugs to treat Parkinson's disease and schizophrenia.

- His work has had significant impact on the treatment of mental illness and neurodegenerative diseases.

- Dr. Wong authored or co-authored 150 scientific publications and book chapters, and is named in 35 U.S. Patents as inventor or co-inventor.

The Prozac Revolution

Dr. David T. Wong is best known as the co-discoverer of Prozac, the first of a class of antidepressant drugs known as *selective serotonin re-uptake inhibitors* (SSRIs) which make serotonin more available to the brain. Serotonin is a chemical that affects mood, and the use of SSRIs has revolutionized the treatment of depression. The "Prozac Revolution" began in 1987 when the FDA approved its use. Almost overnight, the drug became world-famous. It is now prescribed to millions of people worldwide and earns billions of dollars for Eli Lilly and Company.

The antidepressant Prozac enjoys an almost iconic status in American society today. It is among the most well-known prescription drugs ever developed. Its name and importance have so insinuated themselves into popular culture that several books on antidepressants have its name in their titles, among them: *Listening to Prozac* and *Prozac Nation*.

Courtesy of David T. Wong

According to Eli Lilly, its manufacturer, Prozac is the most widely prescribed antidepressant medication in history. Since its introduction in 1986, more than 54 million patients worldwide have been prescribed Prozac for treatment of depression, obsessive-compulsive disorder, bulimia and panic disorder.

Since its launch, Prozac has revolutionized psychiatry's approach to the management of depression. In addition to its clear-cut therapeutic benefits, it has fewer side effects than previously-used antidepressants. It has also generated conflict and spirited discussion, in seminars and in print, on the place of psychoactive chemicals in our society.

Beginnings

On a day like any other in December, 1941, six-year-old David Wong was getting ready for school when he heard explosions. That morning, the Japanese attacked Hong Kong on the same day Pearl Harbor was bombed. The airport down the street from the Wong home was in ruins.

Japan's occupation of Hong Kong temporarily ended young David's formal schooling, but his mother read to her four children in the evenings. He recalls, "She read Robinson Crusoe and biographies of scientists like Thomas Edison and Madame Curie. I wonder now, why did my mother choose these stories? Why not fairy tales?"

The Wong sons were expected to learn the family machinist business. However, when David cut off his right thumbnail while trying out the machines, his brother, Joseph, suspected he was not destined for a machinist's career and that his gifts lay elsewhere.

David began the study of chemistry at National Taiwan University which led to the United States and matriculation to Seattle Pacific University in the summer of 1957.

When David left Hong Kong for the U.S., his father brought him to a tailor and had a suit made for him. The new suit came with this instruction: "Go, and find a career that will benefit humankind."

The Road to Indianapolis and Eli Lilly & Company

His years at his first U.S. alma mater, the Christian-based Seattle Pacific University (SPU), strongly shaped his life. He struggled to pay his tuition by cleaning offices and painting buildings on campus. "The foreman thought the Chinese men did the best work because we used brushes in our writing," he recalls. "We could paint a straight line, so while others made 80 cents an hour, we made a dollar."

He was active in the campus Chinese Christian Fellowship and worked helping the homeless and disadvantaged.

Two professors in SPU's Chemistry Department, Burton Dietzman and Andy Montana, were important mentors: "They were very caring and outstanding teachers," Wong said. "Their sacrifice allowed us to succeed."

Years later, Professor Andy Montana praised Dr. Wong: "I take pride in his scientific achievements. We can take even greater pride in his personal and spiritual development."

Upon graduating SPU, Wong completed his master's degree in biochemistry at Oregon State University. There,

Courtesy of David T. Wong

he met his future wife, Christina Lee, and two years later the couple had the first of their three sons. Wong completed his doctorate work at the University of Oregon, followed by post-graduate studies at the University of Pennsylvania.

Wife Christina remembers: "We lived over a garage and there was a train that went by every night. We roasted in the summer and froze in the winter."

David had dreamed of a biochemistry career with Eli Lilly and Company. He remembered seeing the company's logo on his grandmother's diabetic insulin bottles. Many years later, when he again saw the imprint at a graduate school medical conference, he told himself, "That's the company I'm going to work for."

Mentors, Partners and Colleagues

Eli Lilly hired Dr. Wong as a senior biochemist in 1968. It was the first position he applied for.

Upon being hired by Lilly Research Laboratories, he was taken aback when he asked if there were particular research areas he should focus on. The response from Lilly's Irwin Slater came: "You are a well-trained biochemist. You should be able to decide on your own." Thus emboldened, he "... initiated studies of *uptake processes of monoamines*, and from then on much of my 32 years at Lilly was spent doing what I was interested in and excited by."

Dr. Wong is effective at forging highly productive partnerships with his peers:

Prozac was definitely a team effort. The collaboration between Ray Fuller and I led to many successful projects besides the discovery of Prozac. Throughout my career I have been fortunate to have very effective partnerships with scientists. My colleagues in medicinal chemistry served as mentors to me in many respects.

He has advised younger research biochemists that to transition from academia to industry requires willingness to engage in existing drug discovery projects, and to be an uplifting person with a can do attitude: "You need the ability to focus and persevere and to have devoted associates to understand your research so that they become partners in the projects."

A Biochemistry and Neuroscience Career Illuminated By a Spiritual Path

When Dr. Wong was chosen Seattle Pacific University Alumnus of the Year in 1998, President Philip Eaton praised him, saying: "David Wong is a world-class scientist, yet he's a humble and decent man. He is a wonderful example of our mission. If you want to understand the true SPU vision, just look at David Wong."

Courtesy of David T. Wong

There are critics, many of them devout Christians, who express unease with the philosophy underlying the pharmacology industry's work to ease depression. To those critics, Dr. Wong explains firmly and patiently:

"People have asked me how I can believe in God and also practice a science that affects mood and the human mind. I do not see this as a conflict. I believe that mental illness has a biological origin. Medication is one of God's ways to provide a method of healing and at the same time alleviate suffering."

Quentin Small, the Wongs' minister in Southport, Indiana, for 15 years, says the Wongs are faithful people: "They take the Christian faith very seriously, and believe they have a responsibility to help Asian immigrants whenever they can."

Wong's eldest son, Conrad, a clinical psychologist, sees many of his patients benefit from Prozac: "I am always impressed by how many lives have been improved by this drug. I am very proud of my dad's significant contributions to science and medicine."

Post-Retirement: Consulting and A Professorship

After 32 years of distinguished service, Dr. David T. Wong retired from Eli Lilly and Company in 2000, having attained the status of Lilly Distinguished Research Fellow. Since retirement, he established DT Wong Consulting and accepted an adjunct professor of neurobiology position in the Indiana University School of Medicine Department of Psychiatry.

Son Conrad tells how several decades after Dr. Wong's departure from Hong Kong, he and his father visited the street where Dr. Wong was born: "He told me that his father had a suit made for him to go to America. We found the tailor, who still had my father's measurements."

Courtesy of David T. Wong

Beyond a doubt, Dr. David T. Wong had fulfilled his father's instruction to "Go, and find a career that will benefit humankind."

Dr. Ira Lessor of the Harbor-UCLA Department of Psychiatry generously lent his assistance with this profile.

References

1. Council for Christian Colleges & Universities. (2006). David Wong. Christian Higher Education Month. Science & Technology.
2. McDougall, Connie. (1997). The Faith of a Scientist. Alumnus of the Year David T. Wong Devotes a Lifetime to Neuroscience Research. Seattle Pacific University. Response.
3. Nature Publishing Group. (2007). David T. Wong. drug discovery@nature.com.
4. Oregon Health & Science University. (2004). Department of Psychiatry Annual George Saslow Lecture. Oregon Health & Science University. Department of Psychiatry. Grand Rounds and Presentations Schedules.

An Wang

王
安

Inventor of Magnetic Core Memory, Successful Entrepreneur & Philanthropist

By L.P. Leung

"An Wang's accomplishments, and his desire to repay society for offering him a chance, should inspire all of us to keep America the land of opportunity."

~Robert Noyce, Intel Corporation

"An Wang is...an enterprising innovator whose dedicated idealism has gone beyond the boardroom and given meaning and direction to a host of community, artistic, and charitable organizations.... His story is what the American Dream is all about...."

~Michael Dukakis, former governor, Massachusetts

"The satisfaction of turning an idea into something real never diminishes, and the great gift of change is that it continually replenishes the stock of new ideas that might be brought to life. The thrill of this challenge more than compensates for the setbacks that are the price of learning and growth."

Lessons: An Autobiography by Dr. An Wang

How It All Began

Dr. An Wang's vision and brilliance helped bring our country into the computer age. He made his mark on American society by founding Wang Laboratories (Wang Labs).

Dr. Wang's invention of *Magnetic Core Memory* was foundational in developing the digital information processing technology which followed and continues today.

I never dismiss luck as a factor in a person's destiny. The person who believes that he controls his fate entirely misunderstands the world and sets himself up for situations in which that understanding will cost him dearly.

When I left for the United States, I knew I could acquire whatever skills I needed to survive here. I had heard that there was discrimination against Chinese in the United States, but I came here with no insecurities about what I might try to do. By this time, the notion that there were things I could not or should not attempt to accomplish was utterly foreign to me.

Lessons: An Autobiography by Dr. An Wang.

Dr. Wang came to the U.S. in 1945 after losing most of his family in the Japanese invasion of China. A two-year, $100 a month stipend from the Chinese Nationalist government gave him the opportunity to study physics at

© *Bettmann*/CORBIS

Harvard University. There he saw the first computer ever built in the United States: the *Mark I*, which measured 8 feet tall by 51 feet long. On receiving his PhD in 1948, Dr. Wang accepted a job working with Dr. Howard Aiken of the Harvard Computation Laboratory where he worked on the first purely electronic calculator, the *Mark IV*.

At the laboratory, Dr. Wang invented *Ferrite Core Memory*, a technology widely used in early computers. Harvard was not interested in controlling or promoting the technology, and Dr. Wang was free to pursue a patent on his own. In 1948, Dr. Wang filed a U.S. patent application for a *Pulse Transfer Controlling Device*, which was granted in May, 1955. The device became the cornerstone of digital computer memory.

Chinese immigrants faced all types of discrimination at that time, though somewhat less in academia and high technology research. A professorship in a prestigious university was considered the pinnacle of success by most Chinese scholars in the U.S. A second alternative was a researcher with one of the nation's top technology companies. Dr. Wang did not choose either option.

In his autobiography, Dr. Wang writes: "I founded Wang Laboratories to show Chinese could excel at things other than laundries and restaurants."

When Harvard decided to de-emphasize basic computer research, Dr. Wang took the bold entrepreneurial step of striking out on his own. He formed Wang Laboratories in 1951 as a sole proprietorship to market magnetic core memory and did consulting work in digital computation electronics. Wang Laboratories was incorporated in 1955.

In 1956, International Business Machines (IBM) bought the patent rights for the pulse transfer controlling device from Wang Labs for $500,000, after heavy-handed negotiations. $100,000 of that sum was withheld and later forfeited to IBM due to an interference claim by a third

party. For Dr. Wang, the incident began a strong feeling of rivalry toward IBM in the decades that followed. In *Lessons*, one senses his elation in going head to head with the office machine behemoth.

Success at Wang Labs
"Find a Need And Fill It"
Wang Laboratories was the first and most successful company on the New York Stock Exchange founded by a Chinese American.

From the beginning, when Wang Labs was marketing magnetic core memory, Dr. Wang's vision transcended just selling a commodity. He worked hard identifying his clients' specific needs and marketing his solutions.

Dr. Wang worked for years in the ever-progressing field of digital devices for the office workplace—the foundation of which was his original invention. His motto, "Find a need and fill it," guided his company through its history.

In 1965, Wang Laboratories was one of the first companies to successfully market programmable electronic calculators. Wang introduced the *LOCI* scientific desktop calculator which was based on a centuries-old engineers' and scientists' tool for solving calculations logarithmically. The device was more mini-computer than calculator and was quite an achievement for a machine without integrated circuits. The calculator's electronics used 1,275 transistors. It was considered state of the art at the time and listed at $6,500. Besides being programmable, it was easier to use than other computers of that generation.

When Wang introduced the next-generation Model 300, ten months later, the company's sales revenues skyrocketed. The *Model 300* was a true calculator and sold for $1,700. It housed nearly 300 transistors with a ten-digit display mounted on a desktop unit. Programmable electronic calculators vaulted Wang from an obscure maker of specialized equipment to an internationally known manufacturing company.

In 1976, Wang Labs again revolutionized the office workplace with the introduction of the Wang Word Processing System (WPS) which delivered vast gains in productivity. The *Cathode Ray Tube*-based equipment was so superior to anything available that even with its list price of $30,000, a client ordered one million dollars' worth of the systems. The Wang WPS was hugely successful and broke through IBM's dominance of the office equipment market. The Wang Word Processing System was installed in many Fortune 500 companies and may have forced IBM out of the typewriter business.

Wang Laboratories' word processing system was followed by the equally successful Wang Office Information System (OIS). The multi-user system linked a network of workers to a centralized data storage unit. Wang Labs developed all software for the systems; and the operating systems, file formats, and electronic interface specifications were Wang Laboratories proprietary secrets. By the end of the 1970s, Wang Labs was the largest worldwide supplier of word processing systems. It had joined the prestigious list of Fortune 500 companies.

In 1978, Wang Labs introduced the *VS* minicomputer. It was built for the general marketplace and to compete with IBM's *360 Series* family of computers. Word processing functionality was added to Wang's VS and integrated with its data processing function. Later, telecommunication was added, enabling the VS to network with mainframe computers.

Sales of the VS began to take off. Wang was one of the first computer companies to advertise on television and the first to run an ad during the Super Bowl. The VS minicomputer's high water mark was about 30,000 systems operating worldwide during the mid to late 1980s, providing computing to several million desktop users.

Between the successes, there were numerous setbacks and mishaps. At its prime in the 1980s, Wang had annual sales of $3 billion and employed over 30,000 workers. The company was the darling of Wall Street.

In 1986, in fierce competition with IBM, Wang Labs won a $480 million contract to install *Management Information Systems* at United States Air Force bases around the world. The agreement was eight times larger than any prior Wang Labs contract.

Dr. An Wang retired in 1986 and chose son Fred to succeed him as president. Dr. Wang died of cancer in 1990. The company began to flounder and filed for bankruptcy protection in 1992. Wang Labs never recovered and was sold to a Netherlands network services company in 1999.

President Ronald Reagan awarded Dr. Wang the Medal of Liberty in 1986, along with famed architect I. M. Pei and others.

Dr. Wang was inducted into the National Inventor's Hall of Fame in 1988.

Dr. An Wang, The Generous Philanthropist

Dr. Wang writes in *Lessons*, "When we enter society at birth, we receive an inheritance from the people who lived before us. It is our responsibility to augment that inheritance for those who succeed us. I feel that all of us owe the world more than we received when we were born."

Dr. An Wang is well-known as a philanthropist who believed in sharing his fortune with fine arts, social and educational organizations. He enriched the arts and sciences, especially in Boston, where the Wang Theatre and the Wang Center for the Performing Arts bear his name. His major public interest was education and he believed our nation's success depends on a highly trained, well-educated workforce.

Dr. Wang's Philanthropic Achievements – (Partial List)

- Served on the Massachusetts Board of Higher Education, Massachusetts Board of Regents, as a trustee of Northeastern University and Boston College, and as an overseer of Harvard University.
- Created and funded a school of software engineering at the Wang Institute of Graduate Studies.
- Donated millions of dollars to Harvard University and funded a Massachusetts Institute of Technology program offering fellowships to engineers from mainland China.
- Was a benefactor of Boston's Chinese Cultural Institute which seeks to foster better understanding of Chinese culture through exhibitions and other programs.
- Endowed a $4 million challenge grant that generated a total of $10 million for the Wang Center for the Performing Arts.
- His wife, Lorraine, wanted the family's giving to have immediate, practical benefit for the broadest number of people. She found it in Massachusetts General Hospital's outpatient care unit. The family's donation made possible up to 450,000 patient visits annually.

References

1. Various Internet sources. Dr. An Wang.
2. Wang, An with Linden, Eugene. Lessons: An Autobiography. Reading, Massachusetts: Addison-Wesley Publishing Company, 1986.

Chang-Lin Tien

Distinguished Scientist & Educator Anchored in Both American & Chinese Cultures

By Elaine Woo

- Dr. Chang-Lin Tien made major contributions to U.S. space technology as an expert in thermal radiation science.

- His accomplishments eventually vaulted him to one of the top positions in American higher education: Chancellor of the University of California at Berkeley. He was the first Asian American to head a major research university in this country.

- Dr. Tien championed Affirmative Action when it was under attack, and became one of its strongest champions.

THERMODYNAMICS AND ENTROPY

Mechanical Engineering — Heat Transfer / Combustion

Copyright Peg Skorpinski

A Humble Beginning

Born on July 24, 1935 in Wuhan, China, and raised in Shanghai, Chang-Lin Tien was one of eight children of a well-to-do government banking official who fled to Taiwan with his family before the Communist takeover of Mainland China in 1949. The move forced them into penury as refugees in Taiwan, where they lived crammed together in a 12-foot-by-12-foot room.

Tien dreamed of becoming a basketball star during his youth in Taiwan. He even played as a semi-pro for a year, until he realized that his future would unfold in a far different arena.

The family's prospects improved when Tien's father was named deputy to the governor of Taiwan in 1950. But when his father died of a heart attack two years later, the family's fortunes fell again. Most of Tien's family managed to relocate to the U.S. Tien was the third to arrive.

Racial Prejudice Experienced First-Hand

In 1956, the graduate of National Taiwan University was 21 years old and nearly penniless when he landed in Louisville, Kentucky. There he studied on a teaching fellowship in the University of Louisville's department of mechanical engineering. Stepping into the pre-civil rights South was a shock. Public facilities, including restrooms and drinking fountains, were labeled either "whites only" or "colored." Tien was so befuddled by the segregation rules that he stood up on buses near the driver until he was told to take a seat in the front with the whites. He avoided the bus for a year after that:

"I was really confused and scared," he said in a 1990 interview. "I'm yellow. I don't know if that's colored or white."

"That left a very deep impression on me. This is a tremendous injustice to humiliate any human being that way."

In class, a professor who refused to pronounce his name called him "chinaman" until Tien learned that it was a racial slur and challenged him. "So he'd say, 'Hello, come.' But he never called me 'chinaman' anymore," Tien said.

When Dr. Tien was hired to teach at UC Berkeley in 1959, restrictive covenants prevented him from buying a house in certain neighborhoods. Decades later as chancellor, he encountered racism again when the university's football team won the Citrus Bowl in Florida in 1992 and hecklers greeted him with chants of "Buy American, Buy American."

A Brilliant Academic and Scientific Career

Tien earned a master's degree in mechanical engineering at Louisville before moving on to Princeton University, where he studied heat transfer. After earning a second master's degree and a doctorate at Princeton, he joined UC Berkeley's faculty and quickly earned recognition for his academic talent. In 1962, the 26 year-old Dr. Tien became the youngest professor to receive Berkeley's Distinguished Teaching Award. He was named a full professor in 1968.

At Berkeley he shifted his focus from heat transfer to the new area of thermal radiation. Scientists were being recruited to study the properties of radiant heat so that engineers could alter their designs accordingly. It was not a subject Tien felt confident about. He had missed all the questions about thermal radiation during his PhD orals at Princeton University.

In what he later described as "one of life's twists," he went on to become one of the top experts in the field.

One of his first major projects involved the huge Saturn rocket boosters developed in the 1960s to propel satellites and eventually humans into space. He contributed to the design of the Saturn's exhaust nozzles with work that helped estimate the degree to which exhaust plume would heat the rocket base.

Later he studied ways to alter the design of satellites so that the great variation in temperature between the sunny and shady sides would not interfere with sensitive electronics.

In the 1970s, he was among the scientists asked to address the first crisis of the Space Shuttle program: how to keep some 36,000 insulating tiles glued to the Shuttle despite the extreme heat of reentry. He and other NASA consultants eventually suggested a better way to fire the ceramic tiles that improved their insulating properties and prevented the heat from melting the glue that held the tiles in place. He also conducted research on "superinsulation" materials that could block heat from flowing into the liquid oxygen used in Saturn rocket engines.

His work was applied by the Japanese firm Hitachi in the design of magnetic levitation trains, which rely on low-temperature superconductors to produce powerful magnetic fields.

His research also proved helpful in the design of emergency cooling systems for nuclear reactors. Because of his expertise in this area, he was asked to advise officials dealing with the meltdown crises at Three Mile Island in 1979 and Chernobyl in 1986. He also served as a consultant to the U.S. Nuclear Regulatory Commission.

Among his many honors was the Max Jakob Memorial Award, the highest international award in the field of heat transfer research. In 2000, Chinese astronomers named a minor planet in his honor.

What was unique about Dr. Tien's career in thermal science was that he made fundamental contributions to theory as well as actual applications. Said Richard Buckius, a professor of mechanical and industrial engineering at the University of Illinois at Urbana-Champaign and a former student of Dr. Tien's, "He is a visionary who has always understood where to go [in the field], how to make an impact, which problems need to be addressed."

Becoming the First Chinese American Chancellor in a Premier University

After he became Berkeley's chancellor, Dr. Tien kept a hand in the field by advising graduate students in mechanical engineering. He encouraged them to do what he did himself. "Push yourself a little," he told students. "Always ask yourself, is there anything new here? Are there unsolved questions? Is there an article here?"

The dedicated academic with thick black hair and goggle-sized glasses maintained 20-hour days as chancellor. He was known to pick up litter on campus, pace the sidelines during sporting events, and stop in the campus library at 3:00 a.m. during finals week. That kind of energy propelled him for four decades at Berkeley.

He had headed Berkeley's department of mechanical engineering for seven years before rising to vice chancellor for research, a post he filled from 1983 to 1985. He left Berkeley for only two years, 1988 to 1990, when he led efforts to turn UC Irvine into a nationally prominent research school as executive vice chancellor.

He was on track to become UC Irvine's chancellor when he was chosen to head Berkeley, long considered the flagship of the UC system, in 1990.

Dr. Tien took the reins at a particularly challenging time: Tensions were rising over budget cutbacks and selective admissions policies that angered many whites and Asians, who believed the system was working to their disadvantage.

He was further tested by a series of emergencies. A fraternity house fire killed three students. Later, a deranged gunman took 30 students hostage at a local pub and killed one before police shot him to death. Dr. Tien's campus residence was invaded by a machete-wielding activist who was killed when she lunged at police with her weapon, but Dr. Tien and his wife, Di-Hwa, were unharmed.

The crises showcased Dr. Tien's personal style. After the fire, he spent a day at the fraternity house, soothing students and even helping to identify one victim's body to spare the parents a trip to the morgue. During the hostage crisis, he was the first to embrace the freed students and sent personal notes to their families.

He managed to maintain Berkeley's standing as one of the nation's premier research universities despite the recession of the early 1990s which, within four years, left UC Berkeley with a $70-million shortfall and caused the early retirements of many senior faculty members. Dr. Tien personally recruited top young scholars to teach at the school and sought to ensure that prominent professors would remain on the faculty. He also proved himself a prolific fundraiser, bringing in an unprecedented $975-million during his seven-year tenure as chancellor. His success stemmed in part from a strategy focusing on an untapped pool of potential Asian donors. His efforts netted a $15-million gift from Taiwanese donors for a new East Asian library, the largest international gift Berkeley had ever received.

Ardent Defender of Affirmative Action

When the UC Board of Regents ended affirmative action in admissions and Proposition 209 extended the ban to other sectors of state government, Dr. Tien emerged as one of affirmative action's most ardent defenders. Although friends had hinted that, as he noted in a 1996 *New York Times* article, "it might make more sense" for him as an Asian American to oppose affirmative action, Dr. Tien insisted that the policy was needed until the playing field was level for everyone.

"He was really rather fearless in the way he spoke out on issues, so much against major currents," Berkeley Asian American studies professor, Ling-chi Wang, told the *Los Angeles Times* in 2002. "That's what made him such a great leader and intellectual."

In 1995, after reports surfaced that Dr. Tien was considering other jobs, the regents gave him a $20,000 raise. He used $10,000 of it to start the Berkeley Pledge, a $1-million program to help prepare disadvantaged students to meet admission requirements at UC Berkeley.

In 1997, he stepped down as chancellor but remained on campus as a distinguished professor of engineering. He became the first recipient of UC's presidential medal.

He did not retire from teaching until 2001, a year after he was diagnosed with a brain tumor and suffered an incapacitating stroke. He was 67 at his death on Oct. 29, 2002. In addition to his wife of 43 years, he left behind three highly accomplished children, all UC Berkeley graduates: Phyllis, a UC San Francisco physician; Christine, deputy city manager of Stockton, California; and Norman, dean of engineering at Case Western Reserve University in Ohio.

Dr. Tien's Legacy

Chancellor Tien is remembered on campus for his personable style and inspired interactions with students. His frequent advice to them reflected the lesson he learned decades earlier, when he feared he had flunked all the questions on his doctoral exam in the area that later became his specialty.

"Don't close your mind to the advice and experience of senior people," he told his classes.

Another guiding philosophy was framed on the wall of his office. It was the Chinese character for "crisis," which merges two characters. "One stands for danger," he once explained, "and the other for opportunity." Dr. Tien took it to mean that any obstacle could also be a stepping stone; that in dire times one should always look for a way "to make a difference."

James Wong Howe 黃宗霑

A "True Magician" in Filmmaking, Two-Time Oscar Winning Cinematographer

By Jack Ong

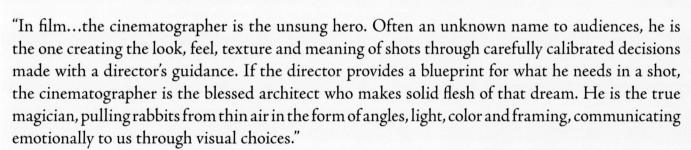

"In film…the cinematographer is the unsung hero. Often an unknown name to audiences, he is the one creating the look, feel, texture and meaning of shots through carefully calibrated decisions made with a director's guidance. If the director provides a blueprint for what he needs in a shot, the cinematographer is the blessed architect who makes solid flesh of that dream. He is the true magician, pulling rabbits from thin air in the form of angles, light, color and framing, communicating emotionally to us through visual choices."

~Grace McKeaney, playwright,
film & TV screenwriter, 2007

Visualize this scene on the wide screen from the 1955 hit movie, *Picnic*:

Kim Novak sashays slowly down the terrace steps to the dance floor, seduction in her eyes, clapping her hands and twisting her hips as she moves toward a hypnotized William Holden to the gentle rhythm of "Moonglow." They dance apart for a few beats before their passions bring them cheek to cheek. As desire burns hotter, violins introduce the "Picnic" theme song in a soulful medley with "Moonglow." The dancers abandon themselves to the moment, oblivious to the pain, longing, envy and desperation their union has unleashed in the lives of those around them.

This unforgettable scene is so charged with romance, sensuality, tension and electricity, that it leaves the theater audience holding its collective breath.

This is just one of countless cinematic triumphs created in the mind's eye of James Wong Howe, filmed through his magical camera lens onto celluloid, and projected onto the silver screen, to be enjoyed and etched in the hearts and memories of film fans, worldwide. That's entertainment in the grand style of master cinematographer James Wong Howe! (1899-1976)

James Wong Howe
More Than An Unsung Hero

James Wong Howe succeeded in becoming the favored cinematographer and director of photography for many directors and stars of his time. He garnered ten Academy Award nominations, two Oscars, and numerous accolades in his illustrious career. Posthumously, the "Jimmie Awards"—honoring people and companies that promote entertainment industry opportunities for Asian Americans—were named in Howe's honor by the Association of Asian Pacific American Artists in 1985. His feat was all the more incredible considering the resistance to racial diversity in the motion picture guilds and unions of that era.

Contrary to the norm, James Wong Howe rose well above the unsung hero ranks of the vast majority of motion picture cinematographers and directors of photography. His name was often as well-recognized as a film's stars when the James Wong Howe credit appeared onscreen. He was both legendary and celebrated in his own lifetime for the professionalism, creativity and unique visual style he contributed to some 135 feature films and television programs between 1923 and 1975.

Howe's career spanned silents and talkies, black and white as well as color, and all image sizes, from TV to anamorphic widescreen. His work in each genre was uncompromising; he believed his job was to help tell the story through imagery, nothing more and nothing less, and he succeeded in doing that for 52 years despite racial prejudice and a reputation for "being difficult".

He was the photographer of demand for many female stars. As he explained, his job was "to make old stars look young, plump stars look thin, ordinary faces beautiful and to convert certain defects into gorgeous assets." He accomplished that with proper angles of lighting, shadows and the desired accent of make-up. He was, indeed, a magician with the camera.

Even viewed alongside today's technology-driven cinematic product, Howe's signature low-key, natural lighting (which earned him the nickname "Low Key Howe"), deep focus images, and his emphatic and sometimes impossible angles, unobtrusively draw the viewer into the moment and mood of the story. His compelling and undistracting shots (which add as much to the feeling of a scene as its performers, dialogue, music, wardrobe and production design) subtly but assuredly elevate the art and enjoyment of movies.

Howe's film titles are apt to evoke visual memories as diverse as the vast, barren Texas landscapes of *Hud*; the fisherman's familiar but threatening ocean in *The Old Man and The Sea*; the desperate and haunting romance of the

Courtesy of the Academy of Motion Picture Arts and Sciences

"Moonglow" dance sequence in *Picnic*, lit by Chinese lanterns reflecting on a lake; the throbbing heartbeat of New York City and the chilling ruthlessness of the lead characters in *Sweet Smell of Success*; the innocence, exuberance and hope in *Yankee Doodle Dandy*; a woman's forlorn isolation at home in *The Rose Tattoo* as well as *Come Back Little Sheba*; the relentless desert vistas in *Hombre*; the menacing play of light and shadows in *The Thin Man* (which anticipated film noir); the stifling claustrophobia in the lightless coalmines of *The Molly Maguires*; the fleeting glamour of a life in the limelight and footlights throughout *Funny Lady*; and the terror of helplessness to resist inevitable doom in *Seconds*.

These and his entire body of work will forever be the magnificent legacy of James Wong Howe.

The Early Years

James Wong Howe was born Wong Tung Jim in Canton (Guangzhou), China. This Chinese American pioneer was brought to America by his stepmother at the age of five. They settled with his father, Wong How, near Pasco, Washington. Wong How had emigrated from China in 1899, working for the Northern Pacific Railroad before operating a successful general store and, eventually, several ranches.

Being the only Chinese in the small Northwestern town, the Wong How family endured much name calling and racist hostility. When young Wong Tung Jim was first enrolled in public school, his teacher quit, refusing to educate a "Chinaman". Another teacher, probably confused by the Chinese method of stating last names first, gave Wong Tung Jim the name James Wong Howe, adding the "e" to How.

He eventually moved to Hollywood, after leaving Pasco to pursue a brief boxing career in Oregon. In Los Angeles, he worked as a delivery boy, busboy, and then janitor of the Jesse Lasky Studios cutting room. By then Howe had an interest in photography and the growing medium of filmmaking. At Lasky Studios he learned about lighting equipment, film processing and how to use the hand-cranked cameras of the day.

Howe's Innovations in Photographic Cinema

In 1919, Howe got his first break as fourth assistant cameraman on the Cecile B. DeMille movie, *Male and Female*, a silent picture starring Gloria Swanson. How that break came about is just one of many stories in the James Wong Howe legend; it is also a testament to Howe's imagination, skills, and creative problem solving ability.

It seems DeMille needed a closeup of a canary singing, but not a single crewmember could get the bird to chirp. Howe volunteered to try, whereupon he placed a small piece of chewing gum in the canary's beak. The bird instantly began twitching its head to dislodge the gum, giving it the appearance of chirping. Problem solved.

Another early Howe legend was born at a time when he earned more as a freelance photographer than he did at the studio. Actress Mary Miles Minter was thrilled that Howe managed to photograph her in a way that made her pale blue eyes appear darker and more alive. She wondered if he could achieve the same effect on movie film; if he could, Minter said, she would request him as her cameraman.

Howe assured the actress he could accomplish this effect, and then began to think of a way to do so. His solution: since the illusion of darkness was the effect of black velvet he reflected off her pale eyes, why not film Minter's close-ups using a similar method with similar velvet? It worked and so began James Wong Howe's career as a cinematographer with Minter's *Drums of Fate* in 1922.

Soon, many a light-eyed actor or actress called for him to perform his "Minter magic." Howe began getting enough studio work to go freelance again, on his own terms this time. He was now doing what he truly wanted: solving problems to achieve the perfect shot by handholding the camera, getting on roller skates, sitting in a wheelchair or using unusual lenses. His renown grew, and with it many a story about this driven, diminutive, persistent, precise and opinionated cameraman.

Howe's Encounter with a Press Photographer

Perhaps the favorite James Wong Howe tale to circulate through the industry came about when he and his wife, writer Sonora Babb (whom he married in 1949 when intermarriage was widely discriminated against), took over a Chinese restaurant in Studio City, near Hollywood, naming it *Ching How*. According to a report on the website anecdotage.com:

The local press sent a photographer … to take some pictures of the Chinese cinematographer and his staff. The photographer, unaware of the specifics of the assignment, lined up Howe and his staff outside the new restaurant. Finding that he could not fit them all into the frame, he backed into the street with traffic whizzing by on either side. Howe, concerned for the man's safety, delicately suggested that he use a wide-angle lens. The pho-

Courtesy of the Academy of Motion Picture Arts and Sciences

tographer was not amused. "Just stick to your chop suey," he replied, "and let me take the pictures."

Ching How Restaurant and Friend & Actor Albert Wong

Actor Albert Wong, a young waiter in Los Angeles Chinatown at the time, worked at Ching How becoming a lifelong friend of "Jimmie and Sonora."

"I was working after school in the early 1950s at Yee Mee Loo," Wong recalls. "It was a real popular place at Ord and Spring, owned by David Yee. Jimmie used to come there to eat and always wanted me to wait on him. He was a small guy, 5'2", but a big tipper! Soon we became friends. He asked me if I wanted to work for him 'because I like you'. When he asked me again, I went to work at Ching How, a remodeled house with two small dining rooms, a private room in back, and a bar."

"If Jimmie didn't want to see someone, he'd tell me to say he wasn't there, then exit out the back. Sonora ran the place; her sister took care of the books. If Jimmie and Sonora had a little argument and she walked out, I'd have to drive him home. On my days off, Jimmie let me drive his custom built car, and he'd use my '46 Ford. He and Sonora were very nice. They gave me a raise even when they knew the restaurant was going to close. They surprised me with a party when I got married up in San Francisco, and we always stayed in touch, up until their deaths. Jimmie and I had a genuine friendship, we spoke Toisanese together, and I respect him and his work to this day."

Wong smiles at the memories of the stars who frequented Howe's restaurant: Clark Gable, Greta Garbo, Sessue Hayakawa, Gary Cooper, Lucille Ball and Desi Arnaz, Al Jolson, Donald O'Connor, Ava Gardner, Kirk Douglas, Helen Hayes, John Garfield, Marilyn Monroe before she was famous, Jane Powell and Piper Laurie.

Tribute from Director John Frankenheimer

The respect felt for James Wong Howe in the film industry is articulated by director John Frankenheimer (original *Manchurian Candidate, Birdman Of Alcatraz, The Train*) on his commentary track for the DVD release of the 1966 cult classic, *Seconds*, starring Rock Hudson in what is widely considered his finest dramatic performance. Frankenheimer says of James Wong Howe: "His contribution to the overall movie was enormous, perhaps more than any other cameraman I've ever worked with. He was a tremendous influence on the rest of my career."

A partial list of James Wong Howe's film credits as director of photography and/or cinematographer include the following:

1. Funny Lady* (1975)
2. The Horsemen (1971)
3. The Molly Maguires (1970)
4. Last of the Mobile Hot Shots (1970) (aka Blood Kin, aka The Seven Descents of Myrtle)
5. The Heart Is a Lonely Hunter (1968)
6. Hombre (1967) (Director of Photography)
7. Seconds* (1966)
8. This Property Is Condemned (1966)
9. The Glory Guys (1965)
10. The Outrage (1964)
11. Biography of a Rookie: The Willie Davis Story (1963) (TV)
12. Hud** (1963)
13. Tess of the Storm Country (1960)
14. Song Without End (1960) (aka Crescendo)
15. The Story on Page One (1959)
16. The Last Angry Man (1959)
17. Bell Book and Candle (1958) (Director of Photography)
18. The Old Man and the Sea* (1958)
19. A Farewell to Arms (1957) (Uncredited)
20. Drango (1957)
21. Sweet Smell of Success (1957)
22. Death of a Scoundrel (1956) (Director of Photography)
23. Screen Directors Playhouse ("Lincoln's Doctor's Dog") (1955) (TV)
24. The Rose Tattoo** (1955)
25. Picnic (1955)
26. Light's Diamond Jubilee (1954) (TV)
27. Jennifer (1953)
28. Main Street to Broadway (1953)
29. The World of Dong Kingman (1953)
30. Come Back, Little Sheba (1952) (Director of Photography)
31. The Fighter (1952) (aka The First Time)
32. The Lady Says No (1952)
33. Behave Yourself! (1951)
34. He Ran All the Way (1951)
35. The Brave Bulls (1951)
36. Tripoli (1950) (aka The First Marines, USA reissue title)
37. The Eagle and the Hawk (1950) (aka Spread Eagle, USA reissue title)

38. The Baron of Arizona
39. The Time of Your Life (1948)
40. Mr. Blandings Builds His Dream House (1948) (Director of Photography)
41. Body and Soul (1947) (aka An Affair of the Heart)
42. Pursued (1947)
43. Nora Prentiss (1947)
44. My Reputation (1946)
45. Danger Signal (1945)
46. Confidential Agent (1945)
47. Counter-Attack (1945)
48. Objective, Burma! (1945) (Director of Photography) (aka Operation Burma)
49. Passage to Marseille (1944) (Director of Photography)
50. The North Star* (1943) (aka Armored Attack, USA recut version)
51. Hangmen Also Die! (1943) (aka Lest We Forget)
52. The Hard Way (1943) (Director of Photography)
53. Air Force* (with Elmer Dyer & Charles Marshall) (1943) (Director of Photography)
54. Yankee Doodle Dandy (1942)
55. Kings Row* (1942)
56. Navy Blues (1941) (dance sequences)
57. Out of the Fog (1941)
58. Shining Victory (1941)
59. The Strawberry Blonde (1941)
60. Fantasia (1940) (uncredited)
61. A Dispatch from Reuter's (1940)
62. City for Conquest (1940)
63. My Love Came Back (1940) (uncredited)
64. Torrid Zone (1940)
65. Saturday's Children (1940) (Director of Photography)
66. Dr. Ehrlich's Magic Bullet (1940)
67. Abe Lincoln in Illinois* (1940)
68. Four Wives (1939) (uncredited)
69. On Your Toes (1939)
70. Dust Be My Destiny (1939)
71. Daughters Courageous (1939) (aka A Family Affair, aka American Family, aka Family Reunion)
72. The Oklahoma Kid (1939)
73. They Made Me a Criminal (1939) (aka I Became a Criminal, aka They Made Me a Fugitive)
74. Comet Over Broadway (1938)
75. Algiers* (1938)

*Academy Award Nomination
**Academy Award

A complete Filmography of Howe's recorded credits is available at www.IMDB.com on the Internet.

Author's Postscript

With a number of James Wong Howe's films now preserved and accessible on DVD and VHS, it is easy to enjoy a personal retrospective and inspire new generations! Seeing his work is guaranteed to invest viewers with newfound respect for this cameraman's particular genius. His composition and lighting are at their zenith when portraying a sense of isolation. This is not to say that Howe's images cannot instantly conjure romance, suspense, joy and gaiety, or abject sorrow, and portray each mood's variations with finesse. When the story calls for isolation, Howe's images are at their most heart wrenching and amazing. His ability to enhance motion picture storytelling is remarkable. Watching his work reminds one of the power of film, and why so many of us are enchanted by this art form.

In addition to the available films of James Wong Howe, his career and life are well-documented in Todd Rainsberger's excellent book, *James Wong Howe: Cinematographer* (ISBN 0-498-02405-9).

Dong Kingman

An American Watercolor Master

By Dong Kingman, Jr.

"Dong Kingman is bold, free and joyous. He paints with soaked light."
~Art critic, Alfred Frankenstein, 1937

Gallery & Studio magazine best describes Dong Kingman's place in the art world: He deserves to be remembered…as a watercolorist on a par with John Marin, Winslow Homer, Charles Burchfield, and very few others….Dong Kingman was not only a famous American artist but an important one as well. Surely the inimitable charm and beauty of his work will endure and continue to delight future generations.

"Most artists are surrealists … always dreaming something and then they paint it."
~Dong Kingman (1911-2000)

Leading American Watercolorist for More Than Six Decades

Two weeks before my father, Dong Kingman, passed away in his New York studio, located just behind the Plaza Hotel, I sat by his bedside and he reached out to hold my hand. After a few moments of silence, he said, "There is no more to be done."

He was right. Considered one of the most accomplished watercolorists of the 20th century, his artistic achievements could fill the pages of several lifetimes. On May 12, 2000, my father's distinguished, artistic odyssey came to an end at age 89.

The next day, I removed the pushpins, which held his unfinished watercolor painting to the easel and placed it with other paintings in the multi-colored flat file. As I sorted his papers, photos and paintings for the next several months, some stored far up in his 20-foot-high studio, the scope of his achievements became evident.

First I noted how many of his paintings are in museum collections, as well as the awards he received. At last count, over 60 museums and private institutions from coast to coast have one or more Dong Kingman paintings, including the Metropolitan Museum of Art; Museum of Modern Art; Whitney Museum of American Art; Museum of Fine Arts, Boston; Brooklyn Museum of Art; Springfield Art Museum; Art Institute of Chicago; de Young Museum of Art; San Diego Museum of Art; Oakland Museum of

Courtesy of Dong Kingman, Jr.

California; San Francisco Museum of Modern Art; and Los Angeles County Museum of Art.

His awards, honors and grants more than matched this impressive number during his lifetime. He received virtually every major watercolor award: the Dolphin Medal (the highest honor from the American Watercolor Society); National Academy of Design 150th Anniversary Gold Medal; Audubon Gold Medal of Honor; Metropolitan Museum of Art Award; Philadelphia Watercolor Club awards; Art Institute of Chicago International Award; and the one that started it all, the San Francisco Art Association First Purchase Prize in 1936 when he was only 25 years old—as well as back-to-back Guggenheim Fellowships in 1942 and 1943.

These accomplishments would have been enough but he pushed his visual arts career further. In the 1960s, Hollywood beckoned. He expanded into the world of films as art consultant for *The World of Suzie Wong* and created stunning, credited title paintings for *Flower Drum Song* (recently reissued with an introduction by Nancy Kwan) and *55 Days at Peking* that evoked the moods of the films. He was fascinated and challenged that this visual medium could transform his paintings into giant moving murals. Additionally, he contributed artwork for films such as *Circus World* and *King Rat*.

From the first time my father saw the silent film, *The Thief of Baghdad*, he was hooked on this visual medium. His close friend and film mentor, the two-time Academy

Award winner, James Wong Howe, directed a documentary on my father in 1954, a 15-minute gem that gained wide distribution internationally. To this day, I am still receiving requests for this short film. My father also produced and animated *Hong Kong Dong*, a short film about his boyhood dreams, Chinese cultural upbringing and mythological environment. This won the San Francisco International Film Festival Best Short Film award in 1976.

My father really had four careers with fine art as the foundation. From there he expanded into the disciplines of teaching, films and commissioned on advertising art. If he were an illustrator alone, he would be ranked among the top ones in the field. Some of his commissioned works are truly works of art, such as the paintings he did for the Hong Kong Tourist Board's posters, the *Fortune* and *Time Magazine* covers and his paintings for the Pan American World Airways first-class passenger menus. In many ways, his art served as a bridge between Chinese and American cultures, and between East and West.

Blossoming of a Celebrated Career in Fine Arts

How he achieved all this began at an early age. Born in Oakland, California, in 1911 as Dong Moy-Shu, his family moved to Hong Kong when he was five. His father opened a haberdashery store on Des Voeux Road in this bustling port city. During his formative years, he studied art, literature and calligraphy at the Lingnan School. His teacher, the Paris-trained painting master, Szeto Wai,

took a keen interest in young Dong and taught him both the Chinese traditional and French Impressionist styles of painting. Another teacher, recognizing Dong's artistic talent, gave him the name King-Man, meaning "scenic composition," and later his name became Dong Kingman. During these years, he drew and painted incessantly. When he ran out of material, he used the crowded sidewalk just outside the family store as his canvas. The influence of Chinese education and culture had a profound effect on his later paintings.

When my father returned to Oakland in 1929 during the Depression, he became co-owner of a Chinese restaurant which failed partly because he painted more than he cooked. In the early 1930s, he moved the family to San Francisco, seeking new opportunities. We lived a block from Nob Hill and seven blocks from Chinatown. Our 4 ½ room apartment at 1 Dawson Place had a distant view of the bay. A framed Picasso print, "Woman in White," and my grandmother's Chinese traditional watercolors of flowers hung in the living room. The rent was about $50 a month. My mother worked as a seamstress and my father worked as a houseboy while painting in his free time. He was determined to make ends meet and to support his relentless quest to become a successful artist.

In 1936, the year I was born, the city's art reviewers acclaimed my dad's exhibition of watercolors at the Art Center Gallery. Critic Junius Cravens noted, "The young Chinese artist is showing twenty of the freshest, most satisfying watercolors

Courtesy of Dong Kingman, Jr.

Golden Gate Bridge Scenario by Dong Kingman

Courtesy of Dong Kingman, Jr.

that have been seen hereabouts in many a day. He handles his color fluently in broad telling masses." At age 25, he also received the San Francisco Art Association First Purchase Prize. At the Association's Second Annual Exhibition, reviewer Alfred Frankenstein wrote, "Dong Kingman is bold, free and joyous as always. He paints with soaked light. He is San Francisco's A-No.1 watercolorist...."

Balancing Career and Family

When the Works Progress Administration (WPA) asked my dad to join an art project for five years, he seized the chance to capture the scenic richness of the West and to explore every facet of the watercolor medium. The $90 monthly WPA stipend enabled him to share a studio at 15 Hotaling Place near the Black Cat Café, a watering hole for Bohemians. The studio was in a deserted part of town. One time, he took me painting near there early on a Sunday morning. I could feel the stillness of the city streets ready to come to life like a Hopper painting. He also loved the mist-shrouded hills and vistas of San Francisco because they reminded him of Chinese landscapes.

I have vague memories of him during my San Francisco years from 1936-1947. Always dressed in tweeds, sometimes he took my brother and me painting outdoors. Occasionally, he brought the family to the Chinese opera at the far end of Grant Avenue, or to see the San Francisco Forty-Niners. He taught me chess and how to hold the paintbrush the Chinese and Western way. The one time he spanked me was for stealing an ice cream bar.

I saw less of him as his career advanced. A pioneer of the "California Style" of plein aire painting, his distinctive watercolors would achieve national recognition quickly. In 1940, the Metropolitan Museum bought the first of its three Kingman paintings. Then back-to-back Guggenheim Fellowships gave him the opportunity to capture the American scene and to build on his mastery of the watercolor medium. The Harmon Foundation funded a documentary film on him. An award at the Art Institute of Chicago's

International Exhibition and an Audubon Artist Medal of Honor in 1946 heralded many more awards to come. Teaching assignments at Mills College, University of Wyoming, the San Diego Art Gallery and other institutions beckoned. During World War II, the Office of Strategic Services in Washington, DC, used his talents in the graphics department. In 1942 and again in 1945, Midtown Galleries in New York exhibited his work to rave reviews, including one from Eleanor Roosevelt. She wrote in her column, "… the young Chinese artist from San Francisco. His pictures are remarkable; he is an artist with a great deal of ability." The de Young Museum had a major exhibition of his paintings later that year and purchased the watercolor, "Nevada."

After the war, we moved to Brooklyn Heights, New York, where we lived from 1947 to 1956. I used to watch my dad paint in his compact studio. It was in the corner of the living room, furnished with George Nelson and Eames furniture, a cigar store Indian, and a mural painted by him. He showed me transparent and opaque techniques, washes for the sky, and how he sometimes created rich, vibrant colors by using color washes on top of each other. One such painting was included in a 1950 exhibi-

Courtesy of Dong Kingman, Jr.

tion and may have contributed to this excellent review by New York Times art critic, Howard De Vree:

Kingman's show at the Midtown Galleries is the liveliest watercolor event of the season … almost Marinesque panoramas of the city and its teeming waterways. He works out a compelling organization with a dominant mood, carefully selective of detail, and vitalizing the commonplace through fresh observation and rearrangement to suit the needs of his pictorial design. Forms, light and color are kept in balance in his stimulating interpretations.

Teacher, University Professor and Cultural Ambassador

For the next ten years, when he wasn't painting, my father taught art five days a week at Columbia University. He taught watercolor painting and Chinese art history at Hunter College for five years, beginning in 1948. In 1954, he became a founding faculty member of the Famous Artists School in Westport, Connecticut, along with Norman Rockwell and Ben Shahn. He exhibited regularly for 14 years at Midtown Galleries, and then at Wildenstein & Co. for the next 10 years. His works during the post-war period became increasingly complex in subject matter and usually had a geometric, abstractionist look. He painted a large number of outstanding cityscapes of New York and

Dong in China   Courtesy of Dong Kingman, Jr.

San Francisco. "The best of these works have exceptional compositions, interesting subject matter and an exciting sense of drama. They are among the finest examples of American watercolor produced during that era," noted the book, *California Watercolors 1850-1970.* Commenting on a ten-year retrospective at Midtown Galleries in 1951, *Time Magazine* wrote that at age 40, "Kingman is one of the world's best watercolorists."

In the ensuing years, the artist's international reputation grew. He became a cultural ambassador when he went on a lecture tour of Asia and Europe in 1954 for the U.S. State Department. In addition to his exhibitions in London and Paris, his many painting trips to the Far East led to a major exhibition in Hong Kong in the early 1970s. *Arts of Asia* in a 1973 article noted,

… not a man to rest on his laurels, he is plumbing new depths to improve and revitalize his work. His latest objects of study, and the subjects of a delightful series of watercolors, are trees … the inclination that led him to this phase may be partially visual, but perhaps it also arises from the Chinese culture that permeates his soul, the Oriental love of the natural world and its creatures that has inspired Dong Kingman to seek (his) own visual communion with … life.

In 1981, the Ministry of Culture, People's Republic of China, hosted a critically acclaimed retrospective of Kingman's paintings in Beijing, Hangzhou, and Guangzhou. The exhibition, attended by well over 100,000 people, was the first, American one-man show since the resumption of diplomatic relations between the U.S. and China. Noted the *China Daily Mail,*

Just as the master painters of the Song Dynasty roamed about mountain and stream to capture the rhythm of nature, Dong Kingman traveled the world capturing the dynamism of modern life … familiar scenes have been transformed into a vibrant new vision of life through color schemes with rhythms that play over the entire surface of the picture. The windswept skies which enliven his watercolors remind us of the pleinairism of the French Impressionists.

Towards the end of his life, the Taipei Fine Arts Museum in Taiwan exhibited "40 Years of Watercolors by Dong Kingman" from November 1994 through January 1995. In 1999, the Taichung Provincial Museum in Taiwan presented a retrospective of Dong Kingman's watercolor paintings. Though he was not in good health, the sheer determination and energy that characterized his artistic life got him to Taiwan and back. This was the last of his own exhibitions that he saw.

The Great Wall   Courtesy of Dong Kingman, Jr.

After his passing, exhibitions and honors paid tribute to the renowned watercolor master. In the summer of 2000, the Academy of Motion Picture Arts and Sciences highlighted Kingman's involvement in films with a special two-month exhibition, "Dong Kingman: An American Master in Hollywood," that commemorated his film-related work in the permanent collection of the Academy's Fairbanks Center for Motion Picture Study in Beverly Hills, California.

Hong Kong Harbor

Courtesy of Dong Kingman, Jr.

Fellowship at Columbia University's School of the Arts; and inclusion in the "Leading the Way" exhibit of pioneering Asian American artists held at Gordon College, Massachusetts. From November 2001 to March 2002, the Chinese Historical Society of America Museum and San Francisco State University's College of Creative Arts co-sponsored a major exhibition, "Dong Kingman in San Francisco", at the Society's new facilities in San Francisco.

A national touring retrospective, "Dong Kingman: An American Master" with venues at the Governor's Gallery, Legislative Building, Olympia, Washington; Chinese Culture Center, San Francisco, California; Louisiana Arts & Science Center, Baton Rouge, Louisiana; and Brooklyn Public Library, New York began in the Fall of 2000 and concluded in March 2002. Then Washington State governor Gary Locke commented,"… I was looking at more than just paintings. The artist deftly brings together elements of his Chinese heritage and life in America. The paintings tell a story of a man's quest to unite the best of both his worlds."

In 2001, activities honoring the artist included the presentation of the first annual American Watercolor Society Dong Kingman award; establishment of a Dong Kingman

At the invitation of the Ministry of Culture, People's Republic of China, a new exhibition, "Dong Kingman: Watercolor Master," opened at Beijing National Museum in 2002, the Exhibition Galleries of the Hong Kong Central Library, and concluded its China tour at the Shanghai Art Museum in early 2003.

For more on the artist, please log onto www.dongkingman.org.

Flossie Wong-Staal

Identified AIDS Virus and Cloned the Genetic Structure of HIV

By Betty Chan Gaw

- Flossie Wong-Staal, PhD, is a pioneer in the field of AIDS research whose groundbreaking achievements include cloning, sequencing and characterizing human retroviruses such as HIV, which causes AIDS.

- Between 1990 and 2000, her AIDS research at UC San Diego led to advances in viral gene therapy, one of the most technologically sophisticated fields of medical research.

- Her ongoing research focuses on new therapies for the hepatitis C virus and cancer.

- In 1990, the Institute for Scientific Information named her the top woman scientist of the past decade, and the fourth-ranking scientist under 45 of either gender.

HIV/AIDS—A Devastating Disease

HIV (*human immunodeficiency virus*) attacks the body's defenses against opportunistic infections. It is life-threatening and transmissible via body fluids and sexual contacts. HIV uses healthy white blood cells to replicate itself, breaks down the immune system, and leaves the body more susceptible to illnesses, including AIDS (*acquired immune deficiency syndrome*).

An HIV-positive person is diagnosed with AIDS when their immune system is so weakened that it can no longer fight off illnesses. People with immune deficiency are much more vulnerable to opportunistic infections such as pneumonia and certain kinds of cancer. Millions of people around the world are infected with HIV.

Courtesy of Flossie Wong-Staal

Wong-Staal at 10th International Conference on AIDS. Yokohama, Japan. August 1994

There presently is no cure for AIDS. While antiviral drugs can improve the quality of life and extend the lifespan of some people, these treatments do not work for everyone and may cause many undesirable side effects.

AIDS symptoms may be hidden after infection. It can take up to several years for the virus to destroy an infected person's immune cells: T-cells and CD4 cells. People infected with the virus may appear perfectly healthy and may pass it on to others unknowingly. It is estimated that one out of four Americans with HIV does not know they have the virus.

Medical research led to development of HIV tests to screen and identify people infected with the virus as well as to screen donated blood. Once positively identified, the further spread of the disease can be better controlled. The identification of HIV as a new viral disease in humans was an important milestone toward its prevention and treatment.

Flossie Wong-Staal's basic research findings on HIV have been fundamental to the worldwide search to develop treatments and vaccines for AIDS.

A Scientist of the Highest Caliber

Dr. Flossie Wong-Staal is a leader in the research of human retroviruses. Prior to AIDS, she studied leukemogenesis by the human T-cell leukemia virus. In 1981, when symptoms of HIV disease were first identified in the United States, Dr. Wong-Staal began to focus her research on this new retrovirus.

Dr. Wong-Staal took a position with the National Cancer Institute (NCI) in Bethesda, Maryland, performing retrovirus research with virologist Dr. Robert Gallo. Drs. Gallo and Wong-Staal identified HIV in 1983, independently but simultaneously with researchers in France. While serving as the section chief in the Laboratory of Tumor Cell Biology at NCI, Dr. Wong-Staal was the first scientist to define the structure of several *oncogene homologues* as well as the genetic structure of HIV. Dr. Wong-Staal not only identified many of the fundamental properties of HIV, but also provided many of the early key reagents for the field of HIV molecular biology.

In 1990, her team discovered the protein of the gene that contributes to Kaposi's sarcoma, the skin cancer that is an initial telltale sign of clinical AIDS.

Dr. Wong-Staal was responsible for the first cloning of HIV in 1985, genetically mapping its structure at the young age of 38. She received several patents for methods of AIDS testing. Her monumental feats place her in the most elite class of molecular virology researchers, worthy of the academic and scientific honors bestowed on her.

Some of the medical boards Dr. Wong-Staal serves on include:

- Health Policy Board of the Institute of Medicine.
- National Task Force on AIDS Drug Development.
- Science Board to the Food and Drug Administration.
- Scientific Counselors for the National Institute of Allergy and Infectious Diseases.

She has been elected a member of the Institute of Medicine of the National Academies, the Academia Sinica of Taiwan, and an honorary member of the American Society of Clinical Investigation.

The United States Pan Asian Chamber of Commerce honored her with its Excellence 2000 award, and she received the T-Sector Innovator of the Year Award in 2001.

Dr. Flossie Wong-Staal's Vision for a Cure

Dr. Wong-Staal works to solve the mysteries of retroviral diseases such as HIV.

At the University of California at San Diego, she held the Florence Riford Chair in AIDS research from 1990 to 2002. Professor Wong-Staal's laboratory focused on human retroviruses as model systems to study gene regulation and pathogenesis, and as targets for genetic intervention. With her scientific team, she led research on finding an HIV vaccine and developing gene therapy to treat the disease.

She is a co-founder of Immusol, a biopharmaceutical company, and leads its drug discovery and development programs. Immusol uses drug target discovery called *Inverse Genomics* to discover therapeutic genes in areas of cancer, viral infections, proliferative diseases of the eye, and metabolic diseases.

Family and Personal History

Flossie Wong-Staal was born in China in 1946 of a businessman father, and a homemaker mother. Her family fled Communist China in 1952 to settle in Hong Kong, where Yee Ching, as she was named, enrolled in a Catholic school. Her father renamed her Flossie, after Typhoon Flossie struck Hong Kong in 1958.

Flossie excelled in science and math and her family was very supportive of her academic pursuits. Graduating from an all-girls high school in Hong Kong, she immigrated to the United States in 1965 and earned a bachelor's degree in bacteriology and a PhD in molecular biology from UCLA.

Dr. Wong-Staal's discoveries and scientific contributions have extended the lives of many and will undoubtedly continue to relieve human suffering on this planet.

Iris Chang

Writer and Historian

Exposed the Forgotten Holocaust in China

By Joyce Mar

- Iris Chang displayed her deep passion for human rights and reconciliation through the impact of her three books.

- Her works often confronted readers with unpleasant events that she felt compelled to bring into the public consciousness.

"During her brief yet remarkable professional career, Iris touched the lives of countless people, shedding light on past injustices and atrocities that had been forgotten or ignored...."

Read into the U.S. Congressional Record by
Michael M. Honda of California, November, 2004.

As a journalist, author and historian, Iris Chang gained recognition for her careful examination of social and historical justice—and her engaging writing style brought her stories to life.

Chang's principal works were *The Thread of the Silkworm* (1995), *The Rape of Nanking* (1997), and her last volume, *The Chinese in America* (2003). Each book weaves together fascinating yet tragic stories of individuals with comprehensive accounts of historical events.

And, Iris Chang accomplished all of this in her brief lifetime of 36 years!

Chang has been described as tall, attractive, confident, vulnerable and dignified. She was a hard worker with an intense drive—totally immersed in her subject matter and never taking much time away from researching yet another book. "She pushed herself to the limit," said her husband. Her books demonstrated her passion for presenting the truth about the exclusions, atrocities, violence and discrimination which have plagued the Chinese and Chinese Americans.

© Jason Jem

her first book, *The Thread of the Silkworm*. The book is the story of Dr. Tsien Hsu-Shen, the top Chinese-born physicist and missile expert at California Institute of Technology's Jet Propulsion Laboratory in Pasadena. Dr. Tsien left America during the 1950s when Senator Joseph McCarthy was holding anti-Communist hearings. The U.S. government accused Dr. Tsien of being a Communist under "flimsy allegations," took away his high security clearance, and forbade him from straying outside the boundaries of Los Angeles for five years. The United States eventually deported Dr. Tsien to China where he subsequently developed that country's missile program. Chang writes in profound detail of the history and science of Dr. Tsien's contributions, even without having had the opportunity to interview him. She recounts how he must have felt upon arriving in the Peoples Republic of China and finding that even items such as tools to repair bicycles were barely available. Yet, the government expected him to build their missile program.

Later, it was discovered that the United States had deported Dr. Tsien as an accused Communist in exchange for the return of American POWs. Many U.S. defense officials had considered him too valuable a scientist to allow him to bring

Her Works

Iris Chang's knowledge of the Chinese language and her master's degree in science writing prepared her to write his expertise to China, but formal deportation proceedings were underway and U.S. Immigration and Naturalization officials won out. The United States' loss was China's gain. The Chinese Haiying-2A missile, developed by Dr. Tsien, came to be known as the *Silkworm* in the 1980s and was later exported to the Middle East. Dr. Tsien never returned to the United States.

Iris Chang's second book, *The Rape of Nanking* (now known as Nanjing), is an account of the massacre that took place during the Sino-Japanese War in the 1930s. Written at age twenty-nine, the book elevated her to the world stage. Her outrage at a series of photographs of mutilated bodies that she viewed at a conference in 1994 became her inspiration to write the book. While her parents had told her about the atrocities committed by the Japanese army against civilians in Nanking, nothing impressed her as much as the photographs. Her rage over the massacre and the untold historical events compelled her to write her controversial book. She later wrote, "… this terrifying disrespect for death and dying, this reversion in human revolution, would be reduced to a footnote of history … unless someone forced the world to remember it." *The Rape of Nanking* sold one-half million copies and was on the *New York Times* bestseller list for several months.

Iris Chang was now speaking at book events and being interviewed on television programs like Nightline and the MacNeil/Lehrer News Hour. *Readers Digest* featured a cover story on her, and *Newsweek* ran an excerpt from *The Rape of Nanking*. She was excited by the opportunity to share her feelings about the book, traveling to over 65 cities in less than two years. Iris challenged the Japanese ambassador to a televised debate on the Japanese military's atrocities against China. She was persistent and steadfast in defense of her book, and accused the Japanese government of never offering an acceptable apology.

To this day, many Japanese government officials and others have refused to acknowledge that the Nanking massacre ever happened. Some suggest the events Iris Chang describes are exaggerations or lies. Despite high praise for her research and professionalism, there are those in the Japanese government who continue to discredit or criticize her work. The human rights abuses described in *The Rape of Nanking* have even been dismissed as a "controversial" incident. Yet, because her writing captures the essence of those horrific acts, and owing to her careful documentation, *The Rape of Nanking* is often used by students researching World War II history and abuses of human rights.

A *Los Angeles Times* editorial (March 7, 2007) prodded Japanese Emperor Akihito, the son of Emperor Hirohito (who commanded the troops in Nanking), to apologize for Japan's wartime atrocities: "The insistence by Japan's extreme nationalists that their country has 'apologized enough' for its wartime atrocities, while its politicians and ersatz historians regularly attempt to downplay or simply falsify historical fact, is supremely self-defeating.…" But, no acceptable apology has been offered and the scars from the Nanking Massacre remain.

Nanking (2008), a documentary film directed by Dan Sturman and Bill Guttentag, is dedicated to Iris Chang. It tells of many Europeans and Americans who remained in Nanking during its siege, creating a two-square-mile safety zone for thousands unable to flee. The efforts of these brave men and women saved thousands of lives. The original grainy film of the events in Nanking was smuggled to Germany and discovered in the 1980s. These grisly images—interwoven with voices of survivors and actors telling the horrors of the bombings, violence, and rape—give viewers a clear look at the uncivilized behavior Iris Chang recounts in *The Rape of Nanking*.

Chang's most recent book, *The Chinese in America* (2003), is a narrative about becoming American. Its stories of immigrants and their lives proves less emotionally charged than her previous volume and is the comprehensive story of a group of people who, over some 150 years, came to the United

States to seek a new life. The author tells of the difficulties that are part and parcel of settling in America and of early immigrants who, despite discriminatory practices and laws, built much of the infrastructure of America. She also traces the lives of later immigrant groups who were instrumental in advances in science and high technology. In addition to these accomplishments by so many groups, she tells of the Chinese, who at times even entered this country by way of smugglers in their pursuit of an uncertain future in America. And she recounts many incidents where Americans of Chinese descent have been viewed as foreigners in their own country.

A round of book signings for *The Chinese in America* brought Iris Chang to Los Angeles in 2004, where she was keynote speaker at the Chinese Historical Society of Southern California's annual banquet. Throughout the evening, she autographed and sold copies of her book, and chatted with many admirers who shared their personal stories of being Chinese American.

Her most recent research, just before her death, focused on the Bataan Death March in the Philippines during World War II. She was determined to interview as many survivors of the March as possible, being keenly aware that many were in their eighties and their experiences might remain forever untold. She would despair upon learning that another of her interviewees had passed away. Again, she wanted to write about important historical episodes and to reveal the injustices and inhumanities that had ensued. Sadly, her research came to an end abruptly, as did her life.

Family Life

Iris Chang was born in Princeton, New Jersey, in 1968 and grew up in Champaign-Urbana, Illinois. Her father was a physicist, her mother a biochemist, and both were university professors. She had one brother, Michael. As a child, she wrote poetry, and in her high school days looked for a sponsor to revive her school's literary magazine. In 1998, she was awarded the Max Beberman Distinguished

Alumni Award from University High School where she graduated in 1985. She received the Peace and International Cooperation Award from the John D. and Catherine T. MacArthur Foundation, and was named Woman of the Year by the Organization of Chinese American Women.

Iris met her husband, Brett Douglas, at the University of Illinois when she was a journalism student and he was pursuing a graduate engineering degree. Iris went on to study playwriting, poetry and fiction, and earned her master's degree in science writing at Johns Hopkins University. She worked briefly as a journalist for the Associated Press and the *Chicago Tribune* before she turned to writing books. After her marriage in 1991, she and her husband moved to California. Her son, Christopher, was born in 2002.

Her Legacy

During Iris Chang's short span of years she deeply touched her readers' lives, bringing to light injustices and atrocities that were previously ignored or unknown. The Iris Chang Memorial Essay Contest publishes some of the essays inspired by her books. Many reveal that their writers knew little or nothing of the injustices and atrocities of which Iris Chang has so eloquently written. Upon reading her books, in particular *The Rape of Nanking*, many have been inspired to learn more. She would no doubt be gratified that young essayists and social activists are so inspired and challenged by her literary works—and likewise are determined to write and fight for truth and justice.

In February, 2007, Iris Chang was honored with a bronze bust at the Hoover Institution on the campus of Stanford University. The bust is one of two donated by the China Foundation for Human Rights Development. The other is displayed at the Nanjing Massacre Museum. The busts were created to honor her for writing *The Rape of Nanking*. Iris Chang's research papers on World War II are in the permanent collection of Stanford University's Hoover Library.

References

1. Benson, Heidi. *Remember Iris.* Chinese American Forum.
2. Chang, Iris. *The Chinese in America.* New York: Penguin Group, 2003.
3. Chang, Iris. *The Rape of Nanking.* New York: Penguin Group, 1997.
4. Chang, Iris. *The Thread of the Silkworm.* New York: Basic Books, 1995.
5. De Pasquale, Sue. *Nightmare in Nanking.* Johns Hopkins Magazine. November 1997.
6. Iris Chang Honored for Her Book *The Rape of Nanking.* Chinese American Forum.
7. Koo, George. *The Iris Chang Essay Contest Perpetuates the Memory of World War II.* Chinese American Forum.
8. Matthiessen, Connie. *Chang, Interrupted. San Francisco Magazine.* March 2005.
9. Wood, Paul. *Author "really cared" for those she wrote about. The News-Gazette.com.* November 12, 2004.

(Please see next page for Addendum)

Addendum

Bringing the *Forgotten Holocaust* to the World Stage

"To forget a holocaust is to kill twice." Nobel Laureate, Elie Wiesel.

Historian and author, Iris Chang, exhibited her courage to champion for justice and truth for millions of nameless, innocent war victims. With her carefully researched and documented book, *The Rape of Nanking*, she was a one-woman Nuremberg panel who brought the world's attention to the Japanese army's atrocities in China during World War II.

The Japanese military, in the service of its Emperor, began its genocide against China in 1931 by occupying Manchuria. Over the next fourteen years, it marched across China, massacring millions of civilians and soldiers alike. Their methods of torture and brutality were beyond human comprehension, but no tribunal equivalent to the Nuremberg Trials was ever convened to expose those crimes to the world.

By contrast, the Nazis massacred about six million Jews during World War II in the "Final Solution"—the Nazi policy to murder the Jews of Europe. The Nuremberg Trials brought those atrocities to the world stage. Since then, hundreds of books and videos have portrayed the cruelty and brutality of Nazi Germany. Germany as a nation has admitted its crimes and asked for forgiveness. However, few journalists outside Asia have written about the Japanese military's atrocities in China.

How many innocent Chinese civilians and soldiers were abused, brutalized, tortured and killed over the fourteen years of Japanese aggression and occupation? In the Nanking Massacre alone, the estimates were between 300,000 to 500,000. The Chinese government did not then have the time or resources to account for the number of victims killed by the Japanese. Thus the Japanese military's killing of Chinese people became the "Forgotten Holocaust."

The Jewish holocaust and the Chinese "Forgotten Holocaust" stand together as two of history's worst atrocities against humanity. Yet, few outside of China were aware of the Nanking Massacre, until Iris Chang researched available archives, discovered the conduct of the Japanese armed forces in China, and documented it in *The Rape of Nanking*.

We do not claim the moral authority to demonize yesteryear's imperialist Japan. However, today's Japan must be reminded that redemption is only possible by redressing the atrocities committed by its predecessors against China and other countries in Asia. Iris Chang waged a campaign for justice by taking the results of her research directly to Japan and the world.

L.P. Leung
Editor-in-Chief

William Shaw

Microsurgery Pioneer
Phenomenally Gifted Surgeon & Dedicated Mentor to Young Surgeons

By Emily Shaw and Bobbi Leung

Dr. William Shaw has been cited for both microsurgery and hand surgery in Best Doctors in America (Woodward/White. 1992 and 1994). Microsurgery requires flawless technique, fine clinical judgment, endurance, and the patience to spend hours repairing a nerve or tiny blood vessel.

"Bill Shaw is an internationally renowned microsurgeon. Before his unfortunate stroke, he had amassed the largest series of microsurgical breast reconstructions in the world.... It was a tremendous privilege to work alongside him over a nine-year period. He is a phenomenally gifted surgeon, yet completely humble—a true gentleman."

~Dr. Neil Jones–UCLA Professor and
internationally famous microsurgeon

The Miracle Workers
New York University-Bellevue Hospital, June 8, 1979

A young flutist, Renee Katz, had been pushed off a New York City subway platform into the path of an oncoming train. She was alive but her left hand was severed above the wrist. A quick-thinking police officer bagged the hand and packed it in ice alongside the girl's stretcher in the ambulance. When emergency room doctors paged the staff surgeon, Dr. Bill Shaw, for a consultation, he knew it would be the last daylight he would see for a long while. He quickly phoned to check on his wife since their second child was due any moment. In the operating room, Dr. Shaw and Dr. Daniel Baker led a team of anesthesiologists, nurses, and technicians—debriding the severed part and using microscopes and miniaturized surgical instruments to carefully reconnect blood vessels, nerves, tendons and skin. They sewed together delicate blood vessels the thickness of a spaghetti strand, using sutures thinner than a baby's hair. Nurses took shifts as the doctors stayed hunched over the table through the night. Sixteen hours later, they unclamped the vessels and watched with relief and exhilaration as Renee's replanted left hand flushed pink with life. The young doctors had completed the longest operation in U.S. medical history to date. Dr. Shaw stated, "Renee may never play the flute again, but her arm will be functional."

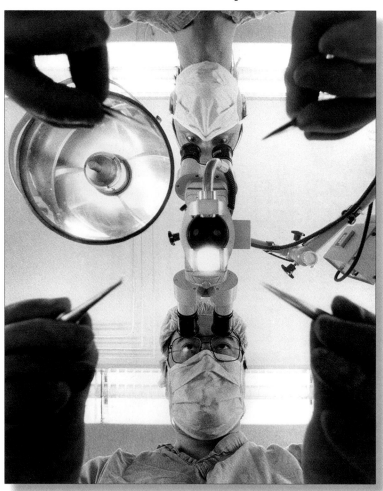

At an earlier time or a different hospital, Renee Katz would have simply been fitted with a prosthetic hand and her amputated hand discarded as biological waste. But the surgical team at New York University (NYU)-Bellevue Hospital replanted her hand. It thus joined the few hospitals in the world with a team trained in the specialty of microsurgery.

Headlines proclaimed the surgeons' pioneering achievement:

- "Doctors Restore Student's Hand Severed by Train." *New York Times*, June, 1979.
- "The Miracle Workers." *New York Post*, June 8, 1979 (photo of surgical team still in "scrubs").
- "Science-Fiction Surgery Now Reality." *Los Angeles Times*, July 11, 1979.

Replantation of Katz's hand in May, 1979, was the third replantation surgery the team performed at Bellevue that month: A policeman crushed between a runaway truck and his patrol car had his left leg replanted. The second was replantation of the severed hand of a New Jersey chemical worker. In September, both legs of lifeguard Manuel Escobar were severed above the ankle by a subway train. The resulting surgery was the first, successful *bilateral leg replantation*.

Drs. Shaw and Baker were interviewed by Walter Cronkite on his TV network news program and for feature articles in *LIFE* and other news magazines. Dr. Shaw was named an honorary member of the New York police and fire departments for the surgical miracles he performed for them.

Who was this brilliant young surgeon and what circumstances led him to this momentous time in the nascent reconstructive surgery field?

An Immigrant Background

William Shaw was born in 1942 in China. His parents, Emil and Rosemarie Shaw, were agricultural scientists, educated in the United States. They moved their family of six from Taiwan to the U.S. in 1957, where they shared a small house in Los Angeles with his aunt's family. When he was 16, his youngest brother, Willy, died from leukemia. This event may have spurred Bill's interest in medicine.

In high school, Bill and his older brother Victor worked part-time at their uncle's store, bagging groceries and stocking shelves. Bill always excelled in math and science, but his English needed work. He was determined to master this difficult language, and luckily he had a diligent English teacher who corrected every detail of his essays. Toward the end of high school, he left home and landed his first job, at a dog hospital, receiving free board for feeding and caring for the animals at night. He often studied while listening to the dogs howling.

College and Medical School

Both Bill and his older brother attended the University of California Los Angeles (UCLA). He immediately gravitated toward the hardcore sciences and astonished his professors with perfect scores in organic chemistry and physiology.

His first year of medical school was grueling. It was the first time his intellect had truly been challenged. Students were warned that their summer break would be their last one. While other students traveled during the summer, Bill and his brother worked in real estate in their neighborhood. He was successful and sold many homes. After his difficult first year, it was refreshing to interact with everyday people again. Bill was well-liked and had an open face that people trusted. In one summer, he earned enough money from sales commissions for the next semester's rent. He considered not returning to medical school but his father had taught him to "finish what you start."

Bill Shaw was the kind of obsessed medical student who remained in the anatomy lab on campus long after his fellow students had left for the night. On a visit with a friend who was attending University of California San Francisco Medical School, all he wanted to see was the cadaver his friend was studying.

After his surgical residency at UCLA, Dr. Shaw took an intensive orthopedics course at the Valley Forge Army Hospital in Pennsylvania. Between 1970 and 1972, he served as chief of orthopedics at the U.S. Army Hospital in Bangkok, Thailand. There he received critical surgery experience working with soldiers wounded in the Vietnam War. He received an honorable discharge from the Army with the rank of major and, in 1975, became a resident in plastic surgery at NYU's Institute of Reconstructive Surgery.

The Microsurgery Department at New York University-Bellevue Hospital

To some, microsurgery sounded like science fiction. Many surgeons in the Bellevue Hospital surgery department were skeptical of the relevance and practicality of the new technology. A traditional surgeon was trained to save lives: amputations on the battlefield, appendectomies, open-heart surgery, mastectomies, and the like—but not to reconnect severed body parts.

Patients with crushed and severed limbs came through New York City's hospitals with grim regularity. Dr. Shaw was aware that a few doctors around the country had reconnected a hand or foot with varying degrees of success. As a resident surgeon, he studied the procedures in use and believed that if the right tools and equipment were available, he could find a better way to replant severed body parts. He wanted to help victims that came through emergency operating rooms not only to stay alive, but to regain a higher degree of functionality and normalcy than prosthetics could offer.

Fortunately, the renowned Dr. John Marquis Converse, Chief of the Surgery Department at NYU-Bellevue, believed in the vision of Dr. Shaw and Dr. Baker. He raised funds to purchase a state-of-the-art microscope and a matching set of miniature surgery tools. Dr. Converse allotted the young surgeons time to train themselves, aside from their obligations as staff surgeons at the city's busiest public hospital. The two doctors used the new tools to practice sewing very thin blood vessels. They were the only plastic surgery residents to devote time to learning the new microscope and miniature tools.

Whenever Dr. Shaw felt overwhelmed by the pressures of a young surgeon's life, his mentor Dr. Converse lifted an eyebrow and reminded him, "Remember, Bill, the most important thing in life … is to decide what is important." Dr. Converse believed that investing in future technologies was critical to advancement of new surgical techniques, and he was glad to have a resident willing to risk his career advancement on it.

Microsurgery originally involved the reattachment or "replantation" of amputated parts such as the thumb, fingers, hands or even the ear and nose, but now refers to the transfer of skin, muscle, bone, or even toes, from part of the body to another area, to reconstruct defects due to traumatic injuries or after cancer.

– Dr. Neil Jones, UCLA

In the late 1970s, Dr. Shaw received approval to initiate NYU-Bellevue Hospital's first microsurgery and replantation program, a service with a remarkable record of achievement. When a person with a severed limb was rushed to Bellevue, the replantation team swung into action, stabilizing the patient and determining the extent of the injury. Based on the damage and the condition of the patient, plans were formulated to salvage the dismembered part or take alternative action if unexpected obstacles arose.

Some of Dr. Shaw's ideas were functional but unconventional. It seemed that by manipulating body parts—a second toe becoming a thumb—he was making a mockery of traditional surgery. It was one thing to seal off a severed leg but another to alter God's design of the human body.

Dr. Shaw's daughter, Emily, recalls:
My Dad had never been part of the establishment, and

perhaps that is why he was able to be so innovative within it. He wasn't caught up in the lifestyle of the rich and famous in New York—he was in it for the fun. He never grew up with riches, so he didn't feel like he needed to sustain that. He didn't have a vested interest in maintaining the status quo. He was grateful for the opportunity, and that there were others who sometimes recognized and got excited by his innovative ideas. He was considered a maverick. He thought differently. He was in it purely for the love and the challenge. The money was nice, but that's not why he was there.

For over ten years, Dr. Shaw honed his craft and performed many more replantation surgeries. The Microsurgery and Replantation Program was now firmly established at NYU-Bellevue Hospital but he was constantly being dragged into the internal politics of the large public hospital. After Dr. Converse's passing, the program received less internal support, and budget priorities favored less time and labor-intensive treatments. Dr. Shaw felt limited by his role at NYU both professionally and personally. He decided it was time to move on.

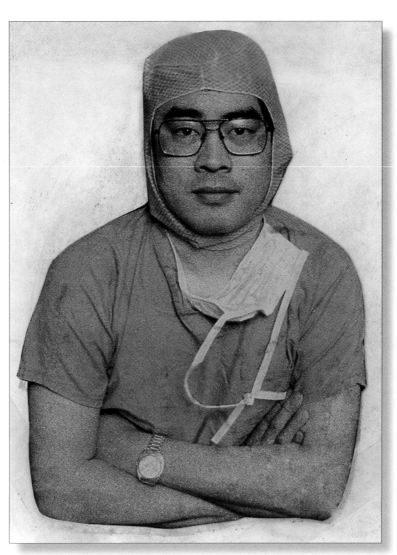

Moving To A Teaching Hospital
Why UCLA Medical School?
In 1989, UCLA School of Medicine offered Dr. Shaw the position of chief of the Plastic and Reconstructive Surgery Department. The offer made him appreciate how far he had come from his days of bagging groceries and sleeping and studying in the dog hospital. He now had many options available, including expanding his lucrative cosmetic surgery practice in New York City, where appointments were backlogged up to six months.

Teaching hospitals had approached him to lead their plastic surgery departments but he had not found an ideal fit. This time, the chance to mentor the next generation of surgeons at his alma mater and his gratitude to UCLA for giving him a full medical scholarship made him strongly consider the position. His passion for teaching, love of microsurgery, and the opportunity to advance the field sealed his decision. Moving to California was a return to his roots.

The Challenge of Leading a Department at a Top Medical School
To meet the challenges of his new position, Dr. Shaw took courses in management administration and learned how to budget and control expenditures. The familiar departmental tensions between cosmetic surgery and reconstructive surgery were still present. What made it worthwhile was his love of teaching, and collaborating with other surgeons.

Dr. Shaw immersed himself in his academic research and tutoring of medical students and residents. He inspired young surgeons to be knowledgeable and compassionate doctors. He loved to tell stories about residents who completed their training and chose to remain to learn and work with him in the hospital.

His program at UCLA rose in the national rankings and became highly sought after by medical students. In selecting students for admission to the UCLA Plastic Surgery Program, he looked at more than their academic achievements. Daughter Emily remembers:

On the Board of Admissions, Dad told me how he evaluated applicants and always identified with students who struggled without pitying themselves and how tears came to his eyes reading their essays. He sought to breed a class of compassionate, thoughtful doctors. He thought the applicants from the big schools weren't necessarily going to become the best doctors—although quality of education was important.

Dr. William Shaw was much in demand as a speaker and presenter at major medical conferences. He published over 100 technical papers in distinguished medical journals and co-authored chapters in 18 medical books and other publications.

Dr. Shaw promoted microsurgery internationally and had many international visitors. He was invited to international conferences, hospitals and universities to deliver lectures, and received numerous international honors and citations. He was proud of being designated chairman of the International Society of Reconstructive Microsurgery Congress held in Los Angeles in June, 1999.

After moving to UCLA Medical Center, Dr. Shaw focused on refining microsurgical techniques to reconstruct women's breasts after mastectomy, using the *free flap* technique. He also performed cosmetic surgeries such as facelifts, breast augmentations, liposuction, and other procedures, to help "pay the bills."

What is Free-Flap Reconstructive Surgery?

A flap is a piece of tissue transplanted from one site to another. It contains skin, blood vessels, tissues, muscle, fat, and fascia. The procedure to transplant a flap varies in complexity. Flaps are used to cover an area in need of tissue which is removed from a less critical area. They are used to reconstruct structures such as a breast or nose.

In 2003, Dr. Shaw suffered a stroke, cutting short his illustrious career. The outpouring of affection was startling. Many of his former residents stopped by the hospital and his home to show their respect and review his care.

Notable Wisdom from Dr. Shaw

On Life: *The most important thing is to feel that you have accomplished something. When you do, you feel alive and vital. It is wonderful.*

On Adversity: *I think part of the fun in life is overcoming problems. There is no way to grow without some pain and anxiety.*

On Success: *Whether in business, science, or surgery, success in general requires three basic elements: vision, knowledge and skill, and hard work. You dedicate your life to being productive, and have a good time.*

On Prejudice: *It forces you to work harder. And once people notice you, they remember you. You just have to overcome that initial barrier.*

(Co-Author Emily Shaw is the daughter of Dr. William Shaw)

Judge Delbert Wong 黃錦紹

World War II Hero and Exemplary Jurist

By Randy Bloch

> • Delbert Wong received the Distinguished Flying Cross for his service in the U.S. Army Air Force in World War II.
>
> • Judge Wong was appointed to the Los Angeles Municipal Court in 1959 by California Governor Pat Brown, making him the first Chinese American named to the judiciary in the continental United States.
>
> • In his twenty-three years on the judicial bench, he was a trailblazer for future Chinese-American legal professionals.

World War II Military Hero

After graduating from UC Berkeley in May of 1942, Delbert Wong joined the war effort by enlisting in the U.S. Army Air Force. At Mather Field in Sacramento, he was trained as a flight navigator and assigned to a crew on a B-17 Flying Fortress, a big, slow, low-flying bomber. After his transfer to Fort George Wright in Washington State, where he was the only Asian American of 360 aviation officers, the Fortress was sent to England, and Delbert began flying bombing missions over Germany, Nazi-occupied France, Holland, Belgium and Austria.

For his heroic service, First Lieutenant Delbert E. Wong was awarded the Distinguished Flying Cross. He was one of three navigators—of eighteen in his training class—to complete thirty bombing missions over Europe.

Remarked First Lieutenant Fred Gong, a distinguished lead bombardier who was also awarded the Distinguished Flying Cross: "Delbert Wong was a real hero. He had to fly without fighter escorts. It is hard to believe he survived thirty combat missions!"

© Jason Jem

Delbert completed his thirtieth mission in June of 1944. He was granted leave to accompany his mother to visit his brother, Ervin, who was completing radio operator training before his transfer overseas. The family briefly met Ervin, and then bid him farewell. Tragically, upon returning home they learned that Ervin and his entire crew had perished in an accident on one of their final training flights. The loss of Delbert's brother on American soil was a severe blow to the family: Earl and Alice Wong, still in their forties, had now lost three of their four children.

In 1945, the Air Corps sent Delbert to the Harvard School of Business for statistical officer training. He served in that capacity at a Southern California air base for the war's duration. Delbert became friendly with the base's chief legal officer who encouraged him to consider a law career upon return to civilian life.

Delbert and his family had assumed he would eventually help manage their grocery business, but that prospect now seemed less than fulfilling. His options finally boiled down to: "… joining my family's grocery business or entering law school." His family did not support his choice of a legal career and asked him, "Who would hire you, a Chinese?" But, he was undeterred, and entered the Stanford University Law School.

Just before his final quarter of law school, Delbert married Dolores Wing, a native of Vallejo, California, working in New Orleans as a psychiatric social worker. The couple met as undergraduates at UC Berkeley. Delbert would later say his second-best decision was attending law school and the first was marrying wife Dolores.

A Long and Distinguished Career as a Jurist

Years later, discussing his job prospects upon graduating from law school in 1948, Delbert recalled: "Civil service was the only available avenue for (Chinese) people interested in law." While his classmates clerked for law firms during summer break, this opportunity was not open to him. On summer break, after his first year of law school, Delbert worked at the District Attorney's office in his home town of Bakersfield.

After graduating and passing the Bar exam, Delbert took a junior counsel position in the Office of the Legislative Counsel (OLC) in Sacramento. He drew the assignment when Governor Earl Warren requested that a revised loyalty oath for public employees be drafted. He also helped draft the California Public Utilities Code, Health and Safety Code, and Business and Professions Code. When his request for a transfer to OLC's Los Angeles office was approved, in 1951, the city became the Delbert Wong family's permanent home. He was just the second Chinese-American lawyer in Southern California.

Delbert passed a promotional exam and accepted a deputy attorney general position under California Attorney General Edmund G. "Pat" Brown. In an important State Election Code case, Delbert successfully argued that the requirement a minority political party have at least one percent of the state's voters in order to appear on the ballot was fair.

When Attorney General Pat Brown ran for governor of California in 1958, Delbert helped deliver the Los Angeles Chinatown business community's vote by co-organizing the *Chinese American Committee to Elect "Pat" Brown*, and a fundraising luncheon. The function was a watershed event for California politics as it was the first time Chinese Americans had campaigned for a candidate statewide.

Pat Brown won the November election by a wide margin. In his second week in office, Governor Brown appointed Delbert Wong a Los Angeles Municipal Court judge. An editorial in the *Los Angeles Examiner* praised the appointment: "The recognition also constitutes a tribute to the democratic process we cherish, because it moves to reward personal merit." The wire services picked up the story and congratulatory calls poured in from across the nation. On January 31, 1959, Delbert E. Wong was sworn in as a Municipal Court judge at the State Building in downtown Los Angeles.

As a new Municipal Court Judge, Wong assessed his role as a jurist, realizing he could neither play social worker nor advocate public policy. He realized if he was known as too severe in sentencing, defendants might plead not guilty in hopes of leniency at trial, further overwhelming the backlogged judicial system.

Governor Brown elevated Judge Wong to the Los Angeles Superior Court in November of 1961.

The definition of obscenity was being carefully re-examined and scrutinized during that period. On numerous occasions, Judge Wong was required to apply the imprecise "community standards" test to determine whether printed material and movies were obscene—or legally protected speech.

Judge Wong heard the case of *People v. Briggs*, 60 Cal.2d 862 (1964), where a standard for admissibility of certain witness statements was tested under a law he disagreed with but was bound to follow. When the law was challenged, the state Supreme Court overturned it, citing reasoning Judge Wong had articulated at the trial level.

Aetna Casualty v. Underwriters at Lloyds of London, 56 Cal.App.3d 791 (1976), was a 1969 oil spill case Judge Wong handled that attracted worldwide attention. Union Oil Company's primary insurance carrier was Aetna Casualty and Surety Company. When Aetna met its liability obligation, its two surplus carriers disavowed any financial responsibility. He devised a formula assigning proportionate responsibility to the surplus carriers, and while both appealed, the state Court of Appeal affirmed his decision which has stood unchallenged in California.

Judge Wong was appointed to the Superior Court Appellate Division in 1968, where he heard appeals from municipal court decisions. Important cases relating to political speech were being decided at that time. One, which Delbert was most proud of, was *People v. Cohen*, 81 Cal.Rptr.503 (Cal.App., 1969). On appeal was the defendant's disturbing the peace conviction for wearing a jacket containing an anti-draft epithet in a Los Angeles courtroom hallway. A panel comprised of Delbert and two other appellate judges reversed the defendant's Municipal Court conviction. Though the state Court of Appeal reinstated the conviction, the United States Supreme Court later affirmed the ruling of Delbert and his associate justices—vacating the original conviction. This landmark freedom of speech case is still taught in constitutional law classes.

Judge Wong retired from the Superior Court on June 30, 1982. He was the senior judge on the 223-judge court,

having served continuously since November of 1961. His fellow jurists honored him with a luncheon at the Los Angeles Music Center that was attended by over two hundred people.

An Independent Referee of Unquestionable Integrity

Delbert Wong's impeccable reputation while a sitting jurist placed him in great demand as an independent referee after he retired. Many of his assignments dealt with civil rights, racial issues, and ethics in government. He also played important roles in local government committees and commissions.

In 1986, the Los Angeles Airport Department retained him to investigate racial discrimination allegations in its Airport Police Bureau. The Department followed his recommendations to revise its promotional practices and implement human relations workshops. In 1987, he was appointed chairperson of the Asian Pacific American Focus Program to address violence against Asian Americans. In 1989, in the wake of allegations of city officials accepting gifts and free travel, L.A. Mayor Tom Bradley appointed Judge Wong to a commission to draft Los Angeles' first ethics code which was later adopted by the voters.

Civic Participation and Community Service

Judge Delbert Wong was deeply involved in community life across the diverse communities of Los Angeles, and in working to build a just and fair society. He strongly supported Los Angeles' Asian Pacific American Legal Center. He and his wife, Dolores, have been ardent supporters of the Chinese Historical Society of Southern California—and civil rights and service organizations such as the Chinese American Citizens Alliance and the Chinatown Service Center. Judge Wong was active in the National Conference of Christians and Jews, participated in the Boy Scouts of America, and supported the Optimists Boys Home. Delbert and Dolores Wong also served on the Board of Governors of the East

West Players theater group. Mrs. Wong is a charter member of the Friends of the Chinatown Library and was its vice-president when it was incorporated in 1977.

Judge Wong received the Cal State L.A. Pat Brown Institute's *Lifetime Community Service Award* in 1996. In 2002, Judge and Mrs. Wong received the Chinese American Museum's prestigious Historymakers Award as outstanding proponents of volunteerism, education and literacy, and as supporters of the Chinatown Public Library. In 2006, the Greater Los Angeles Chapter of the Organization of Chinese Americans presented its Community Achievement Award to Judge Delbert Wong (posthumously) and Dolores Wong.

Family Roots and Early History

Delbert Wong was born in the central California town of Hanford on May 17, 1920. His parents, Earl and Alice, soon moved the family to Bakersfield, an agricultural and oil town, two hours north of Los Angeles. The couple had three more children but only Delbert and his brother, Ervin, survived infancy.

The Wongs lived about seven blocks from Bakersfield's Chinatown in an ethnically mixed, working-class neighborhood. Earl and a partner opened a modern grocery store, the Lincoln Market, which gave the family stability

and a measure of financial security. Despite the Depression, the family grocery business prospered. His father's generosity to his customers during the Depression made a deep impression on Delbert.

Delbert learned of the discrimination suffered by his parents and other Chinese American pioneers. Alice, his mother, was a U.S. citizen by birth but lost her citizenship because her husband was born in China and considered to be an alien. Years later, when the law was changed, she studied the U.S. Constitution and applied to become a naturalized citizen. Delbert's own childhood in Bakersfield was marked by ethnic and race-based restrictions, such as the rule that Chinese and other minorities were only allowed to use the city's public swimming pool on certain days of the week.

Earl and Alice Wong greatly valued education for their sons but could not help with its practical requirements, such as homework. Most of their relatives had limited formal education. Despite these barriers, Delbert excelled as a student, and his high school counselors urged him to attend college. After graduating high school, Delbert fulfilled his general education requirements at Bakersfield Junior College and transferred to the University of California at Berkeley where he earned a degree in business. In December, 1941, the news came that Japan had bombed Pearl Harbor. He graduated from

UC Berkeley the following May, and in June, enlisted in the Army Air Corps with his brother Ervin.

Marshall Wong is Judge Delbert Wong's biographer and his youngest son. He was asked by the editor of *Portraits of Pride* how his father's life influenced him. Marshall replied:

He inspires me daily. In some ways, even more so since his passing. He was an outstanding father: loving, devoted, patient, supportive, and fair. He encouraged his children to not only value education and family, but also to serve the larger community. He taught us about the hardships faced by my grandparents' generation and his own experiences with racial discrimination in the armed forces, public accommodations, employment and housing. Not to make us bitter or resentful, but to make us more compassionate and committed to social justice. I learned from his example what it means to be an exceptional son, husband, friend, jurist, and community leader. And I learned from personal attributes, such as his practicality, generosity, even-temperedness, and sense of humor about how to live a balanced, healthy, and happy life.

Over the course of his career, Judge Wong witnessed changes in the legal profession unimaginable to him when he was appointed to the Municipal Court in 1959. When he attended Stanford Law School in the late 1940s, ninety-five percent of the student body was male—by century's end, over half of U.S. law students were female. Perhaps most remarkably, in one generation, his family had gone from escaping the poverty of Southern China's Guangdong Province to producing the first judge in the United States of America of Chinese ancestry.

References

1. Delbert Wong: Trailblazer. Pi Alpha Phi National Fraternity. Generations. (Spring 2006).
2. Delbert E. Wong. Wikipedia. http://en.wikipedia.org/wiki/Delbert_E._Wong
3. Jason Jem. Chinese American Pioneers in Law, Judge Delbert Wong. Chinese Historical Society of Southern California. (2005). http://www.chssc.org/honorees/2005/2005honorees.html
4. Marshall Wong. Delbert Wong, First Chinese American Judge. Chinese Historical Society of Southern California. (2004). Gum Saan Journal Special Edition 2004.

Andrew Chi

A Forgotten Hero, Atomic Clock Pioneer

By Edgar Wong and Frank Bupp

Dr. Andrew Chi, the NASA Goddard Space Center's 1978 Schneebaum Award recipient, is a forgotten man. A search of his name on the Internet turns up little information other than that he died suddenly in 1982.

Dr. Chi was a pioneer in the atomic clock era that led to today's *Global Positioning System* timekeeping clocks. Fortunately, Dr. Charlie Xie, a member of the Chinese-American Committee of 100, mentioned Dr. Chi in his reply to a letter from President Bill Clinton, inquiring about Chinese-Americans' contributions to America and the world.

We believe there may be many Chinese-American scientists like Dr. Andrew Chi who labored anonymously and made lasting contributions to their adopted country with little or no recognition.

The Editors of Portraits of Pride II thank Edgar Wong and Frank Bupp for their scenario, "Andrew Chi: The Movie." The circumstantial stories may be fictional but the scientific facts are indisputable. We hope this story might bring a smile to Dr. Chi, and perhaps a nod of satisfaction.

Andrew Chi: The Movie

The *Lone Ranger* was a famous radio and television hero of years gone by. In the stories, the masked man's true identity was little-known, except for the silver bullets he left behind. In our movie, the same can be said for our hero, Andrew Chi. He too is a near unknown, except for the marvelous cesium (a silvery-metallic element) clocks that are his legacy.

Return with us now to those thrilling days of yesteryear, when the Lone Ranger's silver bullets were followed, in a fashion, by Andrew Chi's silver clocks. Our Historical Society's movie production of Andrew Chi has six scenes, complete with period costumes and background sets.

Scene 1: Chinese Time (ca. 1930s)

The first "villain" Andy encountered in his young life was "Chinese Time." This was in a Chinatown restaurant where he was with his parents, celebrating his uncle's wedding at the six

An early atomic clock. © Corbis/Bettman

o'clock hour printed on the formal invitation. He was uncomfortable in his starched shirt, but it was pointless to ask for his father's permission to unbutton his collar because of his stern, "one-way" communication style. One hour later, most of the important guests had finally arrived.

They were not really late. On the contrary, they were quite fashionable: they were observing "Chinese Time." After long speeches and toasts, food was served at eight o'clock. For all his squirming, Andy had begun learning about the practice—and perception—of time.

Not so long ago, Chinese event-scheduling made a generous allowance for the always-late crowd. Such loose scheduling is still practiced widely in parts of Asia. Leisurely paced events were common in the United States when the weekend was just Saturday night. With at most one social gathering per week, most folks observed a lazy pace at organized events for the joy of an extended visit, eating, and get-togethers with their families and friends.

But this age-old custom was not to last. After World War II, most Chinese in the U.S. practiced "American Time." This came with the onset of the three-day weekend that included many activities and, concurrently, socialization beyond their own ethnic community. The Chi family was Americanized into the fast-paced, eat and run style of socializing.

Now, and even back in those early years, the perception of time was different for youngsters ("Are we there yet?") and oldsters ("How time flies!"). For little Andy, time was relatively longer because an hour was a far bigger fraction of his young life. On the other hand, Einstein said of "relativity" time that sitting next to a pretty girl for an hour feels like a minute and placing one's hand on a hot stove for a minute feels like an hour.

Scene 2: Arrival Time (ca. 1940s)

In grade school, young Andrew eagerly studied the five senses: sight, touch, hearing, taste and smell. Technically oriented, he was intrigued that in a thunderstorm, three of our senses work overtime when we see lightning flash, feel the ground rumble and hear the clap of thunder.

When Andrew experienced lightning, he counted the number of seconds between what he saw and what he heard, and estimated its distance from the rule: "One mile for every five-second delay." Andrew asked schoolmates who lived on the other side of the tracks what they observed; from these results they "triangulated" the probable location of the lightning. These were smart kids who didn't need an Xbox for mental stimulation!

Although he was only in grade school, Andrew wondered if he could use the arrival time of light, say from reflecting a flashlight beam up the block and back, to determine the distance. Of course, the answer is yes (theoretically) and no (practically); light travels so far in just one tick of a clock that Andrew was faced with dividing that tick into billions of smaller ticks, just for a rough estimate of the distance. Even his track coach's stopwatch—which ticked ten times a second—was far from fine enough to time light over city distances.

Andrew was well acquainted with watches. He was timed by fast-ticking stop watches in intramural track meets. Though not fast enough to make the varsity squad, he qualified for the B team. He tried half-heartedly to best other runners but tried constantly to beat the clock.

Scene 3: Space Time (ca. 1950s)

Now a college graduate, Andrew Chi—along with millions of other people—heard the "beep-beep-beep" of Russia's Sputnik spacecraft. This artificial moon circled the globe every 96 minutes on an earth orbit—hence the space term, "on-orbit."

Navigators know that an earth observer's location—or the on-orbit position of the Sputnik—is known if one knows the time of day (which is just rudimentary navigation). The distance of Sputnik is known if one can measure the travel time of signals from the satellite to earth. From scientific papers by others, Andrew Chi knew that super-fast timers were achievable through atomic-level timing; only they provided the precision necessary in the new age of space travel.

Andrew Chi had studied the papers on C. S. Wu's work on parity. Of course, he reasoned, both conservation and nonconservation of parity exist in nature. As an avid ping pong player, he told his colleagues that the simplest analogy is the ping pong paddle. One can hold the paddle in two ways: (1) horizontally, like holding a racket in tennis or (2) vertically, like holding the pole in pole dancing. Depending on the location of the oncoming ping pong ball, in the first case, the paddle flips over (viewed as asymmetrical) and in the second, the paddle remains vertical (viewed as symmetrical). Dr. Wu proved that parity in nature could switch at the atomic level and low temperatures. These findings increased Andrew Chi's confidence in atomic clocks.

After the beeps of Sputnik, his opportunity to fulfill his passion for clocks came when President Eisenhower formed the National Aeronautics and Space Administration (NASA) in the Space Race between the United States and the Soviet

Union. Chi was at center stage as he and his precision clocks became vital in the Space Age. The demand for precision timing is even greater in today's Information Age.

Scene 4: Atomic Time (ca. 1960s)

Conceptually, Andrew Chi knew that a worldwide navigational system—using artificial satellites for signaling—was feasible if accurate clocks could be made spaceworthy, i.e., small, rugged, and reliable. With the NASA team, Dr. Chi observed that the single line (frequency) radiation from cesium was invariant: it didn't matter what the temperature was, or what chemical and mechanical forces were applied—the "tick-tock" of cesium remained invariant. Dr. Chi determined that despite the conditions, cesium always "vibrates" at exactly 9,192,631,770 ticks per second and was thus the perfect time source for a precision clock.

So it was that Dr. Chi's curiosity and rigorous research led to the cesium second as the new standard for international timekeeping. That was in 1967 when the cesium second replaced the astronomical second, which for centuries had been based on the earth's rotation and its annual trip around the sun.

To keep pace with the true astronomical year, adding a "leap second" to the official time clocks is needed about every 18 months (on a June 30th or a December 31st). Solar calendar users are familiar with adding one extra day—February 29th—in a "leap year." Users of the lesser-known lunar calendar are familiar with adding a "leap month" every few years, with 7 lunar months added in a 19-year solar cycle. The Chinese lunar calendar is an example: it added a leap month 7 in 2006, and adds a leap month 5 in 2009 and a leap month 4 in 2012.

Thus, regardless of the timekeeping method, "leap time" adjustments are necessary to keep annual events—like spring planting and fall foliage—in synchronization with the four seasons. By analogy, adjusting clocks and calendars is like managing multiple checking accounts—with larger additions made to the more active accounts—to stay solvent. Pennies and seconds do count.

Currently, cesium clocks are carried aboard a fleet of over 30 Global Positioning System satellites with the clocks perfectly synchronized with the National Institute of Standards and Technology (NIST) clock in Colorado. Termed NIST F-1, the clocks are accurate to one second in 20 million years. Though called atomic clocks, they are not radioactive because they operate on the resonant frequency property of cesium and not on atomic decay.

The United States Air Force's GPS constellation is deployed so that a receiver can "see" a minimum of six satellites—typically 12—from anywhere on, and above, the earth. A minimum of three satellites is needed for navigational triangulation, but more than three allows greater location accuracy. With a GPS receiver, users receive free "one-way" downloads of atomic clock time and navigation signals. Also, the time readout on our computers is synchronized with NIST time. When you buy something, your sales slip gets an NIST-based time stamp. Next time, think: "Chi Time."

Before GPS, the envisioned NASA Tracking and Data Relay Satellite System was to use a "two-way" round-trip ranging and communication between NASA's first-generation on-orbit satellites. If we were to buy a GPS receiver that relied on the old two-way communications, it would be expensive because these receivers would need to have atomic clock hardware and signal processing software. Apart from being pricey, they would also be big and heavy. It is profound to note that little Andy's father's "one-way" communication method is superior, sometimes.

Scene 5: Quitting Time (ca. 1970s)

It was Monday afternoon at an "all hands" meeting for NASA employees, invited guests, and important dignitaries; Dr. Andrew R. Chi was to receive the prestigious Schneebaum Award for advancing the use of space systems through his creative engineering. He had been instrumental in the establishment of international standards for frequency stability of electronic oscillators—the "heart" of precision timekeeping.

Dr. Chi was comfortable in his starched lab coat at NASA, but as an award recipient, was uncomfortable in his suit and tie (buttoned and starched shirt, and squirming time again). The Schneebaum Award presenters praised Andrew Chi for his contributions and their introductory speeches lasted beyond the allotted presentation time.

After the last introduction, Andrew noticed only a few seconds remained before the 4:30 p.m. scheduled ending. At the podium, he put away his notes, expressed his gratitude, and announced that it was almost quitting time and time to head home. The audience applauded his receiving the award and probably appreciated his short acceptance speech. Now, we wish he said more.

We suspect Andrew Chi would be "ticked" by the following postscript:

Dr. Chi was in a rush to attend a 6:00 p.m. meeting of the Chinese Chess Club at a Chinatown restaurant. The Club met monthly to discuss the feasibility of writing a computer program for chess moves and countermoves. The American chessboard has eight rows and eight columns and there are six chess pieces. Chinese chess has an extra row down the middle and an extra piece called the elephant. Mathematically, the possibilities of solutions are immense. Dr. Chi left this task unfinished.

Scene 6: Epilogue (ca. 1980s)

At NASA, Dr. Chi's Schneebaum Award Recipient listing is: "Andrew Chi (deceased)." On the Internet, we saw a one-sentence obituary indicating that he died in 1982. This last scene must remain unwritten until we can go back in time for an interview.

Today, the legacy of Andrew Chi's work lives on but, sadly, his life story continues untold. We bet that Andrew Chi would say that this movie script outline is "Nuff said."

Authors' Notes

1. Dr. Chien-Shiung Wu pioneered numerous experiments of relevance to the cesium clock. Her award-winning work on the nonconservation of parity is found elsewhere in this Portraits of Pride volume.

2. Jeffrey S. Wong provided the GPS information. He works at the Aerospace Corporation, Space and Missile Systems Center GPS Support, in Colorado Springs, Colorado.

Terence Tao

Mozart of Mathematics

By Randy Bloch

- In 2006, Terence Tao received the world's highest award for mathematics, the Fields Medal, and the MacArthur "Genius Grant" in the space of a month.

- Says John Garnett, former UCLA mathematics chair, "Terry is like Mozart, mathematics just flows out of him . . . he's an incredible talent, and probably the best mathematician in the world right now."

- Dr. Tao is considered the foremost living expert on prime numbers—those whole numbers evenly divisible only by one and themselves.

- In 1999, at age 24, he became a fully tenured UCLA professor of mathematics.

Dr. Terence Tao, who became a fully tenured UCLA mathematics professor at age 24, outdid himself in 2006 by winning the Fields Medal—the world's highest award for mathematics—and the MacArthur "Genius Grant," in the space of a month.

The Fields Medal is the equivalent of math's Nobel Prize. In conferring the honor on Dr. Tao, the International Congress of Mathematicians said this about his selection:

Terence Tao is a supreme problem-solver whose spectacular work has had an impact across several mathematical areas. He combines sheer technical power, an other-worldly ingenuity for hitting upon new ideas, and a startlingly natural point of view that leaves other mathematicians wondering, "Why didn't anyone see that before."

Reed Hutchinson • UCLA

Dr. Tony Chan, Dean of UCLA's Division of Physical Sciences, said he was not surprised by Dr. Tao's selection for the medal, adding: "The best students in the world in number theory all want to study with Terry."

John Garnett, former UCLA mathematics chair, has compared Dr. Tao's abilities to classical music composer Wolfgang Amadeus Mozart: "Terry is like Mozart, mathematics just flows out of him.... He's an incredible talent, and probably the best mathematician in the world right now."

How did the 31-year-old Dr. Tao achieve his doctorate degree at age 20 and a full professorship at UCLA at 24?

A Prodigy Whose Gifts Were Carefully Nurtured

Dr. Terence Tao was born in Adelaide, Australia, in 1975. His father, Billy, is a pediatrician, and Grace, his mother, was formerly a mathematics teacher. Both are first-generation immigrants from Hong Kong.

Terence's mother and father say they encouraged each of their three talented sons to follow his passion. His father tells how two-year-old Terry taught older children to count, using toy blocks, and adds, "He probably was learning those things from watching *Sesame Street*."

Young Terence demonstrated mature and formidable math abilities at an early age. At age eight, he scored 760 on the math portion of the Scholastic Aptitude Test (SAT) and, at twelve, won a gold medal in the International Mathematical Olympiads. Rather than confine him to a restrictive private school environment at a young age, his parents enrolled highly gifted Terry in public school, where they helped his teachers and administrators individualize a program for him. At age 7, Terry began high school-level math classes and his father arranged for math professors to mentor him.

Dr. Billy Tao took care not to push Terence into college too early, knowing the trajectories of some child prodigies who eventually fade into obscurity. "I initially thought Terry would be just like one of them, and graduate as early as possible," Billy Tao said. After talking to experts on education for gifted children, he changed his mind: "To get a degree at a young age, to be a record-breaker, means nothing. All along, we tended to emphasize the joy of learning," his father said. "The fun is doing something, not winning something."

From Adelaide, Australia, to the U.S., Princeton University, and UCLA

14-year-old Terence enrolled at Flinders University in Adelaide, earning his master's degree at age 17. It was then on to the United States and Princeton University where he received his doctorate in 1996, at age 21. At Princeton, he finally felt he fit among a group of peers.

Shortly after receiving his doctorate, Terence Tao accepted a professorship at UCLA and, at the age of 24, became a fully tenured professor of mathematics.

He also added many of math's highest honors to his list of accomplishments, such as the Packard Foundation Fellowship Award in 1999, the Clay Research Award in 2003, the International Mathematical Society's Levi L. Conant Prize in 2005, and the aforementioned Fields Medal.

In 2006, at age 31, Dr. Terence Tao had evolved from a childhood prodigy with great promise to arguably the world's greatest mathematician.

Specialization and Research

Much of Dr. Tao's research is conducted in fields of mathematics considered unknowable and somewhat mysterious by the average person. Some of these are *partial differential equations, combinatorics, harmonic analysis* and *additive number theory*—the realm of pure theoretical mathematics.

Dr. Tao is probably the foremost expert in the world today on prime numbers—those whole numbers evenly divisible only by one and themselves. One of his quests is to reprove the theorem set forth by Greek mathematician Euclid 2000 years ago that "there are infinitely many prime numbers," and to prove the conjecture that this applies also to what are known as "twin primes." Advances in study of prime numbers have significant implications for computer, credit card and Internet security. Dr. Tao's research in compressed sensing could change how digital cameras use sensors to compress an image's data, using less computer power.

Discussing the practical value of theoretical mathematics to society, Dr. Tao said: "Mathematicians often work on pure problems that do not have any applications for 20 years … [but], when Einstein developed his theory of relativity, he needed a theory of curved space. Einstein found that a mathematician devised exactly the theory he needed more than 30 years earlier."

He shares some of his insights into his approach to unraveling the thorniest mathematics problems: "Once you have a strategy, a very complicated problem can split up into a lot of mini-problems. I've never really been satisfied with just solving the problem. I want to see what happens if I make some changes; will it still work? If you experiment enough, you get a deeper understanding."

Dr. Tao shares updates on his current research while encouraging high-level interplay with his peers and students on his Internet blog titled, *What's new. Updates on my research and expository papers, discussion of open problems, and other maths-related topics.* This allows mathematicians from around the world—many his academic peers and co-researchers—to learn, interact and offer perspectives through posting comments and feedback.

Looking Ahead: Future and Family

Dr. Terence Tao has been praised for his natural approach to mathematical theory. He addressed this in this excerpt from his 2006 Fields Medal award interview in Madrid:

How did you get interested in mathematics?

I think the most important thing for developing an interest in mathematics is to have the ability and the freedom to play with mathematics—to set little challenges for oneself, to devise little games, and so on.

How do you look for new problems to work with?

I pick up a lot of problems (and collaborators) by talking to other mathematicians. I was perhaps lucky that my original field, harmonic analysis, has so many connections and applications to other areas of mathematics.... Sometimes I can stumble across an interesting problem by systematically surveying a certain field and then discovering a gap in the literature.

What would you say the relationship is between mathematics and the general public? How should it be ideally?

It probably varies quite a bit from country to country. In the United States, there seems to be a vague consensus among the public that mathematics is somehow "important" for various high-technology industries, but is also "hard," and best left to experts. So there is support for funding mathematical research, but not much interest in finding out exactly what it is that mathematicians do.... I'd like to see mathematics demystified more, and to be made more accessible to the public.

He hopes to teach more non-mathematicians how to think mathematically—a skill that would be useful in everyday tasks like comparing mortgages.

Dr. Tao's wife, Laura Kim, is an engineer at the Jet Propulsion Laboratory in Pasadena, California and they have a four-year-old son, William, who Terence must now consider how to teach math.

Recently, he turned evening snack time into an opportunity to ask his son, "If there are ten cookies, how many does each of the five people in the living room get?" William asked his father to tell him. "I don't know how many," Tao replied. "You tell me." With a little more prodding, William divided the cookies into five stacks of two each.

References

1. Chang, Kenneth. (2007, March 13). Journeys to the Distant Fields of Prime. International Herald Tribune.
2. Ede, Charisse. (2006, August 22). Australian Wins Highest Maths Prize.
3. Gordon, Larry (2006, August 23). UCLA Math Professor Receives Fields Medal. http://www.latimes.com.
4. Interview with Terence Tao. (2006, August 22). News of International Congress of Mathematicians/Madrid 2006, Bulletin No. 9.
5. Mathematics. Wikipedia, The Free Encyclopedia. Peterson.
6. Maugh II, Thomas H. (2006, September 19). Mathematician is Chosen for "Genius" Grant. http://www.latimes.com.
7. Terence Tao. Wikipedia, The Free Encyclopedia. http://en.wikipedia.org/wiki/Terence_Tao
8. University of California at Los Angeles. (2006, August 22). Terence Tao, "Mozart of Math," is UCLA's First Mathematician Awarded the "Nobel Prize in Mathematics." http://www.physorg.com.

Yum-Tong Siu

Internationally Acclaimed Mathematician

By L.P. Leung

"Mathematics is the science of order, and mathematicians seek to identify instances of order and to formulate and understand concepts that enable us to perceive order in complicated situations."

~Harvard University Faculty of Arts
and Sciences student handbook.

Yum-Tong Siu, PhD, of Harvard University is one of mathematics' most internationally acclaimed researchers. His contributions speak volumes to the breadth of his devotion to the mathematics field and its development.

Professor Siu's intellect and abilities have been recognized internationally by visiting professorship requests from France, Germany, Spain, Hong Kong, China. Japan, and major universities in the United States.

Dr. Siu has given three invitational addresses at the International Congress of Mathematicians (ICM). One was a 45-minute presentation at Helsinki (1978). The other two were prestigious plenary addresses (Warsaw 1983 and Beijing 2002). Only the world's foremost mathematicians—those who have made important contributions to the forefront of mathematical research, usually in the four years preceding the Congress— are ever selected to deliver an ICM plenary address. One of mathematics' most coveted honors, it rarely occurs more than once in a mathematician's lifetime. The International Congress of Mathematicians meets once every four years and is the most prestigious body of mathematicians in the world.

Courtesy of Sau Fong Siu

Professor Siu's Overall View of Mathematics

On Being a Mathematician: *At parties, when you mention that you are a mathematician, people usually look awestruck and mumble, 'I was never good at it' or 'I cannot even balance my check book' and then try to change the subject or walk away on the pretext of getting their glass refilled.*

The kind of mathematics the man in the street finds useful is not the kind that present day professional mathematicians do.

The Universality and Appeal of Mathematics: *Mathematics is universal both in terms of space and time. It transcends national boundaries and language barriers. Like music, the language of mathematics is a universal language. Whereas theories in experimental sciences may have to be modified or discarded in the light of new discoveries, mathematics which is valid now is going to be valid in the indefinite future.*

... mathematics is driven by the desire to understand the structural beauty of quantity and space and for this reason it is akin to poetry, music and the fine arts.

Mathematics Research and Applications: *Research in pure mathematics is guided by intellectual curiosity and aesthetic reasons with no specific application in mind. In many cases people in other areas later find applications for the results. One beautiful example is the use of differential geometry by Einstein in formulating his theory of general relativity.*

Many mathematicians … feel that a true and deep understanding of the structure concerning quantity and space will eventually lead to useful applications that promise the material well-being and comfort of mankind.

The research of mathematics requires practically no special equipment…. In terms of return for the investment, financially supporting mathematical research is without doubt a very good bargain.

Mathematics is a field of fundamental research. It investigates structures to provide the tools and models for use in scientific investigations. As the physicist Dirac puts it so well, 'God used beautiful mathematics in creating the world.' Usually the research of a mathematician is several layers removed from the kind of applications we encounter in daily life. The chain of applications goes from mathematics to basic sciences, to applied sciences, to engineering, and finally to products which affect our daily life. Alternative pathways of the chain go through statistics and biomedical sciences or social sciences, and also go through encryption and coding and communication. Other pathways go through financial mathematics to investment vehicles in financial markets.

Within mathematics, research in any one subfield involves more and more techniques and methods of all the other subfields. Scientific investigations are also getting more and more interdisciplinary. An individual researcher's work adds more pieces to the global puzzle which is being put together for us to understand more about the universe we live in. When I carry out my own research, I push forward as much as possible my understanding of known mathematics structures and relations and the discovery of new ones. Like other mathematical researchers I think that a good understanding of mathematics structures and

relations will be useful in the future. There may be a long time lag for applications to come along. Because of the time lag it is very rare for a mathematical researcher to see all the applications of the fruit of his or her labor. Very likely the applications may be something which we can neither expect nor foresee.

About Computers and the Future of Mathematics: *The computer can only help with the computation of examples or the verification of a finite number of cases but cannot help with the development of the mathematical theories themselves.*

The availability of power computer programs that directly manipulate formulas instead of computing numerical values relieves us of tedious routine calculations. The widespread use of such computer programs in the future will profoundly affect mathematical calculation and emphasis will be shifted away from drilling in routine calculations to better calculations in better conceptual mathematical understanding. Such a shift, I believe, would be most welcome by educators and students alike.

Accomplishments in Mathematical Research

For a quarter century, Professor Siu has been the dominant figure in the field of *several complex variables*, which is a subfield of analysis. He has made a broad range of fundamental contributions to several complex variables, *complex algebraic geometry*, and *complex differential geometry*.

Several Complex Variables, According To Dr. Siu

There are many fields inside mathematics. Many high school students are exposed to (1) algebra in solving linear and quadratic equations and (2) calculus in finding velocity and area. Algebra deals with finite processes that are procedures involving a finite number of steps. Calculus is part of analysis that deals with the process of taking limits. For example, the tangent line to a curve is the limit of a line joining two points in the curve as the points get closer and closer to each other in an infinite number of steps until eventually they come together. The taking of a limit is an infinite process, but is described in precise logical arguments expressible in a finite number of sentences. Analysis is divided into real analysis and complex analysis. In real analysis, the only values that variables or unknowns are allowed to take are real numbers, that is, the numbers used in daily life to measure distances. Such variables are known as real variables. There are other numbers, for example, the square root of minus 1, that are not real numbers but are needed to solve equations such as the equation in which one plus the square of the unknown is zero. The numbers that involve the square root of minus 1 are called complex numbers. Variables or unknowns that are allowed to take on complex numbers as values are known as complex variables. When more than one complex variable is used, the complex variables are referred to as several complex variables.

Dr. Siu Discusses How Complex Variables Are Used

Complex variables form the most natural platform for real-world problems. When we use real numbers, a positive number and a negative number represent two forces in opposite directions and can cancel each other when their magnitudes are the same. Most problems naturally require more sophisticated descriptions than can be offered by real numbers. For example, every facet of our daily life is touched by electromagnetic waves, cell phones, televisions, GPS devices, etc. Two waves of the same magnitude coming together cancel each other if their "phases" are precisely opposite, for example, when one wave is going up to the crest (i.e., the peak) of a certain point away from the crest while the other wave is going down to the trough (i.e., the valley) of the corresponding point away from the trough. The "phase" measures the position relative to the crest and the trough of the wave. In contrast to the two polarities of the sign of a nonzero real number, the "phase" of a wave is represented by the angle of rotation in a plane. The phenomenon of a wave gives an important example of a real-world object, which is most naturally described by using complex numbers and complex variables.

Complex variables provide powerful methods for attacking problems that can be very difficult to solve in any other way. It is one of the most diverse branches of mathematics and proves enormously valuable in solving problems of heat flow, signal processing, electromagnetics, image analysis, differential equations, mathematical modeling, fluid flow, astrophysics and modern analytical science.

Dr. Siu's Successful Career Path

Yum-Tong Siu, born in 1943 in China, was educated in Macau and later transferred to Pui Ching Middle School in Hong Kong. There his love of mathematics developed and his talent was nurtured. He received his BA degree from the University of Hong Kong followed by an MA from the University of Minnesota, and his PhD from Princeton University in 1966. He has worked with such outstanding mathematical minds as Professor Eugenio Calabi, Professor Hans Grauert, and Professor Robert Gunning.

Dr. Siu's academic career began with assistant professor positions at Purdue and Notre Dame Universities. He quickly rose to full professorships at Yale and Stanford universities. In 1982, he was invited to join the faculty of Harvard University. He has been Harvard's William Elwood Byerly Professor of Mathematics since 1992, and served as chair of the Mathematics Department between 1996 and 1999. Throughout his academic career he has dedicated himself to mathematical problems considered irresolvable, and as a mentor cultivating young and talented mathematics students.

Professor Siu's fundamental contributions to the fields of several complex variables and the related fields of *complex algebraic geometry* and *complex different geometry* include his work on the *extension theory of coherent analytic sheaves*, the *theory of strong rigidity of compact Kaehler manifolds satisfying negative curvature operator conditions*, and the *theory of multiplier ideal sheaves* and its applications to long-outstanding problems in algebraic geometry, such as *effective algebraic-geometric problems, deformational invariance of plurigenera,* and the *finite generation of the canonical ring.* His contributions stretch the boundaries of intellectual exploration and demonstrate the power of creative thinking.

In 1993 Dr. Siu was awarded the Stefan Bergman Prize by the American Mathematical Society for his contributions to the field of several complex variables.

Siu has published over 100 papers in mathematics journals and authored or edited several books. His academic stature is affirmed by his membership in various American and international academies, including the U.S. National Academy of Sciences, the American Academy of Arts and Sciences, the Chinese Academy of Sciences (foreign member), the Academia Sinica in Taiwan, and the Goettingen Academy of Sciences (corresponding member). He is also a member of the Scientific Advisory Committee of the Clay Mathematics Institute in Cambridge, Massachusetts.

A Partnership of 40 Years and Counting

In 2007, Dr. Siu and his wife celebrated their 40th wedding anniversary in Boston, Massachusetts. They met as undergraduates at the University of Hong Kong and both became university professors. Dr. Sau-Fong Siu is a professor emeritus of social work at Wheelock College in Boston. In 2005 she won the Social Work Educator of the Year Award given by the National Association of Social Workers (Massachusetts chapter). She was also chief editor of a recent resource guide and annotated bibliography on Asian and Pacific Americans, a useful reference work published by the Council on Social Work Education Press.

Hsien-Kei Cheng

Theoretical Aerodynamicist

鄭顯基

By L.P. Leung
with Dr. Cheng's colleagues

Aerospace engineer, Dr. Hsien-Kei Cheng (H.K. Cheng), is well-known for his research and expertise in the fields of theoretical and computational fluid mechanics; flight aerodynamics; hypersonic, geophysical fluid mechanics; and biofluid dynamics.

"His contributions in hypersonic flow research were recognized for modeling and solving key problems in reentry aerodynamics and heat transfer, which helped to validate data from newly developed shock-tunnel experiments needed to lend support and confidence to the safe return of the first Apollo Lunar Mission."

~Citation by the Chinese-American Engineers and Scientists Association. 2005

The Cheng Parameter and the Apollo Mission to the Moon

In 1946, legendary California Institute of Technology professor, Dr. H.S. Tsien, published a paper on the aerodynamics of the space capsule reentry problem, in which he introduced a parameter now known in the literature as the *Tsien Parameter*. Fifteen years later, Dr. H.K. Cheng submitted a scientific conference paper on his work at Cornell University Laboratory—also on the reentry problem. He introduced a variant of the Tsien Parameter, later known as the *Cheng Parameter*, intended to improve the correlation of experimental data of hypersonic flows. Dr. Cheng went on to make numerous other contributions in hypersonic theory, but the Cheng Parameter was unique because of its connection to the Tsien Parameter of fifteen year earlier.

Early in his career, Dr. Cheng researched a variety of problems in high-speed aerodynamics. Describing gas motions within an intense explosion, and the determination of the flow-field about a yawed cone at very high (hypersonic) speed, are just two examples.

© Jason Jem

Most important of these early works was his improved calculation of heat transfer from the nose of a blunt body, such as a space capsule, reentering the atmosphere. The estimate of heat transfer is critical in design of a body shape and size that will successfully return to the earth's surface without destruction by excessive heat.

Dr. Cheng's more accurate calculation of reentry heat transfer rates, published in 1961, came at just the right time to assist in designing the nose cone for the successful Apollo mission to the moon.

In 1988, Dr. Cheng was honored with membership in the National Academy of Engineering (NAE) for his numerous and important contributions to aerodynamics. The citation was "For original contribution to hypersonic flows theory and to the aerodynamics of three-dimensional wings in subsonic and transonic flows."

H.K. Cheng's 2005 CESASC Achievement Award biography stated,

Dr. Cheng's works in aerodynamics cover the entire—subsonic, transonic and hypersonic—speed range ... that helped lay the basis of aero-thermodynamic design for spacecraft atmosphere reentry. His contributions in hypersonic flow research were recognized for modeling and solving analytically several key problems in reentry aerodynamics and heat transfer, which helped to validate data from newly developed shock-tunnel experiments needed to lend support and confidence to the safe return of the first Apollo Lunar Mission. Documented contributions by Dr. Cheng and colleagues are found also in theories on transonic equivalence rule, transonic lifting line, geo-physical fluid dynamics, unsteady aerodynamics, as well as flying and swimming propulsions in nature.

Dr. Cheng was a valued consultant to corporations and aerospace giants such as McDonnell Douglas, RAND, Aerospace Corporation, Northrop, Science Applications, Flow Research, TRW, Zona Tech and others.

Dr. Cheng's Gift for Mathematics

Dr. H.K. Cheng's principal gift was in mathematics. He worked in *applied mathematics* rather than *pure mathematics*, or "mathematics for its own sake." Applied mathematics concerns itself with mathematical techniques used in the application of mathematics to other domains. (Sources: *Wikipedia*: Applied Mathematics; Mathematics.)

Two main attributes distinguished his technical writings over the years. First, his papers were mathematically rigorous. Second—and perhaps more importantly—they always contained the essence of an important physical principle. For example, his work describing physics of high-speed flow over a wing involved many interacting features. Only the most gifted of researchers, however, has the capacity to extract the most salient of these elements and fully describe them mathematically. Dr. Cheng possessed this gift.

A Change of Direction

In the 1980's, H.K. Cheng's interests shifted to the description of wave motions within the earth's atmosphere and oceans and the flapping propulsion of birds and fish in nature. He was particularly interested in the aquatic propulsion and efficiency of large, lunate-tailed fishes such as the oceangoing tuna.

Dr. Cheng's latest focus was describing the underwater sound field produced by an airplane flying overhead at supersonic speeds. He was responsible for the discovery that—in the presence of ocean surface waves—the acoustic wave field of supersonic aircraft does not decay substantially beneath the surface. Indeed, the acoustic field may be of sufficient strength to disturb whales and dolphins.

A Career Dedicated To Academic Research

Professor H.K. Cheng graduated from Chiao-Tung University in Shanghai (now known as Shanghai Jiao Tong University) in 1947. He was recommended for admission to the new School of Aeronautics at Cornell University in Ithaca, New York, by the legendary Dr. Tsien. He met Dr. Tsien while Tsien was visiting Chiao-Tung University in 1947 to deliver a series of lectures on high-speed flow. In 1949, Cheng began graduate studies at Cornell.

At Cornell, he worked with William Sears—one of the most respected theoretical aerodynamicists in the United States at that time. Cheng's doctoral thesis, completed in 1952, was titled "Conical Wings in Supersonic Flow." After graduation, Cheng worked at Bell Aircraft, before returning to Cornell Aeronautical Laboratory in 1959. He spent a year as a visiting lecturer at Stanford University before joining the University of Southern California (USC) in 1965 in its newly formed Department of Aerospace Engineering under the guidance of John Laufer.

Dr. Cheng retired in 1993 to become Distinguished Professor Emeritus at USC. He maintained an office there and continued to do research and publishing, focusing primarily on sonic booms and underwater acoustics.

A Man of Many Interests

As a child, H.K. was interested in airplanes and horses, and was a sprinter in his high school days. Sprinters often excel in the long jump event because speed is so important in the sport, and during his years at Chiao-Tung University, H.K. finished first in an all-China long jump competition.

Dr. Cheng was an enthusiastic model airplane builder and hobbyist. He was founder or co-founder of the Aero Sport Club at Chiao-Tung University, which dominated model airplane competitions in China after World War II. While almost all of his competitors made rubber band-powered model airplanes, he and two other Club members were the first in China to pioneer building of gas engine models.

His two closest fellow club members were Chou Yi Ron, who subsequently came to the U.S. to work at Cal-Tech's Jet Propulsion Laboratory; and Wang Hsueh Jang, who went to the United Kingdom and was a professor of aeronautical engineering at the University of Glasgow.

At one of their early competitions, H.K. and Chou built and entered a free-flight, gas engine model. When launched, it flew straight up, dived straight down, and crashed to smithereens. (The engine had been biased improperly; in free-flight model airplanes, the engine must be biased so the plane will fly in an essentially circular pattern.) Nearly everyone present was certain Cheng's and Chou's chances of winning had ended with the crash. However, the two diehards labored through the night, building a completely new plane but this time with its engine biased properly. The following day, before an amazed audience, their plane captured first prize in its class. Cheng and Chou were the national champions that year. At Chiao-Tung University, H.K. Cheng became the unquestioned leader of the model airplane-building sport during his time.

Cheng's enthusiasm for radio controlled airplanes necessarily lay dormant during his education at Cornell and even his Cornell Aero Lab days. When he moved to California, he resumed his interest in building radio controlled, model airplanes. These planes were large, high-tech, complicated affairs. One of his plane's wingspan exceeded 14 feet. In recent years, he built a number of radio controlled gliders that he flew along the cliffs at Pepperdine University in Malibu, California.

On one celebrated occasion, he was demonstrating one of his models to visiting English aerodynamicist Keith Stewartson, a Fellow of the Royal Society in the United Kingdom. In the course of their conversation, Dr. Cheng's attention strayed briefly from the airplane as it flew beyond radio control range and crashed somewhere in Beverly Hills, lost forever.

As a student at Cornell, Cheng obtained permission to ride horses belonging to the U.S. Army Infantry's *Reserve Officers' Training Corps*. Late one evening, he was thrown off a skittish horse that he was exercising, and was found hours later with a broken hip. His horseback riding thus ended, and H.K. continued writing his doctoral thesis—as a patient in Cornell University's Hospital.

Dr. H.K. Cheng was a kind and humble man who rarely spoke of his accomplishments. Whenever his monumental contribution to the Apollo mission was mentioned, his response was either to attribute the credit to his co-workers or to say that he only did some simple calculations. His colleagues respect him as a great human being and a world-class scientist.

In the words of Dr. Browand, a fellow professor at USC, "In the 40 years I have known him—including 15 in an adjacent office—I have never heard him raise his voice or utter an unkind word to anyone." Dr. Cheng was interested in helping younger researchers. "To me, he is a teacher and father figure," said Dr. C.J. Lee, one of his former students.

Many young researchers around the world share this sentiment.

This Portrait was written with contributions from Dr. H.K. Cheng's distinguished colleagues Dr. Chih-Ming Ho of UCLA, Dr. Fred Browand of USC, Dr. Harvey Lam of Princeton University, and Dr. John Chiu of Columbia University. Dr. Cheng passed away in July of 2007. Editor

Clarence Lee

Graphic Artist
Selected to Design 14 U.S. Postage Stamps

By William Chun-Hoon

- Graphic designer Clarence Lee achieved a cultural and philatelic landmark in the span of twelve years. Beginning in 1992, he designed a series of twelve United States postage stamps, each depicting an animal in the Chinese Zodiac and representing the twelve-year lunar cycle. The final stamp was issued in 2004 and the series was a great financial success for the United States Postal Service.

- In 1994, Clarence Lee was commissioned to design a United States and China joint issue stamp depicting the endangered crane, which is an endangered species in both countries.

- Lee and his staff designed the 2008 Beijing Summer Olympics commemorative stamp, bringing the number of stamps he designed for the Postal Service to fourteen.

- Clarence Lee has received many prestigious awards including the KOA Award for Lifetime Achievement in the Visual Arts (2001). He was selected as a Living Treasure of Hawaii in 2000.

The Chinese Zodiac and Lunar Calendar

In Western Civilization, calendar years are dated from the birth of Jesus Christ, forward. This is a linear perception of time, with years proceeding forward in a straight line to infinity.

In China, traditionally years are cyclical in that the cycle of twelve animal signs is rotated every twelve years. The Chinese lunar calendar started during the reign of Emperor Huangdi, thousands of years ago. The lunar calendar is also known as the "agriculture calendar." It gives specific guidance to farmers on when to plant and when to harvest.

It sets specific dates for the start of the four seasons each year, and suggests suitable dates for certain important tasks and when to avoid doing others. Even today, millions across the globe consult the Chinese Zodiac regularly.

An established folk method, which reflects this cyclical method of recording years, is known as the *Chinese Zodiac*, represented by twelve animal signs. Each year is named after an animal or "sign" according to the following established order: Rat, Ox, Tiger, Rabbit, Dragon, Snake, Horse, Sheep, Monkey, Rooster, Dog and Pig. The same animal name or sign reappears once every twelve years.

Courtesy of Clarence Lee

There are a number of legends telling the story of how the animal signs of the Zodiac were chosen. According to one: "When the Buddha was near death, he invited all the animals to visit him. Only twelve came. The Buddha honored each of them by naming them to represent the twelve years of the Zodiac."

Another legend explains:

The twelve animals quarreled one day as to who was to head the cycle of the years. The gods were asked to decide and they held a contest: whoever was to reach the opposite bank of the river would be first, and the rest of the animals would receive their year according to when they finished the race. All twelve animals gathered at the riverbank and jumped in. Unknown to the Ox, the Rat had jumped upon his back. As the Ox was about to jump ashore, the Rat jumped off the Ox's back and won the race. The Pig, who was very lazy, ended up last.

According to Chinese folklore, people born under different signs of the Zodiac exhibit different character traits. For example, persons born in the year of the Tiger are known to have a quick temper and be sincere, generous, and very affectionate. They are known to possess a good sense of humor.

The Chinese Zodiac is a cultural icon that provides everyday guidance on life's important decisions.

The United States Postal Service Chinese Zodiac Stamp Collection

The inspiration to design a lunar New Year commemorative stamp based on the Chinese Zodiac originated in 1988. Jean Chen, a member of the Organization of Chinese Americans (OCA), Georgia Chapter, believed that America needed to recognize the contributions of Chinese Americans. She brought the idea of a Chinese Zodiac postage stamp

Courtesy of Elsa Lee

to OCA's National Chapter President, Claudine Cheng, who took up the cause and launched a successful campaign on the national level. The U.S. Postal Service approved the idea and settled on the concept of a stamp celebrating Chinese New Year.

Following a nationwide search, graphic designer Clarence Lee of Hawaii was selected to design a Chinese Lunar New Year stamp for 1993, "Year of the Rooster." It was reported that 20 million collectors in China purchased the Rooster stamp. Its phenomenal success in America and Asia led to the U. S. Postal Service commissioning Mr. Lee to create a stamp for each of the remaining Chinese Zodiac animals in the lunar New Year cycle. From 1993 to 2004, a new stamp was issued each year, ending with the Year of the Monkey. A series panel of all twelve of the Chinese Zodiac stamps was released in January, 2005, and the U.S. Postal Service authorized re-creation of the twelve Chinese Zodiac stamps as engraved, solid silver ingots. It was the culmination of one of the most collectible series of stamps issued by the U.S. Postal Service.

The Concept Behind the Design

The Lunar New Year Collection combines the centuries old paper-cut form with an original interpretation by Clarence Lee.

Lee explained his choice of the paper-cut design: "Paper-cut images have a long tradition in Chinese history. Since people had little money to acquire artistic materials, cutting paper became a simple and effective means of artistic expression." The U.S. Postal Service Advisory Board recognized that the paper-cut motif represented a folk art tradition in China that goes back more than 2,000 years and was graphically different than anything else done before. The result is a colorful, culturally inspired depiction of the animal signs of the lunar zodiac—a twelve-stamp collection under the U.S. Postal Service's "Culture & Tradition" category.

On January 5, 1997, Clarence Lee gave the following brief talk on what the stamp project meant to him:

My thanks to the U.S. Postal Service and to the OCA organization for having everything to do with my being on this stage. As I reflect on the past few years, of being part of this celebration, I cannot help but recall the original purpose of the Lunar Stamps: to honor the many Chinese immigrants who came to America, struggled and sacrificed to make our lives fuller and richer.

For myself, I humbly recall my father, Lee Young Fai, a rice farmer from Southern China, who left his family at the age of 18 and came to Hawaii. He found work as a butcher and somehow, along with my mother, made the sacrifices that gave their children rich and rewarding lives.

As I look at the opportunities my children and grandchildren now have in this great country, I want to give thanks to the "Lee Young Fais" for their courage and perseverance in making our lives better.

2008 Beijing Olympics Commemorative Stamp Issue

After Clarence Lee's successful Chinese Zodiac stamp series, in 2007 he accepted a commission from the U.S. Postal Service to design a commemorative stamp for the Beijing Olympics. The postal service dedicated the stamp and it went on sale nationwide on June 19, 2008.

The postal service issued a Bulletin, describing the stamp in detail, on the day of its release:

With the issuance of this stamp, the U.S. Postal Service continues its tradition of honoring the spirit of athleticism and international unity inspired by the Olympic Games. The stamp will be issued to coincide with the games of the XXIX Olympiad, which will be held from August 8, 2008, until August 24, 2008, in Beijing, China.

Designed by Clarence Lee, who served as designer for the recently concluded Lunar New Year series, this stamp features a drawing by artist Katie Doka of a gymnast surrounded by ribbonlike design elements. In the upper right corner of the stamp, the denomination is surrounded by a graphic element that resembles the ink mark created by a Chinese "chop," a carved wooden stamp often used for signatures or seals. The five Olympic rings appear in the lower left corner.

Describing the Beijing Olympics stamp's design, Lee said:
It subtly incorporates various elements from traditional Chinese culture. It was just so energetic and appealing. We did a lot of research for the stamp's design. We found out

there is a very traditional form of paper-cut artwork which was used for over 2,000 years. We took that very traditional art and used it.

Lee said the stamp honors the spirit of the Olympic Games.

Family Support for an Artist in Training

Clarence Lee was born in Honolulu, Hawaii—one of five children in a traditional home where education was highly regarded.

At an early age, Lee began developing an interest in art. This was during World War II and he spent his evenings sketching what was on the minds of many Americans: battle scenes, fighter aircraft, tanks and explosions. His father brought him pink butcher paper from the shop where he worked. His mother enrolled him in a drawing class at the Honolulu Academy of Arts where Lee found himself among adults. He realized that art was something he truly enjoyed doing.

Clarence Lee attended Iolani, a private Episcopal college preparatory school, where Dr. Sun Yat-sen, the Founder of the Republic of China, studied during the 1920s. There, he continued developing his interest in art. However, the school did not offer art classes beyond the eighth grade. His art teacher, Mrs. Bird, noticed his passion for art and she set aside a corner of her classroom exclusively for Lee to paint and draw. Lee was the "artist in residence," and was the school's yearbook editor. Later, Lee returned to Iolani and established the Kathryn Bird Room in her honor.

Lee won a Territorial Scholarship in art and attended Pomona College in California. After his freshman year, he enrolled in a summer art class at the University of Hawaii where he studied under famous graphic design instructor, Josef Albers. Clarence recalled, "The class opened me up to the whole idea of design, the logic of design, and the clarity of design." Albers was a visiting professor from the graphic design department at Yale University and had a marked influence on Lee's future. "The timing was great," says Lee who transferred to Yale after completing a second year at Pomona College. He studied under design legends Paul Rand and Bradbury Thompson who later was on the Citizens Stamp Advisory Committee and possibly recommended Clarence Lee when it was seeking a designer for the lunar New Year stamp.

At Yale's Department of Graphic Design, Lee became engrossed in the art and design curriculum. He recalled that "everybody was studying graphic design. It was a wonderful environment to be able to be with 15-20 students who were all immersed in and loved art."

He graduated from Yale in 1958 with a Bachelor of Fine Arts degree and pursued a career in design in New York City. However, he first fulfilled his military obligation in the United States Army from which he was discharged in 1959.

Clarence Lee spent the next five years in New York. He gained valuable graphic design experience with the studio of Lester Beall and then with IBM before returning to Hawaii in 1965 with his wife and two children. In Honolulu he established a highly successful design studio: Clarence Lee Design & Associates. For over forty years the studio has contributed to setting a level of excellence in design in the community—from corporate logos, annual reports, magazines and books, to packaging and signage.

References

1. Ta, Leanne. (2008, June 26). *Small stamp big on tradition.* www.honoluluadvertiser.com.

Mrs. Lily Chin

An Unlikely Heroine

A Mother's Relentless Courage To Fight Racial Injustice

By Stewart Kwoh
Assisted by Carmina Ocampo

> *There's nothing I can do to bring back Vincent, but I don't want any other mother to go through what I've gone through.*
>
> ~Lily Chin

On June 19, 1982 Vincent Chin, a twenty-seven year old Chinese American man, was killed in Detroit by two white autoworkers. His killers were sentenced to only three years probation and were each given a $3,780 fine (Zia, 60). Vincent's brutal killing and the pitiful sentence that followed shocked Asian Americans throughout the nation who launched a nationwide campaign to demand a just sentencing of Vincent's killers.

My story about the Vincent Chin case is based on my personal experiences and Helen Zia's memoir *"Asian American Dreams, The Emergence of An American People."*

Vincent Chin was brutally murdered in 1982, the year before I started the Asian Pacific American Legal Center (APALC) of Southern California. APALC's founding members had envisioned it as a local organization, so it was by fate that just as we emerged as an organization, there was a well-known civil rights case involving an Asian American that became the first big case we worked on. APALC served as the only out-of-state co-counsel to the Detroit based organization, American Citizens for Justices (ACJ), during the prosecution of Vincent Chin's murderers; and I became associated with Mrs. Chin, Vincent's mother, during my involvement with the campaign. Although the APALC

© Corky Lee

was already underway by the time Vincent Chin was killed, the inspiring community organizing that took place in the months and years after Vincent's tragic death played an important role in shaping the APALC's direction as an organization dedicated to advocating on behalf of the civil rights of Asian Americans. Mrs. Chin's courage and strength in fighting for justice for her son, and the amazing work of all the community members involved, changed many people's lives, launched a movement, inspired countless others in the pursuit of justice, and continues to empower and inspire many people today.

Vincent Chin's Murder

Vincent's murder took place during a climate of intense anti-Asian sentiment in the United States in the early 1980s that no doubt contributed to the circumstances leading up to his death. In 1970, Asian Americans made up around 1.5 million people in the United States and the number of Asian Americans more than doubled by the 1980's. In Detroit, the Asian American population was small, at around 8,000 out of 1.2 million people, but was slowly growing (Zia, 56). Despite the increase of Asian Americans in the country, there was a dearth of national Asian American advocacy groups dealing with civil rights issues; and Asian Americans at the time were in need of greater legal protections.

Suspicion and anger were especially directed towards Japanese people because of the influx of Japanese imports and investments in several industries that had previously been dominated by American companies. Anything that was Japanese or looked Japanese was a potential target (Zia, 58). The climate was especially hostile towards Asians in cities like Detroit, where Vincent Chin lived, that had a huge automobile industry that suffered from massive unemployment of autoworkers. For example, in an angry speech before Congress, Congressman John Dingell from Michigan blamed "those little yellow men" for the hardships suffered by the American automotive industry (Zia, 58). Angry Americans vandalized Japanese cars and Asian American autoworkers faced threats and hostility from fellow workers. In certain parts of America, just being Asian could be dangerous (Zia, 58).

Vincent was out with his longtime friends at the Fancy Pants Club in Highland Park, Detroit, in celebration of his upcoming wedding. Vincent caught the attention of two white men: Ronald Ebens, a plant supervisor for Chrysler, and Michael Nitz, a laid-off autoworker. Ebens taunted Vincent with racial slurs such as "Chink" and "Nip" and was overheard saying, "It's because of motherf*ckers like you that we're out of work." As Ebens provoked Vincent with racist obscenities, the two men became embroiled in a brief fight (Zia, 59-60).

As soon as the fight was broken up, Vincent and his friends left the bar. Once outside, Ebens and Nitz chased Vincent and his other Chinese friend, threatening them with the baseball bat that one of the men wielded. While Vincent and his friend outran the two men and believed they were safe, Ebens and Nitz enlisted the help of another man and searched for almost a half hour before finding Vincent outside a restaurant in the neighborhood. The two men confronted Vincent while his friend managed to escape. Nitz grabbed and held Vincent from behind while Ebens savagely beat Vincent with the baseball bat. Vincent was rushed to the emergency room, but his wounds were fatal. He died a few days later as a result of the beating (Zia, 59-60).

After Vincent's death, the two killers pled guilty to manslaughter. Despite their guilty pleas, the judge sentenced Ebens and Nitz to only three years' probation and a fine of around $3,000 each. The judge, Charles Kaufman, defended the sentence stating that, "These aren't the kind of men you send to jail."

The news of Vincent's tragic death evoked strong emotions from the Asian American community whose members were stunned and outraged that the killers received such a pathetic sentence. Asian Americans who heard about Vincent's death felt that his terrible murder could have happened to them or their loved ones. After all, Vincent was a regular guy and the child of hard-working immigrant parents; and people easily related to him (Zia, 60-61).

Reaction to the Pathetic Sentencing of Judge Charles Kaufman

In reaction to the unjust sentencing of Vincent's killers, a small group of concerned Chinese Americans met in the back of a Chinese restaurant in Detroit one night and set up meetings with Mrs. Chin, who pleaded with them to help her fight for justice for her son. A group of Asian American attorneys did what they could to investigate the facts surrounding Vincent's death, and found numerous legal errors. For example, the police had failed to interview important witnesses, mishandled evidence, and the prosecutor was not present when the judge handed down the sentence. Faced with growing evidence of the mishandling of the case by law enforcement, about one hundred Asian Americans from various occupations and backgrounds in Detroit gathered to discuss whether to form a pan-Asian organization that could seek redress for Vincent's death.

Although the gatherers were mostly Chinese Americans—Japanese, Filipino and Korean Americans from various community groups were also present (Zia, 66).

The group decided to form a pan-Asian umbrella organization called "American Citizens for Justice" (ACJ) that could advocate for justice and coordinate the actions of the various Asian American groups that wanted to get involved. According to Helen Zia, "ACJ marked the formation of the first explicitly Asian American grass-roots community advocacy effort with a national scope." (Zia, 67). Zia describes ACJ as being motivated primarily by the desire to "obtain justice for Vincent Chin, an Asian American man who was killed because he looked Japanese." (Zia, 67).

As time progressed, an ever-widening group of Asian American attorneys, activists and regular citizens from around the state joined ACJ's campaign. National groups like the Japanese American Citizen's League and the Organization of Chinese Americans got involved. Soon the Asian Pacific American Legal Center started working with leaders from ACJ like Helen Zia and Liza Chan. Whites, African Americans, Latinos, and Arab Americans also reached out to lend support, turning the coalition into a multi-racial one.

Bringing the Injustice to the National Stage

The increasing awareness of the case enabled Asian Americans to enter the national dialogue on race relations that had previously been dominated by a focus on white/black relations (Zia 68). By speaking about the Vincent Chin case, Asian Americans engaged the public in conversations about racism and challenged widely held beliefs that Asian Americans were not victims of racially motivated violence.

After reviewing the case with the other attorneys involved, I strongly suggested that we focus our legal attention on getting the United States Department of Justice to bring a civil rights prosecution for a hate crime. Liza Chan and I collectively interviewed some witnesses and wrote a legal memo pointing out different pieces of evidence showing that Ebens and Nitz were motivated by racial animus. The memo listed two counts against Vincent's killers: 1) deprivation of civil rights and 2) conspiracy. Liza and I presented the memo to the Attorney General when several groups met with him, urging the office to go forward with the civil rights prosecution, even though no Asian American had benefited from such a prosecution before. Vincent's case would be the first one involving an Asian American whose rights would be protected by civil rights in the context of a hate crime. Under the conservative Reagan administration, however, the Department of Justice had reduced the number of hate crime prosecutions, so trying to get the DOJ to agree to do so was an enormous challenge.

ACJ undertook massive grassroots organizing to build support for their campaign to pressure the federal government to conduct a civil rights investigation. During the process of reaching out to Asian Americans, grassroots organizers engaged the public in dialogues about why civil rights were significant to Asian Americans. As ACJ proceeded with an intense campaign to raise the profile of Asian American civil rights, they were confronted with many challenges: There was a backlash from critics from various political and ethnic backgrounds who dismissed the idea that Asian Americans needed civil rights protections; it was also very difficult for Asian Americans to publicly and privately confront their experiences and feelings about racism; and lastly, Asian Americans were by and large fearful of making waves and speaking out against hate crimes. Furthermore, the concept of a hate crime was still nascent in the early 1980s and had primarily been recognized as relevant to African Americans, not Asian Americans (Zia, 71-73).

The New York Times' coverage of the story led to even more media coverage. People from across the country and all over the world reached out to support ACJ and join the campaign (Zia, 73). ACJ organized a massive pan-Asian demonstration where hundreds of Asian Americans marched together to demand justice for Vincent Chin. Mrs. Chin spoke during the demonstration and asked hundreds of demonstrators if they would help her seek justice for her son. The demonstrators marched to a Federal Courthouse in Detroit and hand-delivered a petition to the U.S. Attorney with three thousand signatures demanding federal intervention in the case (Zia, 74-75). It surprised almost everyone when the Justice Department finally agreed to conduct a civil rights prosecution of Vincent's killers.

Federal Jury Dismissed Guilty Verdict for Evidentiary Errors

In June 1984, a federal jury acquitted Nitz but found Ebens guilty of violating Vincent Chin's civil rights, sentencing him to twenty-five years in jail (Zia, 78-79). However, the decision was no victory. Unfortunately there was an appeal and re-trial since the appellate court felt that evidentiary errors had been committed. Additionally, the trial was moved to Cincinnati—a city that was much more conservative and had an insignificant population of Asian Americans. Furthermore, the case was hardly known to the Cincinnati public. Potential jurors for the trial were aggressively questioned about their interactions with Asian Americans, and most jurors that were interviewed admitted that they had little interaction with Asian people (Zia, 79). The change in venue was incredibly disheartening.

A jury that was comprised of almost all white, blue-collar men—from backgrounds similar to Ebens—was persuaded by the defense lawyers' framing of Vincent's death as merely a bar room fight with no racial motivation involved. The jury failed to understand the racial dynamics and racial motivation behind the killing and acquitted Ebens of all charges on May 1, 1987—about five years after Vincent was killed (Zia, 80). As an unfortunate result of the jurors' racial insensitivity, Ebens and Nitz never spent a day in jail for Vincent's murder. Although, the Chin family later won a $1.5 million civil judgment against Ebens and Nitz, the former swore they would never get any money. He remained

true to his promise and stopped making payments two years after the judgment was issued (Zia, 80). To say the least, it was a tragic and bitter outcome to the case.

The Legacy of the Vincent Chin Murder

Despite the devastating outcome of the re-trial, Vincent Chin's legacy is one of inspiration, empowerment, and education. The passionate community organizing that took place after Vincent's death was proof of how strong the Asian American community had become. Prominent Asian American community leaders like Helen Zia emerged and have continued to fight for social justice issues important to Asian Americans and people of color.

The Vincent Chin case is taught today in Asian American studies classrooms everywhere, inspiring younger generations of Asian Americans into taking an active interest in Asian American history and activism. Christine Choy and Renee Tajima-Pena filmed a documentary on the Vincent Chin case called "Who Killed Vincent Chin?" The film was nominated for an Oscar, and is regularly shown to students in Asian American studies classes. On the recent 25th anniversary of Vincent's death, over a hundred people showed up to a screening of the documentary in Los Angeles.

Since Vincent Chin's case was the first prosecution involving an Asian American victim, his case brought national attention to the previously invisible issue of hate crimes against Asian Americans. The case increased Asian Americans' concerns about growing anti-Asian violence and Asian American advocacy organizations responded by including hate crimes in their agendas. The Coalition Against Anti-Asian Violence (CAAAV), based in New York, was founded in 1986 as one of the first organizations to organize Asians against anti-Asian violence. Both the National Asian Pacific American Legal Consortium (NAPALC), which is now the Asian American Justice Center (AAJC) based in Washington D.C.; and the APALC in Los Angeles also established hate crimes units as part of their regular work.

The Vincent Chin case also spurred the development of a broad-based pan-Asian movement, bringing together many diverse API organizations in the country with different ethnic backgrounds and priorities. The National Asian Pacific American Legal Consortium (now the Asian American Justice Center), based in Washington D.C., was established and co-founded in 1991—by the Asian Law Caucus based in San Francisco, the Asian American Legal Defense and Education Fund (AALDEF) based in New York, and the Asian Pacific American Legal Center based in Los Angeles—to build the first pan-Asian national legal coalition that had the ability to respond and take unified stances on pressing Asian American civil rights issues.

Vincent's legacy is also about how the fight for justice helped contribute to coalition-building between Asian American groups and other communities of color. There were a lot of African American supporters who came out to support ACJ's efforts. During the Vincent Chin campaign, the Reverend Jesse Jackson, who was busy campaigning for the presidency, stopped by San Francisco's Chinatown to meet Mrs. Chin and speak out against anti-Asian violence (Zia, 76). Detroit's prominent African American organizations issued statements in support of ACJ's campaign for federal intervention in the case (Zia, 74). In fighting for a civil rights prosecution of Vincent's killers, Asian Americans drew upon the legacy of the black civil rights movement, and attempted to use the very laws against hate crimes that black leaders had used to fight for greater protections for black people.

Vincent's Legacy is Also a Story About a Mother's Heroism

One of the most touching aspects of the tragic story of Vincent's death was the inspiring struggle undertaken by Lily Chin. Lily was a very loving woman and had lost her husband just six months before Vincent was killed. Her husband had served in the army during World War II, which made it possible for him to become a U.S. citizen (Zia, 63). He and Lily worked in laundries and restaurants throughout their lives. After Vincent was killed, Lily was compelled by her desire to seek justice for her son. She was convinced that the sentence handed down to his killers was unjust and she was not afraid to speak out in her time of intense grief and join the campaign. She was truly the centerpiece of all the activism, motivating and lending strength and courage to so many people.

Lily was in Los Angeles during the summer of 1984 and there was a big rally. Lily came and spoke in a very crowded Chinatown restaurant. As she had done many times already, she asked people for help in fighting for justice for her son. At one point she fainted and several of us helped her to her feet. That night Lily stayed at my home, where at one moment, I asked her: "Lily are you ok?" She said, "Stewart there's nothing I can do to bring back Vincent, but I don't want any other mother to go through what I've gone through." I was very moved by her words.

After the devastating outcome of the appeal in federal court that resulted in Vincent's killers never spending a night in jail, Lily decided that she couldn't live in the United States anymore and moved back to China. I visited Lily in China in 1995, where she was living with some of her relatives outside of Guangzhou. She could still smile despite having lost so much in her life that was irreplaceable. I will never forget Lily's relentless courage that inspired so many people. To me, she was a true hero and I'm sure countless others feel the same. Many of us have followed in her footsteps to strengthen the ability of our community to stand up for its rights, prevent hate crimes, and strengthen justice in the United States.

Reference

Zia, Helen. (2000). *Asian American Dreams: The Emergence of an American People*. New York, New York: Farrar, Straus and Giroux.

Epilogue

A Tale of Two Cities
from Los Angeles to Detroit

Los Angeles, October 24, 1871—Chinatown Massacre:

Amidst firecrackers and gunfire, two Chinese factions were involved in a dispute over ownership of a woman. Robert Thompson, deputy constable and ex-saloon owner, walked into Calle de los Negros (Negro Alley), firing his rifle at buildings despite warnings from his friend—and was hit in the chest by a bullet. His death unleashed a mob of some 1000 Angelenos into the Alley, armed with guns and rifles and crying for vengeance. Within four hours, 19-21 Chinese had been lynched or hanged by the mob. Those in hiding were driven out of their quarters and shot to death with few able to escape. Calle de los Negros was destroyed and set ablaze. The exact number of Chinese murdered was undeterminable and newspaper reports were murky.

A grand jury indicted over 150 persons connected with the massacre, but few witnesses came forward and as a result there were few convictions. Chinese persons were not allowed to testify under the law. The few convicted were Mexicans who had little or no influence.

In 1871, Chinese people in America had no avenue to fight for justice.

Detroit, June 19, 1982—The Brutal Killing of Vincent Chin:

The verdict was guilty but the sentencing by Judge Kaufman was pitiful: the two killers were set free. His explanation, "These aren't the kind of men you send to jail."

Whether in 1871, 1982, or today, Chinese Americans must fight for justice.

H. S. Tsien

Aviation Engineer and Rocket Scientist

By L.P. Leung

"Dr. Hsue-Shen Tsien was born into a nation of rickshaws and left it a nation of rockets within the span of a single lifetime."

~Iris Chang, author of Thread of the Silkworm.

"He made pioneering contributions to (America's) aviation engineering theory in areas of supersonic and transonic aerodynamics, as well as thin shell stability theory for missile structures."

~Cox Commission Report—105th Congress.

"That this government permitted this genius, this scientific genius, to be sent to Communist China to pick his brain is one of the tragedies of this century."

~Grant Cooper, Dr. Tsien's defense attorney, upon learning of his deportation.

A Distinguished Career in the United States

Dr. Hsue-Shen Tsien was born in Hangzhou, China, in 1911. A brilliant student from grade school through college, he graduated with a degree in railway engineering. He competed for and won a prestigious Boxer Rebellion Scholarship to study at the Massachusetts Institute of Technology (MIT) in 1935, receiving a master's degree.

In 1936, Tsien continued his postgraduate studies at California Institute of Technology (Caltech) at the urging of the legendary Dr. Theodore von Karman. He obtained his PhD in 1939 and would remain with Caltech for almost twenty years. Dr. Tsien rapidly rose to the top of his profession, becoming a full professor at the age of 36 and was one of the founders and directors of Caltech's Jet Propulsion Laboratory (JPL).

Dr. Tsien was a member of "Project Lusty," a team of top U.S. military scientists sent to Germany before World War II ended to interview rocket scientists and recover their research documents. He edited and summarized some three million pages of technical papers in the 800-page *Jet Propulsion*. The work became the classified technical bible for aircraft and rocket research in the post-war United States.

Dr. H.S. Tsien enjoyed a reputation as the pre-eminent authority in mathematical analysis of problems of high velocity phenomena, rocketry, and engineering cybernetics. According to *The United States House of Representatives Select Committee on U.S. National Security and Military/Commercial Concerns with the People's Republic of China* (Cox Commission Report), published in 1999:

… [W]hile at Caltech's Guggenheim Aeronautical Laboratory, he made "pioneering contributions" to aviation engineering theory in the areas of supersonic and transonic aerodynamics, as well as thin shell stability theory for ballistic missile structures.

Tsien's contributions "were essential to the development of high-speed aerodynamics and jet propulsion in the United States," wrote his mentor and friend, Dr. von Karman.

Under Dr. Tsien, JPL's work was concerned primarily with research and development of jet power for peacetime civilian and commercial use. He pioneered the "Dynasoar" concept which combined aerodynamics with space research. In a speech in 1949, he envisioned a future in which Americans would travel to outer space within 30 years, and that a rocket-powered ride from New York to Los Angeles could take less than sixty minutes.

At Caltech, he taught his students original scientific concepts so advanced that textbooks on the subjects had not been written.

"Of all the experts I suggested for the Air Force Scientific Advisory Group in 1945," Dr. von Karman wrote in his memoirs, "my friend, H. S. Tsien … at the age of 36 … was an undisputed genius whose work [provided] enormous impetus to advances in high-speed aerodynamics and jet propulsion." Upon Dr. Tsien's appointment to the advisory group, the Army Air Force conferred the rank of Lieutenant Colonel upon him.

Tsien worked on highly classified U.S. missile programs, including the Titan intercontinental ballistic missile.

Dr. Tsien intended to become an American citizen and pursue his scientific research in his adopted homeland. He applied for citizenship in 1949 but while awaiting final approval from the Immigration and Naturalization Service (INS), a knock on his door from the FBI shattered that dream, turning it into a nightmare. For the next five years, he was subjected to harassment, round-the-clock surveillance, virtual house arrest and solitary confinement in prison.

Dr. Tsien's Deportation and Its Repercussions

The United States had on its soil the acme of China's scientific brainpower from the 1930s to the 1950s. Most of these scientists earned Boxer Rebellion Scholarships prior to the advent of communism in China. They received their educations from some of the United States' best universities and many performed top security research for the military.

McCarthy era witch hunts and the Cold War were largely responsible for the U.S. handing over many of these scientists to China—thereby advancing China's technological progress by at least a decade. Some of them were ordered to remain in the United States out of fear their knowledge might jeopardize U.S. national security. With their top security clearances revoked and financial support withheld, they were made to feel like unwelcome guests and were unable to continue their classified research. Those who reluctantly left on their own knew their work in China would have less than optimal technical support. Many carried a heavy burden of sadness and resentment.

Accused of being a Communist Party member by the nation he aspired to become a citizen of, Dr. Tsien vigorously defended his case in a series of INS hearings. He received the support of his Caltech colleagues but to no avail. In view of his significant contributions to America's war effort, his mistreatment by the FBI and INS for over five years must have changed his view of the United States.

The FBI could not prove his communist affiliation. The INS took over the case and repeatedly questioned his "loyalty" in the hypothetical scenario of a war between the U.S. and China. Five years later, Dr. Tsien was allowed to leave the U.S. (actually deported), ostensibly in exchange for return of American POWs held by China since the Korean War. "In the end," historian Iris Chang wrote, "the case against Tsien hurt rather than helped U.S. national defense. By deporting him, the nation lost a first-class scientist who almost certainly would have been a valued adviser to the American lunar and missile programs."

Just before crossing the Lo Wu Bridge from Hong Kong to China, Dr. Tsien looked back at waiting reporters, "… I have no bitterness against the American people," he said. "My main objective is the pursuit of peace and happiness."

The repercussions were overwhelming. Instead of contributing to the advancement of high technology in the United States, Dr. Tsien, the missile specialist, and Dr. Chung-Yao Chao, the nuclear physicist—with scores of talented Chinese scientists—knew that their forced return to China was in large measure responsible for the rapid development and sophistication of the Chinese nuclear, missile, and space programs.

In an interview with Dr. Tsien's son, Yucon, who is a U.S. citizen, Iris Chang, historian and author of *Thread of the Silkworm*, wrote:

> *One of the first things Yucon told me during the rare interview was that his father still harbored considerable resentment against the U. S. government for their treatment of him during the 1950s. Yucon said, "If my father had committed a crime in this country, then my father would have nothing to say. But my father devoted twenty years of his life to service in the United States and contributed to much of this nation's technology, only to be repaid by (being) driven out of the country."*

Based on her extensive research, Chang concluded that "Dr. Tsien's life is a private story of a shy, introspective, brilliant scientist who wanted nothing more in life than to work in peace but was caught up, not once, but twice, in the vortex of world politics."

Official U.S. Military Commendations Awarded Dr. Tsien for Service in World War II

War Department and Army Air Force: *"Meritorious Civil Service"* and praise for *"Outstanding performance of duty."*

Ordnance Department of the Army Air Force: *"For outstanding performance of duty during the period September 1939 to September 1945 while serving as Group Supervisor, Jet Propulsion Laboratory, Caltech."*

Office of Scientific Research and Development: *A special certificate awarded to Dr. Tsien read: "Participated in work organized under the Office of Scientific Research and Development through the National Defense Research Committee, contributing to the successful prosecution of the Second World War."*

In 1979, Caltech named Dr. H.S. Tsien a recipient of the Distinguished Alumni Award in recognition of his pioneering work in rocket science. On October 31, 2009, Dr. Tsien passed away in Beijing at age 98.

References

1. Chang, Iris. *The Thread of the Silkworm*. New York: Basic Books, 1995.
2. Ryan, William L. & Summerlin, Sam. *The China Cloud*. London: Hutchinson & Co., 1969.
3. *Cox Commission Report* (105th U.S. Congress), January 3, 1999.

Tsien Revisited

The following article on Dr. H.S. Tsien originally appeared in *Caltech News*, Volume 36, No. 1, 2002, the alumni quarterly of the California Institute of Technology, and is reprinted with permission. Dr. Tsien passed away in Beijing on October 31, 2009.

First he was accused, then detained, then deported. Any of this sound familiar?

But there was a twist to this tale. A Caltech professor talks about his long friendship with the Caltech-trained scientist who became the "father of Chinese rocketry."

This past December, Frank Marble, PhD '48, and his wife, Ora Lee, went to China to visit and help honor their longtime friend Tsien Hsue-Shen, PhD '39.

Dr. Tsien with Dr. Marble, boarding ship to China. Los Angeles Harbor, 1955.

they were permitted to leave for China.

Received with open arms in his homeland, Tsien resumed his research, founded the Institute of Mechanics, and, as one of the world's leading authorities in aeronautics, went on to become the "father" of China's missile program, a trusted member of the government and Party's inner circle, and the nation's "most honored scientist."

Many Caltechers, along with Americans who lived through the Red Scare days of the '50s, have at least a glancing familiarity with Tsien's story: a brilliant student and later colleague of aerospace pioneer Theodore von Kármán, commended by the U.S. Air Force for his contributions to its technological development after World War II, the Chinese-born scientist was accused of harboring Communist sympathies and stripped of his security clearance in 1950. Tsien and those who knew him best said that the allegations were nonsense, and no evidence ever came to light to substantiate them. Despite that, and over a barrage of protests from colleagues in academia, government, and industry, the INS placed him under a delayed deportation order, and for the next five years he and family lived under U.S. government surveillance and partial house arrest. In September 1955

Early in the INS saga, Tsien and his wife had planned to visit China so that their parents could meet their American-born grandchildren for the first time. But the INS impounded his luggage and charged him with concealing classified documents—the most "secret" of which, suspected of containing security codes, turned out upon inspection to be a table of logarithms. In the meantime the FBI had decided that Tsien posed a security risk and imprisoned him in San Pedro; he was freed two weeks later after Caltech president Lee DuBridge, among others, flew to Washington to intervene on his behalf. These incidents undoubtedly helped Tsien to conclude, as he confided to friends, that he had become "an unwelcome guest" in the country in which he had spent his whole scientific life. In any case, he was determined to avoid such problems again, and when he sailed to China, he deliberately left all of his research notes and papers behind.

Among the handful of people who saw the Tsien family off in 1955 were Frank and Ora Lee Marble. Marble and Tsien had struck up a warm friendship as aeronautics colleagues, and the Tsien family had stayed at the Marbles' Pasadena home during their final weeks in the United States. After Tsien's departure, he and Marble corresponded intermittently; then, with the onset of the Cultural Revolution in China, Marble stopped hearing from him. In 1979 Caltech named Tsien a recipient of the Distinguished Alumni Award in recognition of his pioneering work in rocket science, but Tsien, although he sent a gracious acknowledgment, did not come to campus to collect it.

Time passes. In 1981, Frank and Ora Lee received an invitation from the Chinese Academy of Sciences to come to Beijing and teach combustion technology and English. Respectively, at the Academy's newly established Graduate School of Science and Technology, a small research institute partly modeled on Caltech. Shortly afterward, the Marble and Tsien families were reunited for the first time in 25 years. Marble recalls his feelings before they met. "We had had very different experiences and lived in such different circumstances. Would our old, easygoing friendship and discussions resume? Or was that something that just wasn't going to happen?" After half an hour, he says, he had his answer. "There was no obstacle."

Photo courtesy of Dr. Frank Marble

Tsien dining with Mao

The two families kept in touch after that and saw each other again in China in 1991. In the years since Tsien had returned to China, Marble had taken on the project of collecting and organizing the extensive research notes—two large file cabinets worth, it turned out—that Tsien had left at Caltech. Tsien repeatedly said he did not want them back, telling Marble at their 1981 reunion, "Frank, American students need them much more than Chinese students." A decade or so ago, however, he had a change of heart, and, with the help of Tsien's colleague Cheng Che-Min, PhD '52, Marble returned the collection to China. Some papers went to the Institute of Mechanics, founded decades earlier by Tsien, and others now form the core holdings of the Tsien Library, which the Chinese government had established at Xi'an Jiatong University, about 600 miles southwest of Beijing. The Chinese Academy of Sciences subsequently brought out selections from the collection as an elegant, coffee table-type book entitled Manuscripts of H. S. Tsien 1938–1955, whose publication coincided with the December 2001 symposium celebrating Tsien's 90th birthday.

When Marble went to visit Tsien for that event, he went both as a friend and as the official emissary of Caltech and President Baltimore, bringing with him the Distinguished Alumni Award that the Institute had presented to Tsien in absentia 23 years ago. Tsien is now permanently confined to bed, so Marble made the formal presentation at his bedside in a ceremony that received widespread coverage in

China, and at last provided a fitting coda to Tsien's long, complicated, and never completely sundered association with Caltech.

Marble, who is Caltech's Hayman Professor of Mechanical Engineering and Professor of Jet Propulsion, Emeritus, spoke with Caltech News editor Heidi Aspaturian about his recent trip and earlier visits with Tsien in China.

Tsien does not speak much English any more, but his family tells me that he still understands it quite well. He was thoroughly aware that I was presenting Caltech's highest honor to him at the official request of David Baltimore, and I think he was deeply impressed with and appreciative of that.

We weren't able to talk much during my most recent visit, but when I saw him in 1991 and again in 1996, we had some very interesting conversations. I think in general we both felt less constrained than we had during our reunion in 1981. One comment he made to me in 1991 particularly stands out: "You know, Frank, we've done a lot for China. People have enough food. They're working and progress is being made. But Frank, they're not happy." He felt very bad about that—almost, I think, a little bit responsible for it, although it was not an area he was involved in at all. His area of activity was military and civilian rocketry, and this was strictly a personal observation. That was about as far as he ever went in saying that things were not ideal.

He obviously has good memories of Caltech. He speaks of the Institute most fondly, and I think that he feels that his time on campus was one of the most enjoyable of his life. In a letter that his wife, Tsiang Ying, wrote us after our recent visit, she said

Photo courtesy of Dr. Frank Marble

Tsien with Marble in Beijing in 1991.

that Tsien still loves to reminisce about Theodore von Kármán and the wonderful times he had at Caltech and to tell the old von Kármán jokes. So I think he stills feels very emotionally tied to the Institute. But it's important to remember that during the entire five-year episode with the INS, Caltech was very good to him. The Institute continued to honor his professorship and to respect his reputation. My understanding is that Lee DuBridge, who vigorously supported Tsien, had difficulties with the Board of Trustees, some of whose members were embarrassed by Tsien's situation.

Once Tsien returned to China, I don't think he ever made another trip West. He did travel once to the Soviet Union. Evidently he did not endear himself to his hosts, and he never went back. Otherwise, so far as I know, he did not leave China. I would guess that this was largely by choice—he never was a great one for traveling. I think that he felt he had so many things to do at home that he had no real desire to go elsewhere.

Tsien never spoke to me about how his life and scientific career in America had ended. He was not a person for looking back or for ruminating about how things might have been. He was very much a realist, and my feeling is that he just tuned those last five years in America out. I do know that he felt, at least when all this started, that he would be able to do better work in the United States than he would initially in China, where research conditions at the time were very primitive. I believe that once he returned to China, what he found there was pretty much what he had expected. But he did have very able people working with him. Many of them had studied in the United States, and they were devoted to him. I met a few of those who had worked with him in the early days, and they had the highest praise for the way he had laid out and directed the program for rocketry development. I think that Tsien also had the great personal advantage of being technically and scientifically on top of things, and he also had the ear of the government. By virtue of his expertise and reputation he could convince officials of what needed to be done and accomplish things that other people couldn't.

He did not talk about his experiences during that era. We were both very careful to avoid discussion about anything that touched on sensitive issues. We would talk about every other subject—family, music, literature, and some scientific work that was mutually interesting. He was very enthusiastic and intrigued about some of the work I was doing on combustion processes in vortex flows and told me, "Frank, you have been more honest to von Kármán than I have." What he meant was that I was still involved in the fundamental research areas that von Kármán had worked in, but that he was now in a very different mode of operation.

Tsien, of course, became a high-ranking, trusted Party official, but it was evident that he had had trouble during the Cultural Revolution. I heard from his colleagues, but never directly from him, that like many leading scientists and intellectuals, he wrote one or two letters of "confession." Ying, his wife, had a very interesting experience. She was head of the Western Vocal Music Department at the Beijing Conservatory, and commuted between work and home on a motorbike. Apparently the Red Guard was after her in some way and so for several months—maybe as long as a year—she just lived at the conservatory until she thought it was safe to go out again. Her students brought her food and other necessities.

I also spoke to one of Tsien's close colleagues, Ch'ien Wei-Zhang. He had earned his doctorate in Canada, was a post-doc at Caltech, and had worked with Tsien at JPL. He also

Photo courtesy of Dr. Frank Marble

In December 2001, receiving Caltech's Distinguished Alumni Award. From left, Tsien, Mrs. Marble, Dr. Marble, and Mrs. Tsien.

went back to China and pursued a very productive career there. During the Cultural Revolution, the Red Guard accused him of all sorts of things, and he wound up spending some time in the countryside, stoking an open-hearth furnace for a time at a steel-manufacturing facility. He had a very difficult time of it. So both Tsien's family and his research circle were affected, although Tsien himself does not talk about that period beyond referring to it as "the 10 lost years."

Many people have said that during his last years in Pasadena Tsien was bitter. I never sensed that. He was no doubt hurt, but I never saw him brooding about it. It was something that had happened, and, as he saw it, he had to react in a way that was appropriate. When he felt he was no longer welcome, he resigned from all the technical societies and sometimes his letters were a bit curt. That was about the extent of it. Apart from the first six months between the cancellation of his security clearance and the INS hearing, he and his family more or less went on with their lives as usual. Their circle of acquaintances and friends did narrow, which must have been hard. A lot of his former colleagues had become a bit afraid of associating with him socially.

His children were both born here, and they have spent time in the United States as adults. His son did graduate work at Caltech. His daughter studied medicine on the East Coast and has had quite a successful practice there, but she recently decided she would return to China this summer. Each of them now has a little boy. One of the tenderest pictures I have of Tsien shows him sitting in the backseat of his chauffeur-driven car with one arm around each little four-year-old grandson.

I do think that after his problems with the INS, Tsien lost faith *in the American government, but I believe that he has always had very warm feelings for the American people. That came through again and again in the public statements he made, both here during the INS hearings, and after he returned to China. But once he went back to China, I don't think he wanted ever to deal with the United States in an official capacity again. When Caltech's former president Harold Brown visited China as secretary of defense in 1980, Tsien avoided seeing him. When I saw him the next year, I said, "Tsien, you made a big error. Harold Brown is a great admirer of yours and a brilliant guy." And he said, "I know. It was a mistake on my part." But that is how he felt about it.*

Looking back, I think the most remarkable aspect of the five years he was detained is the resilience with which he returned to his teaching and research, making this period one of his most productive and innovative. He was instrumentally involved in the development of the Daniel and Florence Guggenheim Jet Propulsion Center, Caltech's academic focus of instruction and research in jet propulsion.

There's always been a kind of single-mindedness about his work. He decides what is to be done and he organizes it and does it. He does not stop to think halfway through, is this really what I should be working on? And I believe he adopted the same attitude once he returned to China. He did not take time to indulge in speculation or fantasies about "what might have been." He never indicated to me that he had. He was confronted with a new set of problems, and he devoted himself to working full time to solve them.

F. K. Lin

Developed First Effective Genetically Engineered Drug to Treat Anemia

By L.P. Leung

• Dr. Fu-Kuen (F.K.) Lin and his research team cloned the gene that produces erythropoietin (EPO), accomplishing one of the most important breakthroughs in the history of genetic engineering. This feat revolutionized the treatment and clinical management of anemia.

• EPO restores what many kidney patients lose: the energy to live a normal life. It also improves the quality of life of AIDS patients and helps cancer patients undergoing chemotherapy to return to a daily routine and more active family life.

• EPO treatment stimulates the bone marrow to produce more red blood cells, thus reducing the need for blood transfusions and the associated risks.

Anemia: A Very Debilitating Illness

Anemia is the most common disorder of the blood. In this condition, there are not enough healthy red blood cells to replenish oxygen in body tissues. People with anemia report feeling weak or fatigued and severe cases may include shortness of breath. Very severe anemia can prompt the body to overcompensate by increasing cardiac output which, in turn, can cause palpitations and hyperthermia that may lead to heart failure in older people.

About 3.5 million Americans suffer from anemia, with millions more around the world.

The three main causes of anemia are: 1) excess blood loss—either acutely as in a hemorrhage or chronically through reduced blood volume; 2) excessive blood cell destruction from AIDS medications, malignancy, or chemotherapy; and 3) deficient production of red blood cells by the kidneys.

Erythropoietin (EPO) is a hormone normally produced in healthy kidneys. People with chronic kidney failure do not produce sufficient EPO. As a result, bone marrow is not stimulated to produce sufficient levels of red blood cells. Without sufficient red blood cells, the supply of oxygen delivered throughout the body is insufficient for rejuvenation.

Before the approval of EPO by the Food and Drug Administration (FDA), treatment of anemia was ineffective, and sometimes required potentially deadly

Photo courtesy of Amgen

Dr. F.K. Lin in his lab at Amgen in 1983.

blood transfusions before adequate HIV testing was available. Other treatments such as testosterone-based therapies were not without risk and had unwanted side effects. Thus, doctors treated only the most severe cases of anemia.

Since 1989, recombinant human EPO has been used to treat anemia in patients with chronic kidney failure, those undergoing kidney dialysis, and anemia in AIDS patients. For surgical patients who may need blood transfusions, EPO is administered in advance to stimulate the bone marrow to produce more red blood cells.

EPO does not cure anemia, and unless the underlying causes can be reversed, treatment with EPO must be continued indefinitely. Left untreated, the fatigue of severe anemia can make it almost impossible to get out of bed, much less carry out daily activities. Worse, anemia is associated with other health problems, such as cardiovascular disease and an increased risk of death. EPO relieves these and other symptoms of anemia.

The Discovery and Synthesis of EPO

The *humoral factor* regulating red blood cell production was first discovered in 1906, based on transfusion experiments in rabbits. In 1950, the still unidentified *erythropoietic factor* was found to be stimulated in rats breathing in a low-oxygen atmosphere, thus establishing the elements of its biological regulation. In the 1960s, its source was identified as the kidneys. T. Miyake, C. K. Kung and E. Goldwasser at the University of Chicago first purified human EPO from human urine in 1977. Limited quantities of the human

EPO protein were used in experiments to treat patients with anemia.

In 1981, Dr. Lin led a research team at Amgen, Inc., aimed at cloning the human EPO gene. The team initially obtained a very small quantity of human EPO from collaborators at the University of Chicago. From this material, they were able to study and determine the sequence of amino acids in part of the EPO molecule.

According to Amgen's 2004 Annual Shareholders Report, paying special tribute to the achievements of Dr. Lin: "Dr. Lin and his associate Chi-Hwei Lin (no relation) spent nearly every waking hour at the lab. Their task was staggering: finding a gene on a single fragment of DNA among about 1.5 million fragments of the human genome."

Their research sometimes led to unsuccessful approaches and disappointments but Dr. Lin never lost his faith or scientific conviction and continued to press on. Such tenacity has become a rarity in biomedical research. As research funds earmarked for their work began to dwindle, Dr. Lin's group was reduced to a team of two consisting of his associate, Chi-Hwei Lin, and himself. He gained the sometimes tenuous support of Amgen's CEO Dr. George Rathmann. After two years of dogged effort, an ingenious method, using multiple short strands of DNA as "probes" to extricate the EPO gene, finally proved effective. In Dr. Lin's words, "It's better to work on a tough project than an easy one. The easy ones may be fun to do, but you can learn a hundred times more on the tough ones."

With the sequence information, Dr. Lin designed very short pieces of DNA called *oligonucleotides*, which he hoped might match the human DNA sequence for EPO. Simultaneously, pieces of human DNA containing the gene for EPO were randomly cloned into genetically altered bacteria. Short pieces of DNA were then used as tags to spot and isolate the human EPO gene in a technique called *autoradiography*.

Recombinant DNA technology was used to express the EPO protein in ovarian cells of Chinese hamsters. The cell line was grown and multiplied under carefully controlled conditions to produce a therapeutically effective form of human erythropoietin. This allowed EPO to be produced in large quantities for the very first time.

The Race for FDA Approval

Dr. F.K. Lin's successful erythropoietin cloning and production methodology created a class of drugs known as colony-stimulating factors—naturally occurring hormones that stimulate the production of red blood cells to combat the effects of anemia. A rival biotechnology startup, Genetics Institute, developed a similar biologic at about the same time. Amgen raced ahead and prevailed in a long court battle over patent rights, leading to its gaining exclusive marketing rights for EPO in the United States.

After identification of the EPO gene in 1983, it took six years to obtain marketing approval from the FDA. EPO was the first drug approved by the FDA in 1989, using recombinant DNA technology, or "gene splicing." It was also the first blockbuster drug developed by genetic engineering laboratories, and has helped millions of patients whose low red blood cell production needed a therapeutic boost to improve their quality of life. Amgen markets EPO under the brand name EPOGEN for treating dialysis, chemotherapy and surgery patients. Johnson & Johnson purchased the marketing rights from Amgen for the same drug using the brand name, Procrit.

FDA approval of EPOGEN was the pivotal event in Amgen, Inc.'s transition from a small, struggling biotechnology startup to a top tier, multibillion dollar business. EPO quickly became the gold standard for anemia management in kidney dialysis patients.

Dr. Lin's Education and Career Background

F.K. Lin received his bachelor's and master's degrees in plant pathology from National Taiwan University in 1967.

In September of that year, he was accepted by the University of Illinois at Urbana-Champaign to study fungi physiology under Professor David Gottlieb, a pioneer in that field, and antibiotics. He received his doctorate in microbiology in 1971. From 1971 to 1981, he was a postdoctoral and research scientist at several academic institutions.

In 1981, with $19.4 million in committed funds from venture capitalists, Amgen brought in a team of research scientists, including Dr. Lin, to work on several projects. Dr. Lin was engaged to develop novel pharmaceuticals and study the molecular mechanisms of their actions. His primary research interests and foci were hematology, hypertension, immune regulation and fungi physiology. He had been involved with the Recombinant Human Erythropoietin Project since his start at Amgen, and became that group's leader. In 1983, Dr. Lin cloned the human erythropoietin gene and subsequently patented a method to produce the first human erythropoietin product. He later patented the name EPOGEN (EPO).

Dr. Lin is the named inventor in seven U.S. patents under the rubrics, "DNA Sequences Encoding Erythropoietin" and "Production of Erythropoietin."

Among Dr. Lin's Major Awards and Honors:

- *1989 Technology Corridor 100 Award* – Technology Corridor Association, and Valley Industry and Commerce Association, California, 1989.
- *Quality of Life Award* (co-recipient) – Nephrology News & Issues, North American, 1990.
- *Achievement Award* – Chinese-American Engineers and Scientists Association of Southern California (CESASC), 1992.
- *Outstanding Science Award* – Chinese-American Society of Nephrology, 1993.
- *PhRMA's 1995 Drug Discoverers Award* – Pharmaceutical Research and Manufacturers of America, 1995.
- *Medal of Excellence Award* (Nominee) – American

Association of Kidney Patients, 1997.
- *Pioneer Recognition Award* – Committee of 100, 2002.

Life After Amgen and Dr. Lin's Thoughts on Organic Gardening

Dr. Lin retired from Amgen as the director of departmental biomedical sciences in 1998. He and his family moved to a rural California town surrounded by farms, orchards and unspoiled nature. He spends much of his time tending to the plants on his two-acre mini-farm and finds gardening relaxing, unlike his previous, high-intensity, scientific work environment. Retirement has allowed him the time to develop a large, flourishing garden and avocado orchard—all grown and sustained through organic methods.

Charles K. Kao

Father of Modern Fiber Optics

By Randy Bloch

- Dr. Charles Kao's breakthrough discoveries in fiber optics ushered in a new era of lightspeed global telephone communications, digital and high-definition television, and split-second transfer of images and sound via the Internet.

- The worldwide communications network based on optical fiber transformed the world, bringing human beings closer than ever before.

- In surgery and diagnostic procedures, fiber optic medical imaging is used universally, helping save hundreds of thousands of lives each year.

- Dr. Kao received the Nobel Prize in Physics in 2009 for his developments in fiber optics. The Royal Swedish Academy of Sciences named Dr. Kao and his Nobel Prize co-recipients, "The Masters of Light."

"I still feel that it is not the invention of something that is important. It is how we can utilize that then to improve life that is important."

~Dr. Kao

Fiber Optic Technology

Fiber optic technology, as refined through Charles Kao's discoveries, uses low-loss transmission of light through glass fiber to send data exponentially faster than was possible earlier through copper wire. Its major application is the efficient transmission of information, including voice, text, graphics, still photos, music, video and movies. Fiber optic cable vastly increases the efficiency of telephone communications, reducing the number of signal-strengthening, repeater stations required for transoceanic cable systems.

Only through Charles Kao's fiber optics breakthroughs were world-changing developments such as the Internet possible. "What the wheel did for transport, the optical fiber did for telecommunications," said Richard Epworth, who worked with Kao at Standard Telecommunications Laboratories in Harlow, England, in the 1960s. But, while the development of high purity optical fiber was as important to communications as Alexander Graham Bell's invention of the telephone, a whole generation remains ignorant of Dr. Kao's achievements and takes their significance for granted.

Fiber Optics Over The Past 150 Years

The core principle of fiber optics—guiding of light through refraction—was described and demonstrated in Paris as early as the 1840s. Practical uses such as illumination during dentistry emerged early in the twentieth century, and the forerunner of modern fiber optic cable was developed by American physicist, Narinder Singh Kapany in 1952. A scientist at Tohoku University in Japan, Jun-ichi Nishizawa, first proposed fiber optic cable's use in communications in 1963 and, in 1964, invented the precursor of the ultra high-speed cable now in use.

© Qi Heng/XinHua/Xinhua Press/Corbis

Modern Fiber Optics: A Technology Remade By Dr. Charles Kao

In 1965, at Standard Communications Laboratories in England, Charles Kao and G. A. Hockham advanced the idea of fiber optics being a practical communications medium, declaring reduction of cable signal loss to below 20 *decibels per kilometer* (required for a quantum leap forward in global communications speed) was achievable.

The underpinnings of Charles Kao's breakthroughs were laid out in a 1966 technical paper, co-written with researcher Hockham. Their collaborative findings were presented by Dr. Kao to the Institute of Electrical Engineers the same year, and publication followed that June.

The theory was now in place for a communications breakthrough of global reach. But to enable a host of new technologies—including the yet undreamed of World Wide Web—a paradigmatic reduction in glass fiber's resistance to light's travel (*signal attenuation*) needed to be realized.

Drs. Kao and Hockham had shown light's absorption and scattering were partial culprits in fiber optic signal losses. More importantly, they determined the underlying and correctable cause was impurity in the glass medium itself. Kao also believed that *fused silica* (a synthetic glass hybrid) could be an ideal production material for a breakthrough in reducing signal resistance, on a mass scale.

Dr. Kao began a quest to bring fiber optics' possibilities to the world's attention. The manufacturing and communications industries scrambled to produce the low-loss glass fiber Kao and Hockham described in 1966. In 1970, a research team at Corning Glass Works in New York State fabricated a prototype and began producing fiber optic cable with the decreased resistance envisioned by Kao and Hockham. Since then, the crucial attenuation benchmark of below 20 decibels per kilometer has been reduced even further.

Applications: How Fiber Optics Changed Our World

By 1975, the first fiber optic communications links were installed in the United Kingdom. More soon followed in the U.S. and Japan. A transatlantic fiber optic cable system was placed in service in 1988 which now carries half a million telephone calls daily from the United States.

Fiber optics are today used universally across the global communications architecture. Almost all telephonic communication relies upon fiber optic technology as do digital and high-definition television. Medical procedures using imaging, such as laparoscopic (keyhole) surgery, ultrasound, and endoscopic procedures, employ slower speed, short distance fiber optic links to transmit photographs and video.

Text, music, photographs and video crisscross the globe in seconds via the Internet. A single optical fiber has the capacity to transmit several terabytes (tera is 1 followed by 12 zeroes) per second—a millionfold increase over what is possible with radio signals.

The Large Hadron Collider at the French-Swiss border—the world's largest and highest-energy particle accelerator—uses a sophisticated fiber optics network to link it to computer centers worldwide and manage the 15 petabytes of data (peta is 1 followed by 15 zeroes) it generates each year.

Education and Personal History

Dr. Charles Kuen Kao was born in Shanghai, China, in 1933 and is a citizen of the United States and Great Britain. He graduated the University of Greenwich in the United Kingdom (formerly Woolwich Polytechnic) in electrical engineering in 1957, and achieved his doctorate in 1965 from Imperial College London. Thereafter, he served as director of engineering at Standard Telecommunication Laboratories in the UK.

Dr. Kao established the department of electronics at Chinese University of Hong Kong in 1970 and accepted a vice-chancellor position in 1987. He is a member of Academia Sinica, Taiwan's most prestigious research institution. An individual of diverse interests, he enjoys pottery making and, in his sixties, took up deep sea diving. Dr. Kao retired in 1996 and lives in Mountain View, California.

Professor Tsui Hung-tat worked with Dr. Kao for four years in the same department at Chinese University of Hong Kong. He recalls: "[Dr. Kao] was always smiling. I never saw him angry. When he first talked about the fiber optics concept, we barely understood, and found his ideas quite inconceivable. He was a friend more than a colleague to me. He was very easygoing and I didn't even feel he was our department head."

An Interview With Dr. Kao

On February 26, 2004, Robert Colburn of the Institute of Electrical and Electronics Engineers conducted an oral history interview with Charles Kao. The following excerpts are used with the IEEE's permission.

Durability Of Fiber

Kao:

[W]hen I was sort of made famous by all of this, I said, "If you ask me how long we will see fiber being used, maybe 1,000 years without a replacement. . . ." The material is very cheap, as I went to the most abundant material on Earth. And it is also that the fiber itself has very, very good durability. . . . It is really the cheapest and strongest material that you can use. Of course I said afterwards also that, "If I say that, don't believe me."

Influence Of Marconi

Colburn:

Did you have the sense of standing on the shoulders of other people, and are there people now who are standing on your shoulders?

Kao:

I suppose all scientific people always find it interesting to see what one could do more to stretch something that we feel could be stretched. . . . So I suppose like all of the interesting stories of science, Newton's Laws are really quite fascinating. Although climbing up on some other giant's shoulder, I don't look at it that way in the sense that I admire the people that do that, but I don't see it as a sort of stepwise progression necessarily. There are sort of spikes of discoveries that really count.

Applications of Fiber Optics

Colburn:

What are some of the uses that fiber optics have been put to that make you proudest or happiest to see them in use that way?

Kao:

I'm an engineer, so my real purpose is something that is useful, and it is interesting to extrapolate how improvement can be made . . . and if it is made, how important it is to serve mankind. . . . I still feel that it is not the invention of something that is important. It is how we can utilize that then to improve life that is important. . . . I think the peripheral ways that people look at it and get very excited are based on very thin evidence. And so I think we should all say, "Here are some useful tools. Are they going to be really helpful for us?"

Education and Childhood Interest In Science

Kao:

I think the most important thing is that I mixed with lots of people that are curious, curiosity-driven people, and so we learned by reading, by experimenting. So that opened our minds in that more flexible way without the constraint of, "You must understand this book before you can move to that book."

The Roles Of Collaboration, Education, and Communication In Fostering Scientific Research

Colburn:

That's something a number of the other Marconi fellows have mentioned, the importance of being with other curious people

Kao:

I think that's why one could say, "is our teaching really effective?" The person that starts without too much constraint tends to do things differently. Some parents will say, "Don't do this. Don't do this." That essentially cuts the possible routes that could be opened to something interesting.

Colburn:

In your travels have you found certain educational systems that seem to [be] better at that, or certain places where that kind of freer thinking is fostered?

Kao:

We cannot put people at risk. At the same time, if you don't risk anything, then nothing will probably be achieved. Hopefully one could say that the human beings are the sensible ones.

2009 Nobel Prize in Physics—Charles K. Kao

Charles Kao received the Nobel Prize in Physics in 2009, "for groundbreaking achievements concerning the transmission of light in fibers for optical communications" (*The Royal Swedish Academy of Sciences*). Please see the Nobel Prize Laureates chapter of this volume for more information on Dr. Kao's award.

Due to Alzheimer's disease, Dr. Kao's acceptance speech was delivered by his wife Mrs. Gwen MW Kao. The *South China Morning Post* reported:

Physicist Dr. Charles Kao received his Nobel prize from Sweden's King Carl Gustaf with a special honor. Because he suffers from Alzheimer's disease, the physicist did not have to approach the king to receive his medal and award. Instead the king came to him, leaving the podium and walking down to the stage where the beaming "father of fiber optics" walked forward a few confident paces to meet him and shook his hand firmly.

Professor Kao's acceptance speech, delivered on December 8, 2009 at Stockholm University, is reprinted here by permission of The Nobel Foundation.

SAND FROM CENTURIES PAST
SEND FUTURE VOICES FAST

1. Introduction
It is sad that my husband, Professor Charles Kao, is unable to give this lecture to you himself. As the person closest to him, I stand before you to honour him and to speak for him. He is very very proud of his achievements for which the Nobel Foundation honours him. As are we all!

In the 43 years since his seminal paper of 1966 that gave birth to the ubiquitous glass fiber cables of today, the world of telephony has changed vastly. It is due to Professor Kao's persistence in the face of skepticism that this revolution has occurred.

In the 1970s, the pre-production stage moved to ITT Corp, Roanoke, Virginia, USA. Whilst Charles worked there, he received two letters. One contained a threatening message accusing him of releasing an evil genie from its bottle; the other, from a farmer in China, asked for a means to allow him to pass a message to his distant wife to bring his lunch. Both letter writers saw a future that has since become past history.

In the 1960s, our children were small. Charles often came home later than normal—dinner was waiting as were the children. I got very annoyed when this happened day after day. His words, maybe not exactly remembered, were:

"Please don't be so mad. It is very exciting what we are doing; it will shake the world one day!"

I was sarcastic, 'Really, so you will get the Nobel Prize, won't you!"

He was right—it has revolutionized telecommunications.

2. The Early Days
In 1960, Charles joined Standard Telecommunications Laboratories Ltd. (STL), a subsidiary of ITT Corp in the UK, after having worked as a graduate engineer at Standard Telephones and Cables in Woolwich for some time. Much of the work at STL was devoted to improving the capabilities of the existing communication infrastructure with a focus on the use of millimeter wave transmission systems.

Millimeter waves at 35 to 70 GHz could have a much higher transmission capacity. But the waters were uncharted and the challenges enormous, since radio waves at such frequencies could not be beamed over long distances due to beam divergence and atmospheric absorption. The waves had to be guided by a waveguide. And in the 1950s, R&D work on low loss circular waveguides—HE-11 mode—was started. A trial system was deployed in the 1960s. Huge sums were invested, and more were planned, to move this system into the pre-production stage. Public expectation for new telecommunication services such as the video phone had heightened.

Charles joined the long-haul waveguide group led by Dr. Karbowiak at STL. He was excited to see an actual circular waveguide. He was assigned to look for new transmission methods for microwave and optical transmission. He used both ray optics and wave theory to gain a better understanding of waveguide problems—then a novel idea. Later, his boss encouraged him to pursue a doctorate while working at STL. So Charles registered at University College London and completed the dissertation "Quasi-Optical Waveguides" in two years.

The invention of the laser in 1959 gave the telecom community a great dose of optimism that optical communication could be just around the corner. The coherent light was to be the new information carrier with capacity a hundred thousand times higher than point-to-point microwaves—based on the simple comparison of frequencies: 300 terahertz for light versus 3 gigahertz for microwaves.

The race between circular microwave waveguides and optical communication was on, with the odds heavily in favour of the former. In 1960, optical lasers were in their infancy, demonstrated at only a few research laboratories, and performing much below the needed specs. Optical systems seemed a non-starter.

But Charles still thought the laser had potential. He said to himself: "How can we dismiss the laser so readily? Optical communication is too good to be left on the theoretical shelf."

He asked himself the obvious questions:

1. Is the ruby laser a suitable source for optical communication?
2. What material has sufficiently high transparency at such wavelengths?

At that time only two groups in the world were starting to look at the transmission aspect of optical communication, while several other groups were working on solid state and semiconductor lasers. Lasers emit coherent radiation at optical frequencies, but using such radiation for communication appeared to be very difficult, if not impossible. For optical communication to fulfill its promises, many serious problems remained to be solved.

3. The Key Discovery

In 1963 Charles was already involved in free space propagation experiments: the rapid progress of semiconductor and laser technology had opened up a broader scope to explore optical communication realistically. With a helium-neon laser beam directed to a spot some distance away, the STL team quickly discovered that distant laser light flickered. The beam danced around several beam diameters because of atmospheric fluctuations.

The team also tried to repeat experiments done by other research laboratories around the world. For example, they set up con-focal lens experiments similar to those at Bell Labs: a series of convex lenses were lined up at intervals equal to the focal length. But even at the dead of night when the air was still and even with refocusing every 100 meters, the beam refused to stay within the lens aperture.

Bell Labs experiments using gas lenses were abandoned due to the difficulty of providing satisfactory insulation while maintaining the profiles of the gas lenses. These experiments were struggles in desperation, to control light traveling over long distances.

At STL the thinking shifted towards dielectric waveguides. Dielectric means a non-conductor of electricity; a dielectric waveguide is a waveguide consisting of a dielectric cylinder surrounded by air. Dr. Karbowiak suggested Charles and three others to work on his idea of a thin film waveguide.

But thin film waveguides failed: the confinement was not strong enough and light would escape as it negotiates a bend. When Dr. Karbowiak decided to emigrate to Australia, Charles took over as the project leader and he then recommended that the team should investigate the loss mechanism of dielectric materials for optical fibers.

A small group worked on methods for measuring material loss of low-loss transparent materials. George Hockham joined him to work on the characteristics of dielectric waveguides. With his interest in waveguide theory, he focused on the tolerance requirements for an optical fiber waveguide; in particular, the dimensional tolerance and joint losses. They proceeded to systematically study the physical and waveguide requirements on glass fibers.

In addition, Charles was also pushing his colleagues in the laser group to work towards a semiconductor laser in the near infrared, with emission characteristics matching the diameter of a single-mode fiber. Single mode fiber is optical fiber that is designed for the transmission of a single ray or mode of light as a carrier. The laser had to be made durable, and to work at room temperatures without liquid nitrogen cooling. So there were many obstacles. But in the early 1960s, esoteric research was tolerated so long as it was not too costly.

Over the next two years, the team worked towards the goals. They were all novices in the physics and chemistry of materials and in tackling new electromagnetic wave problems. But they made very credible progress in considered steps. They searched the literature, talked to experts, and collected material samples from various glass and polymer companies. They also worked on the theories, and developed measurement techniques to carry out a host of experiments. They developed an instrument to measure the spectral loss of very low-loss material, as well as one for scaled simulation experiments to measure fiber loss due to mechanical imperfections.

Charles zeroed in on glass as a possible transparent material. Glass is made from silica—sand from centuries past that is plentiful and cheap.

The optical loss of transparent material is due to three mechanisms: (a) intrinsic absorption, (b) extrinsic absorption, and (c) Rayleigh scattering. The intrinsic loss is caused by the infrared absorption of the material structure itself, which determines the wavelength of the transparency regions. The extrinsic loss is due to impurity ions left in the material and the Rayleigh loss is due to the scattering of photons by the structural non-uniformity of the material. For most practical applications such as windows, the transparency of glass was entirely adequate, and no one had studied absorption down to such levels. After talking with many people, Charles eventually formed the following conclusions.

1. Impurities, particularly transition elements such as iron, copper, and manganese, have to be reduced to parts per million or even parts per billion. However, can impurity concentrations be reduced to such low levels?

2. High temperature glasses are frozen rapidly and therefore are more homogeneous, leading to a lower scattering loss.

The ongoing microwave simulation experiments were also completed. The characteristics of the dielectric waveguide were fully defined in terms of its modes, its dimensional tolerance both for end-to-end mismatch and for its diameter fluctuation along the fiber lengths. Both the theory and the simulated experiments supported the approach.

They wrote the paper entitled, "Dielectric-Fibre Surface Waveguides for Optical Frequencies" and submitted it to the Proceedings of Institute of Electrical Engineers. After the usual review and revision, it appeared in July 1966— the date now regarded as the birthday of optical fiber communication.

4. The Paper
The paper started with a brief discussion of the mode properties in a fiber of circular cross section. The paper

then quickly zeroed in on the material aspects, which were recognized to be the major stumbling block. At the time, the most transparent glass had a loss of 200 dB/km, which would limit transmission to about a few meters—this is very obvious to anyone who has ever peered through a thick piece of glass. Nothing can be seen. But the paper pointed out that the intrinsic loss due to scattering could be as low as 1 dB/km, which would have allowed propagation over practical distances. The culprit is the impurities: mainly ferrous and ferric ions at these wavelengths. Quoting from the paper: "It is foreseeable that glasses with a bulk loss of about 20 dB/km at around 0.6 micron will be obtained, as the iron-impurity concentration may be reduced to 1 part per million." In layman terms, if one has a sufficiently "clean" type of glass, one should be able to see through a slab as thick as several hundred meters. That key insight opened up the field of optical communications.

The paper considered many other issues:

- The loss can be reduced if the mode is chosen so that most of the energy is actually outside the fiber.
- The fiber should be surrounded by a cladding of lower index (which became the standard technology).
- The loss of energy due to bends in the fiber is negligible for bends larger than 1 mm.
- The losses due to non-uniform cross sections were estimated.
- The properties of a single-mode fiber (now a key technology especially for long distance and high data rate transmission) were analyzed. It was explained how dispersion limits bandwidth; an example was worked out for a 10 km route—a very bold scenario in 1966.

It may be appropriate to quote from the Conclusion of this paper:

The realization of a successful fiber waveguide depends, at present, on the availability of suitable low-loss dielectric material. The crucial material problem appears to be one which is difficult but not impossible to solve. Certainly, the required loss figure of around 20 dB/km is much higher than the lower limit of loss figure imposed by fundamental mechanisms.

Basically all of the predictions pointed accurately to the paths of developments, and we now have 1/100 of the loss and 10,000 times the bandwidth then forecast—the revolutionary proposal in the 1966 paper was in hindsight too conservative.

5. Convincing The World

The substance of the paper was presented by Dr. Kao at an IEE meeting in February 1966. Most of the world did not take notice—except for the British Post Office (BPO) and the UK Ministry of Defense, who immediately launched major research programs. By the end of 1966, three groups in the UK were studying the various issues involved: Kao himself at STL; Roberts at BPO; Gambling at Southampton in collaboration with Williams at the Ministry of Defense Laboratory.

In the next few years, Dr. Kao traveled the globe to push his idea: to Japan, where enduring friendships were made dating from those early days; to research labs in Germany, in the Netherlands and elsewhere to spread his news. He said that until more and more jumped on the bandwagon, the use of glass fibers would not take off. He had tremendous conviction in the face of widespread skepticism. The global telephony industry is huge, too large to be changed by a single person or even a single country, but he was persistent and his enthusiasm was contagious, and slowly he converted others to be believers.

The experts at first proclaimed that the materials were the most severe of the intrinsic insurmountable problems. Gambling wrote that British Telecom had been "somewhat scathing" about the proposal earlier, and Bell Labs, who could easily have led the field, simply failed to take notice until the proven technology was pointed out to them. Dr. Kao visited many glass manufacturers to persuade them to produce the clear glass required. He got a response from Corning, where Maurer led the first group that later produced the glass rods and developed the techniques to make the glass fibers to the required specifications.

Meanwhile, Dr. Kao continued to pour energy into proving the feasibility of glass fibers as the medium for long-haul optical transmission. They faced a number of formidable challenges. The first was the measurement techniques for low-loss samples that were obtainable only in lengths of around 20 cm. The problem of assuring surface perfection was also formidable. Another problem is end surface reflection loss, caused by the polishing process. They faced a measurement impasse that demanded the detection of a loss difference between two samples of less than 0.1%, when the total loss of the entire 20 cm sample is only 0.1%. An inexact measurement would be meaningless.

In 1968 and 1969, Dr. Kao and his colleagues Davies, Jones and Wright at STL published a series of papers on the attenuation measurements of glass that addressed the above problems. At that time, the measuring instruments called spectrophotometers had a rather limited sensitivity—in the range of 43 dB/km. The measurement was very difficult: even a minute contamination could have caused a loss comparable to the attenuation itself, while surface effects could easily be ten times worse. Dr. Kao and the team assembled a homemade single-beam spectrophotometer that achieved a sensitivity of 21.7 dB/km. Later improvements with a double-beam spectrophotometer yielded a sensitivity down to 4.3 dB/km.

The reflection effect was measured with a homemade ellipsometer. To make it, they used fused quartz samples made by plasma deposition, in which the high temperature evaporated the impurity ions. With the sensitive instrument, the attenuation of a number of glass samples was measured

and, eureka, the Infrasil sample from Schott Glass showed an attenuation as low as 5 dB/km at a window around 0.85 micron—at last proving that the removal of impurity would lower the absorption loss to useful levels.

This was really exciting because the low-loss region is right at the gallium-arsenide laser emission band. The measurements clearly pointed the way to optical communication—compact gallium-arsenide semiconductor lasers as the source, low-cost cladded glass fibers as the transmission medium, and silicon or germanium semiconductors for detection. The dream no longer seemed remote. These measurements apparently turned the sentiments of the research community around. The race to develop the first low-loss glass fiber waveguide was on.

In 1967, at Corning, Maurer's chemist colleague Schultz helped to purify the glass. In 1968, his colleagues Keck and Zimar helped to draw the fibers. By 1970, Corning had produced a fiber waveguide with a loss of 17 dB/km at 0.633 micron using a titanium-diffused core with silica cladding, using the Outside Vapor Deposition (OVD) method. Two years later, they reduced the loss to 4 dB/km for a multimode fiber by replacing the titanium-doped core with a germanium-doped core.

Bell Labs finally got on the bandwagon in 1969 and created a programme in optical fiber research after having been skeptical for years. Their work on hollow light pipes was finally stopped in 1972. Their millimeter wave research programme was wound down and eventually abandoned in 1975.

It was during this time of constant flying out to other places that this cartoon joke hit home: "Children, the man you see at the breakfast table today is your father!"

We saw him for a few days and off he went again. Sometimes he flew off for the day for meetings at ITT Corp headquarters in New York. I would forget he had not left to go to the office and would phone his secretary to remind Charles to pick up milk or something on his way home.

His secretary was very amused: "Mrs. Kao, don't you know your husband is in New York today!"

6. Impact on the World

Since the deployment of the first-generation, 45-megabit-per-second fiber-optic communication system in 1976, the transmission capacity in a single fiber has rapidly increased a million fold to tens of terabits per second. Data can be carried over millions of km of fibers without going through repeaters, thanks to the invention of the optical fiber amplifier and wavelength division multiplexing. So that is how the industry grew and grew.

The world has been totally transformed because of optical fiber communication. The telephone system has been overhauled and international long distance calls have become easily affordable.

Brand new mega-industries in fiber optics including cable manufacturing and equipment, optical devices, network systems and equipment have been created.

Hundreds of millions of kilometers of glass fiber cables have been laid, in the ground and in the ocean, creating an intricate web of connectivity that is the foundation of the world-wide web.

The Internet is now more pervasive than the telephone used to be. We browse, we Skype, we blog, we go onto YouTube, we shop, we socialize on-line. The information revolution that started in the 1990s could not have happened without optical fibers.

Over the last few years fibers are being laid all the way to our homes. All-optical networks that are environmentally green are contemplated. The revolution in optical fiber communication has not ended—it might still just be at the beginning.

7. Conclusion

The world-wide communication network based on optical fibers has truly shrunk the world and brought human beings closer together. I hardly need to cite technical figures to drive this point home. The news of the Nobel Prize reached us in the middle of the night at 3:00 a.m. in California, through a telephone call from Stockholm (then in their morning) no doubt carried on optical fibers; congratulations came literally minutes later from friends in Asia (for whom it was evening), again through messages carried on optical fibers. Too much information is not always a good thing: we had to take the phone off the hook that night in order to get some sleep!

Optical communication is by now not just a technical advance, but has also caused major changes in society. The next generation will learn and grow up differently; people will relate to one another in different ways. Manufacturing of all the bits and pieces of a single product can now take place over a dozen locations around the world, providing huge opportunities for people especially in developing countries. The wide accessibility of information has obviously led to more equality and wider participation in public affairs.

Many words, indeed many books have been written about the information society, and I do not wish to add to them here—except to say that it is beyond the dreams of the first serious concept of optical communication in 1966, when even 1 GHz was only a hope.

In conclusion, Charles and I want to thank the Professors at The Chinese University of Hong Kong, namely: Professor Young, Professor Wong, Professor Cheung and Professor Chen for their support in compiling this lecture for us. Charles would like to thank ITT Corp where he developed his career for 30 years and all those who climbed on to the bandwagon with him in the early days, as without the legions of believers the industry would not have evolved as it did.

Charles Kao planted the seed; Bob Maurer watered it and John MacChesney grew its roots.

References

1. Colburn, Robert. (2004, February 26). Oral-History: Charles Kao. Institute of Electrical and Electronic Engineers Global History Network.
2. Guo, Jiaxue. (2009, October 8). Chinese University Honors Charles Kao.
3. Mesher, Kelsey. (2009, October 15). The Legacy of Charles Kao. Mountain View Voice.
4. Mok, Danny. (2009, December 11). Kao Gets Special Royal Treatment at Nobel Awards Ceremony. South China Morning Post.
5. The Royal Swedish Academy of Sciences. (2009, October 6). The Nobel Prize in Physics 2009. Press Release.
6. The Royal Swedish Academy of Sciences. (2009, October 6). The Nobel Prize in Physics 2009. Scientific Background.

Nobel Prize Laureates

By L.P. Leung

© ® The Nobel Foundation

Each year since 1901, five Nobel Prizes have been awarded to people who perform outstanding research, invent innovative processes or equipment, or make outstanding contributions in the fields of physics, chemistry, literature, peace, medicine or physiology. A sixth Nobel Prize for economics was added in 1969.

The Nobel Prize Committee of five members is entrusted with the research and selection of the prize winners, who are regarded as the best in their fields.

Alfred Nobel, a Swedish chemist and industrialist who was the inventor of dynamite, established the Nobel Prize awards as his final will and testament. It is said that Nobel was increasingly troubled by the military use of his invention, and that an erroneously reported obituary published by a French newspaper condemned him as a "merchant of death." He left 94% of his net worth to the establishment of five Nobel Prizes, perhaps in a desire to seek redemption.

According to Nobel Prize.org, between 1901 and 2009, 802 individuals and 20 organizations were awarded Nobel Prizes. Each winner receives a gold medal, a diploma, the extension of Swedish citizenship and a sum of money. Chinese-American scientists have received or shared eight awards: six in physics and two in chemistry.

1957 Nobel Prize in Physics
Tsung-Dao Lee and Chen-Ning Yang
李政道 和 楊振寧

Drs. Tsung-Dao Lee and Chen-Ning Yang shared the 1957 Nobel Prize in Physics for radically questioning one of its basic tenets—the Parity law of nuclear physics. Their hypothesis led to the publication of their historic paper, *Question of Parity Conservation in Weak Interactions*. The Merriam-Webster dictionary defines "Parity" as "The symmetry of behavior in an interaction of a physical entity (as a subatomic particle) with that of its mirror image." The principle had been accepted as a fundamental concept for the previous 30 years. However, during the 1950's, observable phenomena were found in high-energy physics that could not be explained by existing Parity theories.

In 1956, Dr. Lee (of Colum-

bia University) and Dr. Yang (of the Institute of Advanced Study in Princeton, New Jersey) further pursued the question they had raised by reviewing results of all known particle decay experiments involving weak interactions, concluding that the fundamental law of Parity Conservation might have been violated. Confirmative experiments by Dr. Chien-Shiung Wu, the "First Lady of Physics," concluded that the principle of Parity is violated at least in weak nuclear reactions, commonly known as "Parity Non-Conservation."

The "fall" of Parity cleared the way for a reconsideration of physical theories and led to new, far-reaching discoveries regarding the nature of matter and the universe.

At age 31, Dr. Tsung-Dao Lee was the second-youngest scientist to earn the Nobel Prize, which he shared with his one-time mentor, Dr. Chen-Ning Yang. Dr. Lee earned his PhD from the University of Chicago in 1950 with his thesis entitled *Hydrogen Content of White Dwarf Stars*.

At age 29, Lee became the youngest Professor of Physics on the Columbia University faculty. He was a research associate and lecturer at UC Berkeley during 1950 and 1951. The following two years, he was awarded a

Credit: Allan Richards, courtesy AIP Emilio Segre Visual Archives

L-R: Chen-Ning Yang and Tsung-Dao Lee

fellowship at the Institute of Advanced Study in Princeton where he collaborated with Dr. Yang.

Dr. J. Robert Oppenheimer, father of the atomic bomb, considered Dr. Lee one of the most brilliant theoretical physicists then known. Lee's work was characterized by a remarkable freshness and versatility. He is noted for his achievements in statistical mechanics, nuclear and subnuclear physics, astrophysics and turbulence. Many honors were bestowed upon Dr. Lee, including the prestigious Albert Einstein Commemorative Award in Science.

Dr. Chen-Ning Yang shared the 1957 Physics Nobel Prize with Dr. Lee. Dr. Yang's interests in physics were twofold: statistical mechanics and symmetry principles. He was introduced to these fields by Professor Edward Teller, the father of nuclear physics.

Drs. Chen-Ning Yang and Robert Mills, a physicist specializing in quantum field theory, collaborated to develop a new "gauge theory." Gauge theory is the cornerstone of quantum field theories, used in the Standard Model of elementary particle physics. The "Yang-Mills theories" are now a fundamental part of the Standard Model of particle physics.

Yang entered the University of Chicago in 1946 on a Tsinghua University Fellowship and received his doctorate in 1948 under the guidance of Edward Teller. He became a Professor in 1955 at the Institute for Advanced Study.

Dr. Yang is a prolific writer who has published many physics and mathematics articles in professional journals. He was elected a Fellow of the American Physical Society and the Academia Sinica in 1958 and was awarded an honorary doctorate by Princeton University in 1958.

1976 Nobel Prize in Physics
Samuel C. C. Ting
丁肇中

Dr. Samuel C.C. Ting and his research team conducted experiments at Brookhaven National Laboratory in Long Island, New York, in search of new high-mass particles. In 1974, Dr. Ting's team discovered evidence of a new "subatomic heavy parent particle," generally now known as the J/psi particle. Since then, a whole new family of particles has been discovered.

The discovery of the J/psi particle, which is thought to be composed of a "charmed quark and its antiquark," led to a significant expansion and refinement of the quark model. For his discovery, Dr. Ting was awarded one-half of the 1976 Nobel Prize for Physics jointly with Burton Richter,

Courtesy of Brookhaven National Laboratory

Samuel C.C. Ting

who made the same discovery independently at almost precisely the same time.

Samuel C.C. Ting received his doctorate degree from the University of Michigan in 1962. After spending three years as a Ford Foundation Fellow at the European Organization for Nuclear Research, he returned to teach at Columbia University's Physics Department. In 1969, Dr. Ting joined the Physics Department of the Massachusetts Institute of Technology (MIT) and, in 1977, was appointed the first Thomas Dudley Cabot Institute professor at MIT.

Dr. Ting has received numerous honors and awards in the United States as well as Europe and Asia.

1986 Nobel Prize in Chemistry
Yuan T. Lee
李遠哲

Dr. Yuan T. Lee shared the 1986 Nobel Prize Award in Chemistry with Professor Dudley R. Herschbach of Harvard University and John Polanyi of the University of Toronto. The three-man team devised techniques for cross-directing molecular beams for more precise study of processes involved in a variety of chemical reactions.

Lawrence Berkeley National Library

Yuan T. Lee

The new understanding made possible by Dr. Lee's team's findings, "could have profound applications in such varied areas as improving the efficiency of industrial chemical reactions, improving the ability to burn coal and other fuels cleanly, and understanding reactions in earth's atmosphere such as the depletion of the protective ozone layer by various chemicals," according to Eric Leber of the American Chemical Society.

Yuan T. Lee entered UC Berkeley as a graduate student from Taiwan in 1962. He carried out his thesis research on "chemi-ionization processes of electronically excited alkali atoms" under the tutelage of the late Professor Bruce Mahan. In 1967, he joined Professor Dudley R. Herschbach at Harvard University as a post-doctoral fellow.

In 1968, Dr. Lee became an assistant professor in the Department of Chemistry of the University of Chicago, beginning his illustrious academic career. He constructed a new-generation, state-of-the-art crossed molecular beam apparatus, enabling him to conduct many exciting and pioneering experiments with his students. Professor Herschbach described Lee as "the Mozart of his field, extraordinarily talented."

Since 1974, Dr. Lee has been a chemistry professor at UC Berkeley and a principal investigator at the Lawrence Berkeley laboratory. His world-class laboratory utilizes very sophisticated molecular beams apparati, which were specially designed to pursue problems associated with reaction dynamics, photochemical processes and molecular spectroscopy.

1997 Nobel Prize in Physics
Steven Chu

朱棣文

Dr. Steven Chu won one-third of the 1997 Nobel Prize in Physics by using six intersecting laser beams to create an effect known as "optical molasses." This phenomenon traps and cools sodium atoms down to 240 millionths of a degree above absolute zero. Chu and his fellow researchers reduced the speed of the target atoms from nearly 4,000 kilometers per hour to about one kilometer per hour—as if the atoms were moving through thick molasses. Dr. Chu and his team developed an "atomic trap," using lasers and magnetic coils that enabled them to capture and study the chilled target atoms. These procedures enabled a quantum leap in the study of the relationship between matter and energy. The Chu research team's new laser techniques now enable scientists to do a host of things, from improving the accuracy of atomic clocks in space navigation to designing atomic lasers that manipulate electronic circuits.

Dr. Chu was a professor in Applied Physics at Stanford University for 17 years prior to moving over to UC Berkeley. His research interests at Stanford included atomic physics, biological physics and polymer physics. In 2004, he became the sixth Director of Lawrence Berkeley National Laboratory. One of Lawrence Berkeley Laboratory's chief objectives is developing technologies to reverse climate change.

Dr. Chu campaigned for and won an unprecedented research pact to build a $500 million biofuels institute on the UC Berkeley campus—a collaboration between oil giant British Petroleum, Lawrence Berkeley Lab, and the University of Illinois. The $160 million Energy Biosciences Institute—to be funded and built by British Petroleum—will include Dr. Chu's separate solar energy program. These research pacts place the Lawrence Berkeley Lab and UC Berkeley at the center of the quest to find environmentally friendly alternatives to fossil fuels.

His devotion to the search for new solutions to our energy challenges and reversing global climate change inspired President Obama to appoint him the twelfth U.S. Secretary of Energy in 2009.

1998 Nobel Prize in Physics
Daniel C. Tsui

崔琦

Dr. Daniel C. Tsui shared one-third of the 1998 Nobel Prize Award in Physics for using powerful magnets and extremely low temperatures to

Linda A. Cicero/Stanford News Service

Steven Chu

show that thin sheets of electrons behave as a frictionless superfluid on a macro scale. His discovery has inspired a new area of research that holds the promise of revolutionary technological applications.

Dr. Tsui's research specialties include electrical properties of thin films, microstructures of semiconductors, and solid-state physics.

Daniel Tsui was born to illiterate parents in China and began his academic career aiming to study medicine. The 1957 Nobel Prize, awarded to Chen-Ning Yang and Tsung-Dao Lee, inspired him to change his course to physics. He earned his doctorate from the University of Chicago and took a research position in solid-state physics at Bell Laboratories. Instead of following the mainstream in semiconductor physics, he wandered into a new frontier: the physics of two-dimensional electrons. In February, 1982, Dr. Tsui was appointed a professor of engineering at Princeton University, beginning his teaching career.

Daniel C. Tsui

In his Nobel Prize autobiography, Dr. Tsui explained his reasons for leaving a comfortable research position at Bell Labs to return to the world of academics: *"Perhaps it was the Confucius in me, the faint voice I often heard when I was alone, that the only meaningful life is a life of learning. What better way is there to learn than through teaching?"*

2008 Nobel Prize in Chemistry
Roger Y. Tsien
錢永健

A bioluminescent jellyfish is the agent that helped three scientists earn the Nobel Prize.

Professor Roger Tsien of the University of California, San Diego (UC San Diego), shared the 2008 Nobel Prize in Chemistry with two other American chemists—Osamu Shimomura and Martin Chalfie—for the discovery, expression and development of the green fluorescent protein (GFP) from the jellyfish, *Aequorea victoria*. Jeremy M. Berg, Director of the National Institute of General Medical Sciences, stated, "It is an essential piece of the scientific tool box.... It is impossible to overstate the impact of these investigators' work on scientific progress."

The remarkable, brightly glowing, green fluorescent protein, GFP, was first observed in the beautiful jellyfish in 1962. Since then, this protein has become one of the most important tools used in contemporary science. With the aid of GFP, researchers have developed ways to watch processes that were previously invisible, such as the development of nerve cells in the brain or how cancer cells spread.

~The Royal Swedish Academy of Science
(entrusted with awarding the Nobel Prize)

Professor Tsien contributed to the general understanding of how GFP fluoresces. He and his colleagues studied the color-producing protein of the GFP and mutated the color palette to produce variants that glowed yellow, cyan and blue. Other researchers soon followed to extend the spectrum of dazzling fluorescent colors, including red, as markers for different proteins and cells. Its development as a tagging tool enabled scientists to follow several different biological processes simultaneously. Now, researchers can peer inside living cells and see the movements, positions and interactions of the tagged proteins in real time.

Roger Y. Tsien   Getty Images

Dr. Roger Y. Tsien was born in New York in 1952 and is from an extended family of scientists. His father was an engineering professor at MIT and his brother is a scientist at Stanford. Dr. H.S. Tsien, co-founder of the Jet Propulsion Laboratory and a renowned rocket scientist, was his father's cousin.

At age 16, Tsien won the Westinghouse talent search with a project investigating how metals bind to organic compounds. He graduated from Harvard University on a National Merit Scholarship and received his PhD in Physiology from the University of Cambridge.

In 2004, Dr. Tsien received the Wolf Prize in Medicine, "for his seminal contribution to the design and biological application of novel fluorescent and photographic molecules to analyze and perturb cell signal transduction."

Dr. Tsien has received numerous other awards and honors. He served on the faculty of the University of California, Berkeley, from 1982 to 1989 and has been on the faculty of UC San Diego as Professor of Pharmacology, and Professor of Chemistry and Biochemistry, since 1989.

2009 Nobel Prize in Physics
Charles Kao
高錕

Dr. Charles K. Kao received the 2009 Nobel Prize in Physics for developments in fiber optics—the low-loss transfer of light through ultra pure glass fiber.

Dr. Kao's breakthroughs have dramatically increased the efficiency and affordability of worldwide telephone communications. Fiber optic cable allows near-instantaneous global transfer of voice, photos, video, music, text and other data. The technology has important medical applications in diagnostic and surgical procedures: it conveys real-time images from inside the body through fiber optic cable to a video screen.

The Nobel Prize in Physics award generally recognizes achievements in theoretical rather than applied physics.

An award in the latter instance is uncommon. Moreover, crossing disciplines to select an engineer to receive the Physics prize is rare.

Charles Kao received half the $1.4 million prize with the other half shared between Willard S. Boyle and George E. Smith, co-inventors of digital sensor imaging technology.

For more information on Dr. Charles Kao's education, training, and contributions to fiber optics, please see his expanded profile listed in the Table of Contents.

Yo-Yo Ma

Super Virtuoso Cellist and Messenger of Peace

By Wing Mar and Randy Bloch

- Yo-Yo Ma is an international concert soloist who also performs on television and in movies.

- He is the winner of numerous Grammy Awards for his performances and albums.

- Ma was a founding member of the *Committee of 100*, an organization that monitors Chinese- American political and community issues and U.S.-China relations.

- He was appointed a United Nations Messenger of Peace in 2006 by former UN secretary general Kofi Annan.

Ambassador Traveling with a Cello

The world's premier classical cellist, articulate and debonair Yo-Yo Ma, builds bridges of friendship wherever he travels. His engaging personality and virtuosity qualify him as an ambassador traveling not with a portfolio—but a cello.

Few musicians, classical or otherwise, have successfully bridged as many styles and genres as Yo-Yo Ma. The cello virtuoso has recorded with jazz musicians Bobby McFerrin and Chick Corea, bluegrass musician Edgar Meyer, Argentinean tango composer Astor Piazzolla; and played "Silent Night" at a fictional White House Christmas dinner on the TV drama, *West Wing*. He has appeared on the children's shows *Sesame Street* and *Mister Rogers' Neighborhood* and won Grammy Awards in nearly every classical category.

Silk Road Project Linking People and Cultures

As his arc as a soloist before the world's great orchestras began to rise, Yo-Yo Ma gradually embraced musical traditions well beyond the traditional classical repertoire. This led to his vision of music linking peoples and cultures, which found expression

Kevin Mazur—Getty: WireImage

in founding the *Silk Road Project* in 1998. The Project is named for the network of trade routes that for two thousand years connected the cultures and countries of East Asia to the Mediterranean. Ma metaphorically describes the historic Silk Road as "the World Wide Web of its day." *The World & I* magazine described his Silk Road Project as "An ambitious project exploring exchanges between lands of the Silk Road and the West through concerts, festivals, exhibitions, educational outreach, recordings, publications and the commissioning of new musical works." Festivals are the project's cornerstone, and appearing at them all is cellist Ma himself, the Project's Artistic Director. Again quoting Yo-Yo Ma: "There is no culture in the world we have not benefited from. Every time I open a newspaper, I am reminded that we live in a world where we can no longer afford not to know our neighbors."

Committee of 100 Humanitarian Endeavors

Whenever possible, Yo-Yo Ma uses his global standing as an artist to further his humanitarian endeavors. He is a founding member of the Committee of 100 which was organized in 1990 by accomplished Chinese Americans from a wide range of professions. The Committee keeps a watchful eye on issues in the

Chinese-American community and U.S.-China relations. Early on, its founders initiated a landmark survey and focus group study, to analyze perceptions of Chinese Americans and Asian Americans by non-Asian Americans. The results showed troubling and negative stereotyping still prevalent in our communities, particularly in the high-tech and defense sectors.

United Nations Messenger of Peace

Yo-Yo Ma was appointed a United Nations Messenger of Peace in 2006 by then UN secretary general Kofi Annan. UN Messengers of Peace help to focus worldwide attention on the goals of the United Nations and are selected for their prodigious career achievements and participation in humanitarian causes. Yo-Yo Ma's vision for the Silk Road Project—creating bridges of understanding through sharing music and cultural traditions across international boundaries—is akin to his role as a UN Messenger of Peace. Some of his fellow Messengers have been Nobel Prize laureate Elie Wiesel, actor Michael Douglas and primatologist Jane Goodall.

Path to Success

A classical music "super-virtuoso," Yo-Yo Ma was born in Paris on October 7, 1955 to a musical family from Hong Kong. He was a prodigy who began violin and cello study at age four. After his family moved to New York City when he was seven, he began formal studies at the Juilliard School of Music, and was a featured soloist with the Harvard Radcliffe Orchestra at the age of fifteen. He later attended Columbia University and earned an undergraduate degree from Harvard University in 1976. In 1991, he received an honorary doctorate degree from Harvard and, in 2004, received the 10th Annual Harvard Arts Medal for his contributions to education and the public good.

I.M. Pei

One of the World's Premier Architects

By Yvonne Chang

The 1983 laureate of the Pritzker Architecture Prize (the world's most prestigious architectural award), I.M. Pei is one of the most successful architects of the 20th century. He is known for embracing Eastern and Western approaches in his designs. This fusion testifies to how the convergence of two cultures, Chinese and European, can create distinct aesthetic design standards.

"I belong to that generation of American architects who built upon the pioneering perception of the modern movement, with an unwavering conviction in its significant achievements in the field of art, technology and design…. Architects by design investigate the play of volumes in light, explore the mysteries of movement in space, examine the measure that is scale and proportion, and above all, they search for that special quality that is the spirit of the place as no building exists alone."

~From I.M. Pei's Pritzker Architecture Prize acceptance speech

"He has given this century some of its most beautiful interior spaces and exterior forms."

~Citation from the Pritzker Prize Jury

When I.M. Pei was awarded the Pritzker Architecture Prize—widely considered the architecture field's Nobel Prize—he had designed over fifty projects in the U.S. and internationally, many of them award winners. The Pritzker award medal bears the inscription, "Commodity, Firmness, and Delight"—three conditions set forth more than 2,000 years ago by Marcus Vitruvius in his *Ten Books of Architecture.*

In 1986, I.M. Pei was awarded the Medal of Liberty by President Ronald Reagan as one of twelve persons considered to be among the most distinguished naturalized citizens in the United States of America.

© Jason Jem

Ieoh Ming Pei was born in China in 1917, the eldest son of a prominent banker. Until age 17, his entire world was the coastal area of China. He recalls playing in the family garden in Suzhou with its caves of rock, stone bridges, ponds and waterfalls. In this garden, he learned to appreciate how man and nature complement each other. He has said, "Man creates to complement nature and nature has an effect on man's creations."

Early Career—an Architect of Quality Public Housing Projects

At age 17, I.M. Pei came to the United States to study architecture at MIT and the Harvard Graduate School of Design. He later took a position as assistant professor at Harvard and, in 1948, was recruited as director of architecture at Webb and Knapp, a major New York City real estate development firm. He learned the importance of local and state politics to real estate development there from William Zeckendorf, one of the most prominent developers in the United States, who purchased Webb and Knapp in 1949.

One of Pei's first major projects was renewal of the Society Hills district of Philadelphia. His project helped turn the district from a slum into a desirable residential neighborhood. Another low-cost housing project—the Kips Bay Apartments in the heart of New York City's Manhattan borough—was designed by Pei's firm in 1961 and consists of three, high-rise towers with a large, private park, within. During this period, I.M. Pei and William Zeckendorf replaced parcels of substandard urban housing in many U.S. cities with low-cost, quality housing.

The Road to Becoming a World-Renowned Architect

In 1955, Pei formed his own partnership: I.M. Pei and Associates. The Pei firm was chosen in 1961 to design the National Center for Atmospheric Research in Boulder, Colorado—his first important project independent of William Zeckendorf. The project site was in the foothills of the Rocky Mountains, requiring harmonization with the dramatic backdrop of the mountain range. Pei and his wife drove to Colorado, Arizona, and New Mexico to acquaint themselves with the area. His design achieved a remarkable congruence between the building and the natural setting, making it appear the edifice had been carved out of the mountains. The result was perfect harmony.

In 1964, Jacqueline Kennedy considered retaining I.M. Pei to design the John F. Kennedy Presidential Library and Museum in Boston, Massachusetts. At that time, Pei worked out of a modest-sized studio, and lacked an impressive portfolio of museums or concert halls to show clients. Up to that point, his work was relatively unglamorous—largely consisting of slum clearing and low-cost housing projects. In preparing to receive Mrs. Kennedy, he repainted his studio and purchased flowers which he placed in the tiny reception area. Mrs. Kennedy noticed the beautiful flowers immediately and asked if he always kept flowers in his studio. She inquired about his previous work and his involvement with low-cost housing projects. In the end, Mrs. Kennedy chose Pei over a number of well-established architects, many with international standing.

The Kennedy Library project was completed between 1965 and 1979; ten years alone were spent finding and securing a site. Robert Kennedy died in 1968, and Jacqueline Kennedy left the project shortly afterward. Teddy Kennedy was preoccupied with his own problems. The project was orphaned spiritually, and Pei himself became emotionally and creatively exhausted. The site finally selected was an unseemly location that had originally been a garbage dump. Pei remade the site, and placed the building at the tip. Due to circumstances beyond his control, the project was a success but not in quite the way Pei had imagined. The Kennedy Library was a partial disappointment, but also a turning point for I.M. Pei.

In 1983, the restoration of the Louvre Museum in Paris was another project of I.M. Pei's that was fraught with difficulties. It had the enthusiastic support of French president François Mitterrand but there were protests from many. Eventually, the work took thirteen years to complete. When Pei proposed a glass pyramid for the new central courtyard that he said would appear like a sparkling diamond, the *Commission Superieure des Monuments Historiques* suggested it would look like a cheap, fake diamond. The mayor of Paris at the time, Jacques Chirac, was also not in favor of Pei's plan. After seeing a full-scale mock-up, however, he decided it was "not bad." The battle over the design of the pyramid lasted 18 months. Chirac's acceptance was crucial. But, President Mitterrand kept his private promise to Pei that he would not be sent home in disgrace.

In 1990, Pei retired, but continued accepting commissioned projects outside the United States. In 2006, at age 89, his Suzhou Museum project—in Jiangsu, People's Republic of China—opened to great fanfare. This was a project very important personally as his family had lived in the area for hundreds of years, and he spent summers there as a boy. The Suzhou Museum is a combination of contemporary and traditional Chinese motifs. Pei's hope is that this type of design will encourage and inspire China to preserve its rich heritage without being a slave to it.

I.M. Pei's Advice to Young Architects

When two of Pei's sons decided to become architects, he cautioned them that they must have a great love of the profession and success would not come quickly. He told them a 25 year old architect is rarely selected to design an office building, and an unknown architect would be lucky to be chosen even to design a small house. When asked what he enjoyed most about his world-class projects, he said it was the process of overcoming great obstacles with the assistance of his collaborators and his clients.

References

von Boehm, Gero. Conversations with I.M. Pei. Munich, London: Prestel, 2000.

Maya Ying Lin

Architect and Artist: Visions with Unlimited Boundaries

By Bobbi Leung and Margie Lew

Maya Lin changed how America grieves with her design of the Vietnam Veterans Memorial.

"'I meant for people to cry,' she says. 'Memorials are about honesty and acceptance of death—only then can you experience a catharsis.'"

~Asian Week, November 1995

The Vietnam Veterans Memorial (The Wall)

As a young Yale University student, Maya Lin's life was never touched by the horrors of war or its aftermath. It therefore seems inconceivable that her intuitive vision enabled her to create a memorial touching the very souls of America's war veterans. Maya was a 21-year-old undergraduate architecture student when she designed the Memorial as a project for a funerary architecture class. When she visited the proposed site, she envisioned "cutting into the earth ... opening it up, an initial violence and pain that in time would heal ... leaving a pure, flat surface in the earth with a polished, mirrored surface." (*Boundaries, 2000*) From the image in her mind's eye evolved the dynamic and emotionally searing monument. The design was complete before she even thought to enter it into the nationwide competition.

Maya Lin's design was chosen from a field of 1,421 blind entries. It was controversial, and some critics called it a "black gash of shame." The fact that she was a young Chinese-American woman added to the controversy. The criticism and opposition continued for months and could have derailed the project. Despite the unpleasantness, Lin stood her ground, defended the design, and "fought like hell." Her determination and conviction made it certain the memorial

© Adam Stoltman/Corbis

was built as originally conceived. Dedicated in 1982, the ensuing years have shown the impact of the Vietnam Veterans Memorial as it continues to bring people together and foster emotional healing.

Since its dedication, millions of people have visited the Memorial. Vietnam veterans have come by the thousands to honor their comrades-in-arms, find healing for their spiritual pain, and to form unbreakable bonds with other veterans and visitors. In remembrance, innumerable mementos and tokens of love have been left at the Wall. Even more poignant are the images of the visitors themselves:

A woman's hand reaches up to touch a name on the shiny black granite. Reflected in the wall, her face expresses grief and remembrance. Her eyes on the name, she quietly speaks, then touches her fingers to her lips and to the name again. Before stepping away, she places a card and a flower at the base of the wall;

A sweet-faced little boy is held high enough to reach and kiss his daddy's name;

A mother, in tears, holds a photo of her soldier-son;

An elderly couple holds each other as they gaze at their grandson's name;

A woman in a wheelchair wipes her eyes as a rubbing is made of her son's name;

A Marine with medals and insignias on his cap and jacket, with a faraway look in his eyes, holds a photo of his buddy—missing in action;

Groups of veterans share long, tearful embraces;

Veterans sit in wheelchairs, sharing memories of the war and enjoying each other's company;

A lone veteran sits a distance away from the Wall, lost in his own thoughts and with emotions too painful to bring him closer to the site;

Family members console a young widow whose deep sense of loss is etched in her grief-stricken face.

These images, seen time and again, are a testament to the power of the Memorial to bring solace and a measure of relief from the painful memories of a war that affected so many Americans.

The Vietnam Veterans Memorial Changed the Language and Form of Memorial Architecture

The Memorial is not a traditional monument, commemorative statue, or political statement:

Two polished walls of granite, composed of seventy panels, stand starkly alone in Constitution Gardens. Where the outer ends of the two walls meet, the visitor is below ground level, looking up at a wall of granite etched with names 10.1 feet in height. The structure is highly polished and reflective so that one reading the names will find his or her own image cast, as through smoked glass, upon the Wall. On this polished, reflective surface are 58,183 (as of 2007: 58,256) names, etched chronologically in the order of their

deaths—the men and women of the Armed Forces of the United States, who died or remain missing as a result of having served in the Vietnam War.

Steve Lew, Vietnam Veteran

Maya Lin's Early Years

What circumstances in her early life gave rise to this unique young woman's artistic sensibility? Maya Lin is from a close-knit family. Both her parents are Chinese immigrants, educated in the United States. They were professors at Ohio University in Athens, Ohio, where her father, Henry, was dean of the art school and her mother, Julia Chang Lin, was a professor of Asian and English literature. Maya has an older brother, Tan Lin. She grew up surrounded by land and the sounds of nature. The family home was filled with books, magazines, and arts and crafts. Education was emphasized, not only to learn, but to experiment and be creative. It was an atmosphere of learning that encouraged her to make choices, develop her mind and improve upon her abilities. There were always many opportunities to explore and create art at home and while attending college. Lin did well in school and took university classes while a high school student.

Maya was accepted to Yale University and began her freshman year in 1977. She was informed she could choose to study sculpture or architecture, but not both. She admits that as an architecture student, she would sneak over to the art school for sculpture classes. Being unable to choose between two disciplines, studying both proved to be an asset that makes her creative work unique.

Maya Lin is not only an architect: her diverse works and projects cross the boundaries of architecture, art, landscape and sculpture. She has said, "The difference between architecture and art can be likened to the difference between prose and poetry." Architecture is functional, and yet a single theme or idea underlies her designs. Artwork, however, stems from a "pure inspirational idea."

Her Creative Process

Once Lin determines the purpose of a project, especially a memorial, "purpose becomes the soul of the work," determining the outcome. "I have always used nature and the environment for inspiration," says Lin. Consequently, her designs develop as a response to the natural surroundings of a specific location. As the design emerges, it is not static; it progresses and changes as construction continues, never deviating from the original purpose or vision. "My idea appears very quickly and is fully formed when it arrives. I do not work and rework the ideas. And in looking at the final work, I think it is most successful when it captures the spirit of those first sketches or models."

The Montgomery Civil Rights Memorial

After designing the Vietnam Veterans Memorial, Maya was commissioned to design the Civil Rights Memorial (1989) in Montgomery, Alabama. For months she researched and educated herself on all facets of the Civil Rights Movement. Only then did she visit the location planned for the memorial—the church where Dr. Martin Luther King served as pastor during the Montgomery Bus Boycott in 1955-1956. She was inspired by Dr. King's "I Have a Dream" speech: "... we will not be satisfied until justice rolls down like waters and righteousness like a mighty stream...." She knew that water would form an integral part of the memorial; a thin film of water ripples over the names of 40 civil rights activists.

The Women's Table at Yale University

In 1993, Lin completed The Women's Table at Yale University, celebrating the presence of women at Yale since they were first admitted to Yale College in 1969. She researched and read about these pioneer women for months before conceiving the work's elliptical shape, and the design of the text and graphics. After this project, not wanting to be known solely as a monument builder, she retired from the "memorial business." Her subsequent public and private works, from Groundswell (1993) to the present, exist "somewhere between art and architecture."

The Confluence Project
Commemorating The Lewis and Clark Expedition

In 2000, around the time of publication of her book, *Boundaries*, Lin was approached about a new project: a series of memorials commemorating the Lewis and Clark Expedition of the American West. She has become the "visionary guide of ... the Confluence Project—a grand collaboration between Lin, the Confederated Tribes of the Umatilla, the Nez Perce Tribe, the Lewis and Clark Commemorative Committee of Vancouver/Clark County, and the Friends of Lewis and Clark of Pacific County."

Maya Lin sees the Confluence Project as a "restoration and reclamation project," a transformation that offers people the opportunity to "look to the past, see where we are today and then look to a different future, perhaps a greener future." The word *confluence* is defined as a place where rivers flow into one another but also as a coming together, meeting, or gathering in one place. The Confluence Project highlights sites along the Columbia River and its tributaries that were points of contact between the Lewis and Clark expedition and Native Americans.

There are seven Confluence Project sites along a 450-mile course of the Columbia River Basin, each marking a place of confluence between rivers, peoples and cultures along the River. As of August 23, 2008, three of the sites had been completed.

The natural settings at each Confluence Project site, as well as the permanent art installations, create a sense of place and bring together the past and present. Environmental issues and history are integrated to create awareness of and sensitivity to the changes that have occurred in the 200 years since Lewis and Clark made contact with the culture and homelands of Native Americans. The Project involves unprecedented interpretive artwork by Maya Lin. At each site, her own work, and those of local artists and architects, incorporate historical facts and information on plants and animals that existed 200 years ago.

The *Cape Disappointment State Park* site, dedicated November 18, 2005, is located at the mouth of the Columbia River where it flows into the Pacific Ocean. *The Sandy River Delta* site, dedicated on August 23, 2008, is near the confluence of the Columbia River and the Sandy River. *The Vancouver Land Bridge project site* in Vancouver, Washington, was also dedicated on August 23, 2008, and reconnects the historic Fort Vancouver area with the Columbia River at its confluence with the Klickitat Trail.

Lin is less about stunning artworks than overall message. "I'm a restorer: If I was successful, you'll barely know I was there," she says. "The art is about helping people get in touch with the land. Maybe if you realize what's gone, you think more about the future."

The News Tribune of Tacoma, Washington
October, 2008

"Missing"—One Last Memorial

The subject of Maya Lin's final memorial is one she cares deeply about and is the only theme that Lin herself initiated. The memorial is a commentary on the environment and humanity's relationship to it. Entitled "Missing," it focuses on the disappearing species on planet Earth. Its installations, involving multiple sites, include photography, video, and lists of names of extinct or near-extinct birds, animals and plant species. With a satellite link connecting all the sites, it is a way to monitor the health of the planet. "Missing" was launched on Earth Day, April 22, 2009, with the placement of a memorial table, commissioned by the California Academy of Sciences, in Golden Gate Park in San Francisco, California.

Sometimes I think creativity is magic; it's not a matter of finding an idea, but allowing the idea to find you.

Maya Lin

Maya Lin Career Timeline (Highlights)

- 1982: The Vietnam Veterans Memorial, Washington, DC
- 1989: Civil Rights Memorial, Montgomery, Alabama
- 1993: Women's Table, Yale University, New Haven, Connecticut
- 1993: Groundswell, Ohio State University, Athens, Ohio
- 1994: Eclipsed Time, Penn Station, New York, New York
- 1994: The Wave Field, University of Michigan, Ann Arbor, Michigan
- 1999: Langston Hughes Library, Haley's Farm, Clinton, Tennessee
- 2000: Publishes her book Boundaries
- 2000: Confluence Project—first site dedicated in 2005
- 2000: Timetable, Stanford University, Palo Alto, California
- 2004: Interfaith Chapel, Clinton, Tennessee
- 2005: Elected to the American Academy of Arts & Letters
- 2005: Elected to the National Women's Hall of Fame
- 2005: Arts Plaza, University of California, Irvine
- 2006: Maya Lin: Systematic Landscapes
- 2008: Renovation of Museum of Chinese in America (MOCA), New York, NY

References

1. Jack Magazine. http://www.jackmagazine.com/issue9/essayksands.html.
2. Lashnits, Tom. (2000) Asian Americans of Achievement. New York: Chelsea House.
3. Lin, Maya. (2000) Boundaries. New York: Simon & Schuster.
4. Lopez, Sal. (1987) The Wall: Images and Offerings from the Vietnam Veterans Memorial. New York:

Collins Publishers.

5. Maya Lin: A Strong Clear Vision. American Film Foundation. Mock, Freida Lee.

6. Maya Lin Interview—Academy of Achievement. (2000) http://achievement.org.

7. O'Connor, Anne Marie. Earthly Concern. Los Angeles Times.

8. Remembering Vietnam: The Wall at 25. (2007) Video. Smithsonian.

9. Scruggs, Jan. (1985) Reflections on the Wall, The Vietnam Veterans Memorial.

10. The Confluence Project. http://www. ConfluenceProject.org.

11. The News Tribune. Tacoma, Washington. October 12, 2008.

The World of
Nancy Kwan

A Fortune Teller's Prescience?

By Jack Ong

"Like the ocean, life is ever-changing. I learned to go with the flow. I live for the day and I live in the moment."

~Nancy Kwan, leading actress in major Hollywood films, including *The World of Suzie Wong* and *Flower Drum Song*

A Fortuneteller's Prescience?
The World of Suzie Wong

Born in Hong Kong and educated in England, her childhood dreams focused on a career as a ballet dancer, Nancy Kwan—quite by chance—found herself catapulted into the world spotlight when she was chosen to star in Paramount Pictures' The World of Suzie Wong opposite William Holden.

Chance? Most definitely, it seems!

"I went to a fortune teller as a kid," Kwan recalls. "They told me I was going to be an actress, a famous actress. But I always wanted to be a ballet dancer. Ballet was my big passion. I took lessons once a week. But acting? I never considered acting. So it was in the stars, as they say."

In addition to the global box office success of Suzie Wong, Nancy herself won rave reviews and earned Hol-

Courtesy of Nancy Kwan

lywood Foreign Press Golden Globe nominations as Best Actress (Drama) and International Star of Tomorrow for her enchanting, heartbreaking performance as a resilient Hong Kong prostitute struggling to raise a baby boy, who meets an American artist. Nancy Kwan also won the hearts of filmgoers everywhere—none more so than those in the Asian American community, thrilled at last to discover a beautiful, talented superstar in the making!

"Well, I was definitely in the right place at the right time," Kwan says modestly, again referring to the matter of chance. She elaborates:

France Nuyen was playing the Suzie role on Broadway, where the musical, Flower Drum Song, was also a big hit at the time. Ray Stark, Suzie Wong's producer, was on a worldwide search for an actress to do the movie version. When they got to Hong

Courtesy of Nancy Kwan

Kong, the auditions were held in a studio that my father (a prominent architect) had designed. I went there to watch my favorite Chinese movie stars audition, that's all. They saw me sitting there and asked if I wanted to audition. That's when I met Ray Stark. I auditioned and I giggled throughout the test.

About six weeks later, I got this letter from Ray Stark offering to send me to America to study acting. I thought, "Hmm, I've never been to America. That would be nice, and I'll be paid to do it." So I went. I came to Los Angeles, staying at the Studio Club, where lots of out-of-town actresses stayed. Well, I didn't get the role. France got it and she went to do the movie in Hong Kong. Ray Stark advised me to join the Suzie Wong stage touring company if I was really interested in acting, so I did. I was in Toronto doing the show when he called me from London and asked me to test again for the movie. I said I thought they were already filming with France Nuyen. He said, "No, no, no. We're letting her go and we're letting the director go. Come over and do another screen test." I asked who with, and he said, "William Holden."

Nancy packed her bags and left the Toronto stage company, flew to London for her second screen test, and got the part.

"So you see, it's all timing in life," she reflects; "being at the right place at the right time."

Then Came "Flower Drum Song"

The time was right for Nancy Kwan and her growing legion of fans. The time also was right for her to bring her considerable dancing skills to the big-budget, motion picture version of Rodgers and Hammerstein's hit Broadway musical, *Flower Drum Song*. The international success of that Universal Pictures movie, produced by Ross Hunter, more than validated the fortune teller's prescience: Nancy was now a very famous actress!

She recalls being at a party in Los Angeles after the release of "Suzie Wong" when a gentleman approached her:

Courtesy of Nancy Kwan

"Nancy Kwan?" he asked. I said "Yes." "You're perfect for Linda Low!" he said. "It was Ross Hunter. He told me he was producing the movie version of *Flower Drum Song* and that I was perfect for the part. And that's how I got it. No audition or screen test, none of that. Again, I was in the right place at the right time."

Nancy had not read the *Flower Drum Song* novel nor had she seen the stage musical; so she was able to offer her own, unforgettable, onscreen interpretation of the sassy, thoroughly modern Linda Low.

The filming of *Flower Drum Song* gave new life to the Rodgers and Hammerstein stage production and established Nancy's lifelong friendship with C. Y. Lee, author of the book. "C. Y. is amazing," she said. "He is so prolific. In fact, he wrote a new play in 2007 and asked me to be in it. Even in his advanced years, he continues to write and do ballroom dancing."

Another relationship developed during Nancy's *Flower Drum Song* experience: "We had six weeks of dance rehearsals at Universal. Our choreographer was the legendary Hermes Pan. One day, we were working, and I looked up to see a familiar man standing by the piano. Soon all of us were looking at him. It couldn't be! But it was … Fred Astaire! We freaked out! He couldn't have been nicer as I got to know him."

After "Flower Drum Song"

After *Flower Drum Song*, marriage and motherhood took center stage in the world of Nancy Kwan. Following the birth of her son, Bernie, she divided her time between Europe and

America, starring in such films as *The Main Attraction* with Pat Boone; *Honeymoon Hotel* with Robert Goulet and Robert Morse; *Tamahine*; *Fate is the Hunter* opposite Glenn Ford; *Lt. Robinson Crusoe USA* with Dick Van Dyke; *The Wrecking Crew* with Dean Martin; *Arrivederci Baby* opposite Tony Curtis; *Nobody's Perfect* with Doug McClure; and *The McMasters* with David Carradine, Brock Peters and Jack Palance.

The 1970s in Hong Kong

Nancy moved to Hong Kong in the 1970s with her son (the late Bernie Pock, a stunt performer and writer). There, she entered film production as the managing director of Nancy Kwan Films, which specialized in TV commercials for the Southeast Asia market. In addition to running the business, which included a recording studio and a motion picture equipment rental division, Nancy directed a number of commercials. She also continued her acting career, starring in numerous films made in Southeast Asia, including *Wonder Woman*; *The Pacific Connection*; *Fortress in the Sun*; *Project Kill*; *Fear*; and *Spring Comes Not Again*, which won her rave reviews.

Returning to the U. S. in the 1980s

Nancy appeared in the TV pilot of *Hawaii 5-0* with Jack Lord and the two-part "Cenotaph" episode of *Kung Fu* with David Carradine.

Returning to the United States, Nancy starred in numerous television episodes of *ER*, *Fantasy Island*, *Trapper John* and *Knots Landing*; TV movies such as *Noble House* and *Miracle Landing*; the feature films *Dragon: The Bruce Lee Story*, *Walking the Edge*, *Keys to*

Freedom, and the Sundance-developed *Mr. P's Dancing Sushi Bar*; and, the live stage dramas *Love Letters, Arthur and Leila* and *Who's Afraid of Virginia Woolf*. She also recorded a variety of audio books.

Nancy also produced (with husband Norbert Meisel) *The Biker Poet*, a movie written by her son; co-produced and starred in *Ray of Sunshine* (directed by Meisel); narrated the documentary, *Anna May Wong, Frosted Yellow Willows: Her Life, Times and Legend*; appeared in *Hollywood Chinese*, an Arthur Dong documentary and Toronto International Film Festival selection; and is the central subject of *Ka Shen's Journey*, a documentary feature by Brian Jamieson. She also starred in and narrated a TV special, *My Hong Kong*, which won two Telly Awards; collaborated as a writer on several screenplays; and developed the concept for *Tai Chi Chuan—Touching the Clouds*, her bestselling instructional video.

The World According To Nancy

"I've stayed in the movie business all this time because I really love films and I love the whole business of making them," Nancy says. "I love being part of it all!" Often asked by aspiring actors, young and old, for her advice, Nancy has this to say: "If it's really important to you, if it's really what you want to do, then you just have to stay in there and work

for it. In the long run, if you work for something, especially considering the big disappointments, it will be worth it. Hang in there! Believe in what you're doing!"

It is very apparent that Nancy Kwan believes in everything she

embraces—acting, dancing, producing, directing, writing, running a business, and giving of her talent and resources in any number of charitable endeavors. She is extremely comfortable being a role model, and is happy when youngsters approach her with admiration.

"At a party following the premiere of Arthur Dong's *Hollywood Chinese*," she recalls with a smile, "a 12-year-old girl came up to me, happily telling me that she watches *Flower Drum Song* every day. Every day! I think it's wonderful when your efforts can inspire new generations."

As inspired as she is inspirational, Nancy accepts her many tributes (like the Hawaii Chinese Chamber of Commerce Lifetime Achievement Award (2008)) with gratitude and humility, transcending the Hollywood star persona with charm and dignity, and fortified with the courage and determination of a world-class champion.

What fuels Nancy Kwan's drive? What's the philosophy behind this enduring, endearing international star?

Good question. My philosophy changed after my son's death. That's when I truly realized how fleeting life is. It's very fleeting. Nothing stays the same. Like the ocean, life is ever-changing. I learned to go with the flow. I live for the day and I live in the moment.

Michelle Kwan

World Champion Figure Skater

By Marian Chew

關
穎
珊

- Michelle Kwan is the only woman in figure skating history to reclaim the World Championship three times (1998, 2000, and 2003).

- She holds the record at the U.S. Nationals for the most 6.0 rankings by the tournament's judges.

M ichelle Kwan is considered one of the greatest figure skaters in the history of the sport.

Extraordinary Record

Known for her consistency, accuracy, and expressive artistry on ice, figure skater Michelle Kwan set U.S. records with her eight consecutive U.S. Championship titles (1998-2005) and 12 consecutive U.S. Championship medals (1994-2005). She is the only woman in figure skating history to reclaim the World title three times (1998, 2000, and 2003). At the U.S. Nationals alone, she holds the record for the most 6.0 rankings by the tournament's judges. But regardless of the records she holds or the number of gold medals she wins, Michelle Kwan has realized her dream of going to the Olympics, and will always be considered a true champion.

The Spark to a Young Skater's Dream

After watching Brian Boitano win the gold in the 1988 Olympics, Michelle determined to pursue her dream of competing in the Olympics. Michelle was born July 7, 1980 in Torrance, California into a modest, middle-class family as the youngest of three children. She began skat-

Photo credit: Proper Marketing Associates

ing at the age of five, after seeing older brother Ron play ice hockey, and sister Karen figure skate on the ice. To deal with the hardship of their daughters' increasing skating rink time and coaching fees, their mother, Estella, took on a second job and their father, Danny, worked extra hours. Eventually, Michelle and her sister were offered financial assistance by a member of the Los Angeles Figure Skating Club, allowing them to train at the Ice Castle International Training Center in Lake Arrowhead, California.

"Work Hard, Be Yourself, and Have Fun"

Michelle's motto, "Work hard, be yourself, and have fun," originated from her parents. She began home schooling at age 13, and practiced her skating routines three to four hours a day, rising at 3:00 a.m. to skate before her school day began, and returning to the rink after school to skate again. Despite the disapproval of her coach, Frank Carroll, she applied in 1991 for senior status in the United States Figure Skating Championships and was accepted. In 1994, Michelle was sent to Lillehammer, Norway, for the Olympic Games. She placed eighth in her division, assuring the U.S. Team of two places the following year. It was a year filled with valuable experiences, and later that year she won the World Junior title.

Metamorphosis

After placing second in the 1995 U.S. Championships and fourth in the World Championships, Michelle realized the judges wanted to see the image of a young lady rather than a girl. Besides a makeover to a more mature look, she worked long and hard developing an artistically expressive skating style. With the debut of her Salome program, she brought a new, exotic style to her routine, improved her speed and jump techniques, and performed more difficult choreography. Michelle went on to win the 1996 National and World championships. The judges and the world were enthralled by Michelle Kwan's new image—one of maturity and beauty.

High Expectations

1996 was Michelle's dream year. She reached elite status and was deemed unbeatable. She finished first in nearly all her competitions, including the U.S. Championship and the World Title. It was also the year Michelle debuted her signature move, a *change-of-edge spiral*. With the entire country's expectation behind her to win, Michelle was under immense pressure, and moved her emphasis from skating to winning.

Temporary Setbacks

After a year of peaks in 1996, the next year was one of valleys. Mental and physical changes distracted her focus: First, she had to confront the tragic deaths of her close friend, Harris, and another friend, Carlo Fassi, as well as figure skater Scott Hamilton's serious illness. Secondly, under the terms of an endorsement contract, Michelle was required to switch skating boots but never felt comfortable in the new skates. Lastly, in August 1997, a diagnostic test revealed Michelle had sustained a stress fracture in a toe of her left foot. After she stumbled during her free skate at the 1997 U.S. Nationals, and lost the Champion Series Final and World titles that season, she came to understand that being a figure skating champion is not ultimately about winning, but the true love of the sport and being an artist on the ice.

Comeback Season

By November, Michelle's cast was removed. Though her toe was not fully healed, she triumphantly regained her World title with an outstanding performance in the long program at the 1998 U.S. Nationals. From a technical and artistic standpoint, that performance was considered the high point of Michelle Kwan's career. The same year, at the Olympic Games in Nagano, she was the overwhelming favorite. Even though Michelle Kwan didn't win the gold, she displayed the grace and elegance of a true champion as she held her head high, and accepted her silver medal with maturity and dignity.

Michael Chang

French Open Tennis Champion

By Randy Bloch

- At age 17 years and 3 months, Michael Chang became the youngest player and first American in 34 years to win the French Open Grand Slam tournament.

- Michael was elected to the International Tennis Hall of Fame on January 23, 2008.

- He established the Chang Family Foundation in 1999—promoting youth and community outreach, and tennis camps in the United States and overseas.

1989 French Open Tennis Tournament
David Versus Goliath

One of the biblical characters Michael Chang identifies with most is David—and the story of David and Goliath. Without a doubt, Chang's and Ivan Lendl's battle royal in the 1989 French Open Grand Slam evokes the epic clash of the biblical titans: Lendl was ranked No. 1 in the world, was the tournament's top seed, and laid claim to three prior French Open victories. By contrast, Michael was ranked No. 18, seeded No. 15, and had never won a Grand Slam tournament.

Having defeated Eduardo Masso, Pete Sampras and Francisco Roig in his first three rounds, Michael next drew Ivan Lendl, undoubtedly the tournament's most feared competitor that year.

Chang lost to Lendl in the round's first two sets but prevailed in the third. In set four, ravaged by leg cramps, he consumed vast quantities of water and ate bananas to fight his cramps. Racked and screaming with pain, he continued fighting. Then, hitting slow-moving "moon balls," he shattered his opponent's equilibrium—and won the set.

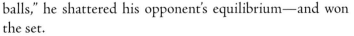

© Dimitri Lundt/TempoSport/Corbis

In the climactic fifth set, he fought with all his being to stay alive in the match. He cramped so badly that he began to walk, as he wrote in his autobiography, "…like Charlie Chaplin." Lendl then lost a point when Chang threw him off balance with an almost unheard of underhand serve. With Lendl spewing profanity, Michael inexplicably approached the T-line at center court to await his opponent's serve. Lendl then *double-faulted*, serving into the net twice. The set and Round Four belonged to Michael Chang. The round had taken 4 hours and 37 minutes—and David had slain Goliath!

A Danish journalist wrote: "The youngest one ate bananas and poured water into himself while he crushed the biggest one. Afterwards, Paris went totally bananas."

In Round Five of the match, Michael dispatched Stefan Edberg to capture final victory in the 1989 French Open. At age 17 years and 3 months, he had become its first American winner in 34 years. At the conclusion, he fell to his knees in tears.

A Sixteen-Year Run on
the Pro Tennis Circuit

Michael Chang was born in 1972 in Hoboken, New Jersey. He moved to Southern California with his family when his professional tennis star began to rise. Michael then burst to the international tennis community's attention in 1987 by turning professional at age fifteen. In his sixteen years on the professional circuit, he logged an average of 200,000 air miles a year, signed a long-term endorsement contract with Reebok, and won tournament prize monies totaling near $20 million.

Besides becoming the youngest player ever to win the French Open tournament, Michael Chang's pro

© Evan Hurd/Sygma/Corbis

tennis achievements include ranking in the World Top 10 for seven years, a career-high world ranking of No. 2, and capturing 34 singles titles.

Michael also achieved seven career victories in *Association of Tennis Professionals* events, was on the winning United States team in the 1990 *Davis Cup* competition, and was a member of the victorious U.S. Team in the *World Team Cup* competition in 1993.

Perhaps more edifying than a list of those accomplishments is a look beneath the surface at how Chang developed as an athlete, a relentless competitor, and a man of deep religious faith at the pinnacle of professional tennis.

Parental Support and Strong Family Values Guide His Early Career

In his autobiography, *Holding Serve, Persevering on and off the Court*, Michael Chang said of his childhood: "We were a close-knit, Asian-American family that believed children should have dreams, and dreams should never be discouraged."

In many important ways, his parents, Joe & Betty Chang, shepherded young Michael's career. Chang explains in *Holding Serve* that his father, Joe, " … built my strokes from the ground up." Research chemists by profession, the Changs were "geniuses of commitment" when it came to helping Michael and brother Carl, a talented tennis player in his own right, pursue their dreams. Mr. Chang guided Michael's career from its inception; Mrs. Chang accompanied Michael to tennis competitions around the world—arranging travel, looking after his nutrition requirements, tracking finances, and managing a thousand important details.

Michael also discussed the financial pressures on his family. "Now I understand why I can never remember my folks taking any kind of vacation for themselves. Everything they did was for Carl's and my benefit." Joe Chang purchased a racket re-stringing machine so Michael and Carl could trim expenses by doing this task themselves. As the brothers matured, important family decisions were submitted to "family councils" (usually over a sumptuous Chinese dinner) until consensus was reached.

Carl Chang was deeply involved in his brother Michael's career and, after graduating from UC Berkeley, was his coach for several years. Carl knew Michael's strengths and weaknesses better than any human being and was the natural choice to guide his game. Michael and Carl collaborated with the Prince tennis racket company to develop a new model, the *Longbody*, that better fit Michael's specifications, and extended the standard tennis racket length by an inch. The Longbody gave Michael an additional ten to twenty miles per hour of speed on his serve, and in 1996 and 1997 was the world's top-selling tennis racket.

Faith—His Beacon in Dealing with Adversity

In a 1989 *Los Angeles Times*, article, "The Kid Isn't Nasty Enough to Become a Tennis Champion," legendary sports journalist Jim Murray wrote of Michael's exemplary character:

> *Watch him when a call goes against him.... No outbursts. No shrieks. He never approaches the chair, the neck cords standing out in his throat, his face red, his language X-rated.... Michael, you see, is not one of your Long Island sons of riches who got into tennis because his yacht sank.... Temper tantrums do not run in the family.... [And] if Michael Chang uses the Lord's name, he's praying, not cursing.*

Michael Chang reached the summit of professional athletics while remaining untainted by stardom and privilege. Strong family values and his religious faith cannot be downplayed as factors making him such an exceptional person. Michael states that his faith allowed him to face down debilitating injuries, a precipitous career slide, and negative and destructive elements that lurk in the world of professional sports. The Chang Family Foundation's *Christian Sports League* seeks to foster, "...sports as an avenue through which individuals can see, hear, and experience the Christian faith."

At 36, Michael continues to develop athletically, educationally, and spiritually. He is also a keen golfer with a "ferocious swing," a highly skilled fisherman, and raises *African cichlid* tropical fish in freshwater aquariums at his home in Washington State. Michael Chang was named to the USA Today list of "Most Caring Athletes" in 1995. In 1997, *A Magazine* conferred a leadership award upon him as a role model for Asian-American youth.

References

1. Michael Chang and Mike Yorkey, *Holding Serve—Persevering On and Off the Court*. Nashville: Thomas Nelson, Inc., 2002.
2. E. Trier Hansen. Copenhagen, Denmark: Politiken.
3. Jim Murray, *The Kid Isn't Nasty Enough to Become a Tennis Champion*. Los Angeles: *Los Angeles Times*, 22 September, 1989.
4. *Wikipedia, The Free Encyclopedia*. Michael Chang. http://en.wikipedia.org/wiki/Michael_Chang.

Part II

Group Portraits of Pioneers

Why Group Portraits of Chinese in America?

By Edgar Wong

Yearbook Analogy

History books are like school yearbooks: group portraits are included along with individual portraits. Looking at group portraits is usually boring, sometimes interesting, and occasionally agonizing (i.e., remember flipping through your high school yearbook?).

Like it or not, the group's character sets a standard from which following generations, or classes, are measured. Within groups, the notion that "the whole is greater than the sum of its parts" is true, especially, when the parts therein include known star qualities. Our group portraits consist of well-known superstars and their under-recognized counterparts.

Group Portrait Scope

This PoP book section is intended to fill the "missing gap" in U.S. history of the lasting contributions made by faceless immigrant Chinese groups. During a racially difficult era in American history, amazing achievements were made through the Chinese tradition of hard work and perseverance. Nevertheless, while hidden in plain sight, they made a visible difference in many fields.

Chinese laborers helped build our railroads, reclaimed millions of acres of fertile farmlands, and pioneered the California fishing industry. More recently, the engineers and scientists contributed in a major way to the technology of space exploration and national defense. Men and women have served—and are serving—with distinction in the U.S. military. Educators are found at all levels of educational institutions.

Reconciliation

Our purpose is to make another step towards reconciliation and recovery from a dark period early in American history. To achieve genuine reconciliation, it is compelling to create genuine historical memory. Imagination is an imperfect substitute for real, but often unavailable, historical records. But the ability by compassionate people to imagine the pain and anguish that the Chinese experienced is an essential first step.

It is not enough to vilify the bigots and their racism; we must never forget to celebrate the heroism of those who stood up to them and advocated equal rights. Legislative reconciliation began in 1943 with the formal repeal of the Chinese Exclusion Act of 1882 (see the Appendix herein). It is the love of liberty and justice by many that brings us to this period of reconciliation. Though we have not yet achieved perfection, we are making progress.

Chinese-American Legacy

Yes, America is by no means perfect. But the opportunities it offered—and still offers—are unique on this planet. Logically we know that America is no better than any other country; but, emotionally we're sure she is better than every other country.

Our successes were due in part to some people of goodwill in this land that lent us a hand by providing the opportunities to excel. Hopefully, the group portraits will make the Chinese immigrants, and parts of their culture, an inclusive legacy in a wider Americana heritage.

Note: Reconciliation lessons learned from the wisdom of former Washington Gov. Gary Locke.

Transportation:
Iron Rail to Golden Spike

~

The Blood and Sweat
of the
Nameless Railroad Builders

By William F. Chew

"Without them (the Chinese railroad workers) it would be impossible to complete the Western portion of this great national enterprise within the time required by the Acts of Congress."
~*Governor Leland Stanford of California reporting to President Andrew Johnson,*
October 10, 1865

"D–O–N–E" tapped the telegraphed message to cheering dignitaries and guests who had gathered in Washington, DC, to herald completion of the first Transcontinental Railroad. The date was May 10, 1869.[1]

Chinese immigrants played a key role in the building of railroads in America:

Transcontinental Railroad: from Sacramento to Promontory Summit in Utah. It is estimated that more than 30,000 Chinese laborers worked in the western section of the railroad, suffering an estimated 1200 to 1300 casualties. In 1869, the East Coast of the United States was joined with the West with the opening of the Transcontinental Railroad. Trains began to bring settlers and goods from the East; the Transcontinental Railroad would bring 142,000 people West in its first year.

Northern Pacific Railroad: joining Seattle with Duluth, Minnesota. Many thousands of Chinese worked on building the tracks.

Southern Pacific Railroad: from Los Angeles to New Orleans. The Chinese worked to complete the final tracks.

Canadian Transcontinental Railroad: the seasoned Chinese workers contributed to the building of this railroad from 1881 to 1885.

In the South, Chinese immigrants were hired to build railroads in Alabama and Tennessee.

© Bettman/CORBIS

Chinese laborers on a hand car.

Building the Transcontinental Railroad

From its inception, building a Transcontinental Railroad had a few elite and influential supporters including President Abraham Lincoln.

The eastern cities were overcrowded with Europeans and Irish immigrants. Pioneers were moving west to new territories, traveling by horse and wagon for as long as a year. The Mormons walked and moved their possessions westward by pushing handcarts. People of means sailed around Cape Horn, South America, to reach San Francisco, requiring six months at sea. Others would disembark at the Isthmus of Panama; travel overland to the shores of the Pacific, and risk malaria and death, before reaching their final destination. The country, in dire need of expansion, was ready for a western railroad linking the East with the West, but finding the best route would take years.

Theodore Judah, a young Eastern civil engineer and surveyor with proven expertise in railroad building, did a survey as early as 1854, but it was not accepted by the Senate and the House. In 1860, Daniel Strong of Dutch Flat pointed out an easier passage through the Sierra Nevada Mountains. Having received financing from seven men, four of whom represented the Central Pacific Railroad Company,

Judah drew new plans and maps for a Pacific railroad, which were incorporated into the Pacific Railroad Act and signed into law by President Abraham Lincoln on July 1, 1862.[2]

The established and experienced Union Pacific Railroad Company would build the eastern route starting from Omaha, Nebraska. The upstart Central Pacific Railroad Company (CPRR), headed by the "Big Four", Charles Crocker, Leland Stanford, Mark Hopkins, and Collis Huntington, would build the western route from Sacramento, both linking up in Utah.

On January 8, 1863, at 54 "K" Street, in front of the Huntington and Hopkins Hardware Store, the official groundbreaking of the Central Pacific Railroad took place.[3]

A year later, only 18 miles of tract had been laid. Lack of manpower was becoming critical. It was back breaking labor, too grueling to stay on. Men would work a short time and move on to other, hopefully, more profitable and less arduous projects.

Charles Crocker needed dependable workers. He had hired a small group of local Chinese miners to clear the Dutch-Flat-Donner Lake Wagon Road. Impressed by their discipline and efficiency, he proposed to Supt. James Strobridge to hire these Chinese workers. Strobridge, however, strongly objected because he believed that "the Chinese were too small and inexperienced". He was soon silenced when Crocker supposedly rebuted: "They built the Great Wall, didn't they?"[4]

Employment Date of the First Chinese Railroad Workers

The Central Pacific Payroll sheets No. 26 and No. 34, respectively dated January and February 1864, record the first Chinese railroad workers.[5] Ah Toy is listed as railroad foreman, and Hung Wah as supervisor of a crew of 23 unnamed workers. Hung Wah later became the largest labor contractor known as The Hung Wah Company. It is be-

lieved that Hung Wah may have been among the few workers who remained to the completion of the Transcontinental Railroad.

These two payroll sheets are undisputed proof that the Chinese started to work for the Central Pacific Railroad as early as January 1864, and not in spring 1865, as previously published by several well-known authors.[6]

Only the names of Chinese Gang Bosses or Headmen, and labor contractors are listed on the payroll sheets. A few other independent workers, not assigned to specific crews, such as cooks, waiters, water boys and blacksmiths are also named. Crewmembers' names were too numerous to list. Tragically we will never know the names of the thousands of workers.

A meticulous accounting of the total man-days paid to each gang boss or headman helped with estimating the total number of Chinese railroad workers employed by the Central Pacific, between January 1864 and December 1867, to be 30,000. The critical loss of 29 months of payroll records from this period, as well as all the payroll records from January 1868 through May 1869 would have changed this total dramatically. An explanation for the large number of workers is that the average tenure of the Chinese crews consisting of about 28 workers, was 1.6 months. A rapid turnover was experienced because of the grueling task. New immigrants and families replaced the workers.[7]

Fortunately, it appears that all 12 months of 1866 payroll sheets are complete. This is particularly important because April 1866 recorded the peak monthly employment of 6,191 Chinese workers. This was the time when the workers were digging thirteen tunnels through solid granite at a rate of a foot per day, working three shifts, six days a week.

The premise that some of these workers may have been counted more than once, by switching from one Gang Boss to another, incorrectly inflating the total count, is doubtful.

When Gang Bosses selected crewmembers, they would pick men who came from the same village and spoke the same dialect, ensuring clear communications and cooperation with one another. Men from different villages followed an established cultural division and would not intermingle. The Gang Bosses kept a running account of payroll deductions for transportation debts incurred by their crew workers. Crossovers would sabotage the orderly accounting system they were responsible for; therefore, it was not practiced.

These historical payroll records also reveal no less than sixteen different, skilled trade jobs -- not just "coolies" of the pick-and-shovel type labor. Chinese worked as blacksmiths, lumberjacks, carpenters, teamsters, masons, etc. Their wages varied from a low $0.63/day for a waiter, to $1.34/day for a blacksmith.[8]

Naming the First Chinese Railroad Workers

Railroad history documents that some Chinese workers were hired from the Dutch Flat area. The 1860 Dutch Flat census, fortuitously provided by local historian Douglas Ferrier, demonstrates that many Chinese names, listed as miners, were also listed on the early payroll records of the Central Pacific Railroad as Gang Bosses. A further study of the 1870 Dutch Flat census reveals some of the same Chinese residents, now listed as railroad workers, leading to the logical conclusion that the following men, entered in the payroll sheets of January and February 1864, were the first Chinese workers of the Central Pacific and members of Hung Wah's crew:

Ah Chung, Ah Wong, Ah Kung, Ah Chin, Ah Fong, Ah Quong, Ah Chow, Ah Lim, Ah You, Ah Henge (Ah Hen Gee), Ah Wah, Ah Ming, Gee Tong, Ah Jim, Ah Hing, Ah Tou, and Ah Low.[9]

Bloomers Cut

In 1865, at Bloomers Cut in Auburn, the workers literally had to remove a mountain of dirt by hand, pick and shovel and one-horse-dump wagons. They opened a trapezoid shape cut sixty feet deep by eight hundred feet long. This is the place where the Chinese established themselves as men of unyielding tenacity, replacing other white workers who would leave after a day or two of exhausting labor.[10]

A plaque placed at the entry of Bloomer's Ranch commemorates this achievement declaring:

"Bloomer Cut" so named because of its location on the Bloomer Ranch remains virtually unchanged since its original construction in 1864. The overwhelming task of construction was undertaken by the diligent hard-working efforts of a small band of Chinese laborers. Using picks, shovels, and black powder, they inched their way through the conglomerate rock cemented together with rock-hard clay. At the time of its completion, Bloomer Cut was considered the Eighth Wonder of the World. The first Central Pacific train rolled into Auburn on May 11, 1865. Dedicated by the Native Sons of the Golden West, October 12, 1991, Thomas W. Perazzo, Grand President.

Secret Town Trestle Project © Corbis/Bettman

That the Chinese worked and completed Bloomers Cut, had many local detractors, who believed that no Chinese were employed on the Railroad until the spring of 1865. But the undisputed evidence inked on the Payroll sheets of January and February 1864, has now convinced them of the truth.

Cape Horn

Half a mile out of Colfax, Cape Horn, named after Cape Horn, South America, because of the similar difficulty in circumventing the landmass, is another landmark where the Chinese workers distinguished themselves with their ingenuity.

The roadbed required the laying of three miles of track around a promontory, at a slope of seventy-five degrees, starting at 1,400 feet above the American River. Without even a goat trail to lead the way, a grade had to be dug and sculpted from the sheer cliffs.

Cape Horn became one of the most romanticized and publicized accomplishments, as well as the most disputed. It has been written that the Chinese foremen, eager to reinforce their crews' exceptional skills approached Strobridge and assured him that their workers were up to this challenge, because they were familiar with similar work done along the Yangtze River by their ancestors. To further convince Strobridge, the Chinese foremen started to detail a plan.

Bloomers Cut   Courtesy William F. Chew

They would weave reeds into baskets, which would be used to lower the men over the cliffs. The men would chisel holes in the mountain, stuff them with black powder and blast a roadbed.

Having no other option, a reluctant Strobridge approved the plan and the Chinese workers did as promised. After pounding black powder in the mountain and lighting the fuse, the men above would furiously pull up the suspended workers - hopefully out of harms way. Many reached safety. Others were injured or killed by falling rocks or were caught in the explosions blasting the mountain and worker. This event may be the origin of the saying: "you don't have a Chinaman's chance" to describe a hopeless situation.

That the Chinese were lowered in baskets over Cape Horn has been romantically depicted in many artistic drawings. Because no photographs of this fete have been found, there are many individuals who claim that this, in fact, has no truth.

These detractors support their denials by stating that the seventy-five degree slope would preclude the use of (round) baskets, because they would be uncontrollable during the descent and ascent. Could the baskets be of rectangular shape to prevent rolling? Or were Bosons chairs used as some historians believe?

In the spring of 1866, the grading and tracking of Cape Horn

191

was completed.[11] Because of its much-publicized controversy, this is one of the most talked about achievement of Chinese labor. Today, overlooking the American River, another stone monument with a bronze plaque designates Cape Horn as a California Historical Site with these words:

View of Cape Horn Promontory, North Fork American River Canyon. Dedicated to the memory of thousands of Chinese who worked for Charles Crocker on the Central Pacific Railroad. They were lowered over the face of Cape Horn Promontory in Bosun's chairs to a point 1332 feet above the canyon floor. The ledge created for this rail bed was completed May 1866. They are honored for their work ethic, and timely completion of the transcontinental rails ending in Promontory, Utah, May 1869. Dedicated May 8, 1999, Colfax Area Historical Society, Inc.

About thirty guests and members of the Chinese Historical Society of Southern California attended this dedication.

Thirteen Tunnels

Nineteen tunnels dot the transcontinental route between the Union Pacific terminus at Omaha, and the Central Pacific terminus in Sacramento. The Central Pacific workers built thirteen tunnels through the Sierra-Nevada Mountains. The first tunnel was called Grizzly Hill, west of Cisco, 77 miles from Sacramento.

The most impervious and longest tunnel of the Transcontinental was Summit Tunnel #6, measuring 1659 feet long, 26 feet wide, 20 feet high, and 120 feet below the surface. Progress was painfully slow—six to twelve inches per day—

because of the solid granite material. Hoping that it would be more efficient, nitroglycerine was briefly used, but the inexperienced handling of it was killing many needed workers and injuring others. Blasting continued with black powder.

A central vertical shaft was made to penetrate deep into the earth to allow the excavation from four locations. The digging started from both entrances from the west and east directions, and two diggings from the center out in opposite directions toward each entrance.

By August 1867, Summit Tunnel #6 was pierced from opposite sides with almost perfect alignment. The majority Chinese labor force, under white supervision, completed the grading and tracking on November 30, 1867.[12]

Snow Sheds

Records show that the winters of 1866 and 1867 were the most inclement in history. Snow drifts as high as forty feet were recorded. The work force was at the mercy of unforgiving weather. Avalanches were frequent, burying workers alive. Many bodies were never recovered. To keep the tracks cleared, an engine was converted into a giant snowplow with three more engines pushing it along the snow-covered tracks. But frequent derailments demanded a more effective solution: build thirty-seven miles of timber snow sheds covering the tracks. Chinese and Irish workers joined forces in order to finish this construction as quickly as possible.

Ten Miles a Day

The Chinese endured years of backbreaking labor, in both freezing and torrid temperature. As the terrain leveled and

A study of major projects reveals that the Chinese builders of the Transcontinental Railroad suffered the largest number of accidental deaths.

Project	Year	Number of accidental fatalities
Transcontinental Railroad[14]	1869	1,346
Panama Canal	1905	8
Moffet Tunnel	1913	28
Hoover Dam	1936	336 (112 recorded)
Golden Gate Bridge	1937	11
Mount Rushmore	1941	0
Total:		1,729

work became easier, many workers were laid off. Fewer workers were needed to lay track across the flat Nevada-Utah desert on the approach to the Utah promontory.

With the worst behind them and the completion of the Railroad in sight, a relieved Charles Crocker of the Central Pacific Railroad and vice-president Durant of the Union Pacific Railroad each boasting of their crew's superior abilities, challenged each other to a race over whose side could lay the most tracks in one day. Spurred on by a wager of $10,000 to the winner, on April 28, 1869, the Chinese and Irish crews of the Central Pacific feverishly pounded twenty-seven tons of spikes, and laid down a record breaking 10 miles of track in one day.[13]

Today, a primitive wooden sign in the small community of Rozel, Utah, near the linking site of the Transcontinental in Promontory, marks the spot where this frenzied competition came to rest.

The Insignificance of Life

The Chinese who died while building the Transcontinental died in relative anonymity. Their deaths were not reported nor memorialized nor mourned. In general, there was little, if any, news of the Chinese workers who perished – as if their life had been insignificant. If the headman knew the deceased, he would tag the body with his name and village of origin for later shipment of the bones back to China.

Deaths were caused by blasting accidents, avalanches, land slides, falling trees, rail accidents, falls, pneumonia, and freezing to death. Most of these workers came from a semi tropical region unprepared for the freezing weather. In contrast, with these circumstances under their control, not a single death from sun or heat stroke was reported, because of the protection of their wide-brimmed straw hats, nor were there any deaths caused by dysentery, as many of their white counterparts had suffered, because of the Chinese custom of boiling water to make tea while white workers drank water directly from the ground.

Allowing for the span of time and technological progress between these projects, the number of deaths of the Chinese workers is staggering. The Transcontinental Railroad accounts for approximately 78% of the total fatalities; these numbers, however, do not include the hundreds lost from avalanches, and landslides whose bodies were never found, nor counted.

A newspaper article in the Sacramento Reporter dated June 30, 1870, under the headline "Bones in Transit", accounts for this single largest number of deaths.

> The accumulated bones of perhaps 1,200 Chinamen came in by the eastern train yesterday from along the line of the Central Pacific railroad. The lot comprises about 20,000 pounds. Nearly all of them are the remains of employes (sic) of the company, who were engaged in building the road. The customs of the Celestial Empire require that, wherever possible, the bodies of its subjects shall be interred upon its own soil, and the strictness with which this custom is observed is something remarkable.

A second article appeared in the Elko Independent newspaper on January 5, 1870, entitled

Dead Chinamen – Six cars are strung along the road between here and Toano, and are being loaded with dead Celestials for transportation to the Flowery Kingdom. We understand that the Chinese companies pay the Railroad Company $10 dollars for carrying to San Francisco each dead Chinaman. Six cars, well stuffed with this kind of freight, will be a good day's work. The remains of the females are left to rot in shallow graves, while every defunct male is carefully preserved for return to his homeland.

It is uncertain that this trainload is the same train as reported in the Sacramento Reporter in June, 1870, six months later. An article by J.P. Marden from the Book Club of California may explain the time delay. He writes

In March 1870 the Chinese funeral car was working in Winnemucca on a siding near Bridge Street grade crossing preparing the deceased for their final trip home. Two carloads of bones, prepared and boxed in the most approved manner, and labeled with the appropriate Chinese characters, which gave the name, date of death, and tong to which they belonged, were shipped from Winnemucca to San Francisco at that time.

It is believed that both these articles refer to the one and same train, because if it were an additional train, the poundage of the bones and the number of bodies would be doubled.

Some critics attribute the majority of these deaths to an as yet undocumented story of a smallpox epidemic in 1868-1870. Medical statistics reveal that the mortality rate from smallpox is approximately 30 % of those infected. If the majority of the 1200 Chinese died from smallpox, it would mean that about 4,000 workers were infected during this period. It seems doubtful that these many workers were still active, because after the work on the Sierra Nevada was completed, many workers were laid off. In addition, the last payroll record of December 1867 shows only 428 workers remaining. The December payroll records, however, may be incomplete since the adjusted total would approach the estimated 4,000 workers.

Iron Road Pioneers statue in San Luis Obispo's Railroad Square

The Completion

At Promontory Summit, Utah, as the official ceremony was being photographed for posterity, Leland Stanford, President of the Central Pacific Railroad Company and former Governor of California, was handed a ceremonial golden spike engraved with the words "May God continue the unity of our country, as this Railroad unites the two great oceans of the world".[15]

Chinese railroad workers then laid the last rail and drove the last spike uniting the rails of the Transcontinental Railroad. Three of the eight workers, Ging Cui, Wonk Fook, and Lee Shao, brought up the last rail at Promontory Summit on May 10, 1869.

These Chinese adventurers came to "Gum San" to work unaware of the daunting undertaking or life-threatening dangers they would face. They accepted employment hoping to earn enough money to return to their homeland with newly attained riches and live the rest of their lives in relative comfort.

Even though the building of the western route of the Transcontinental has been somewhat romanticized and some episodes have become legendary, it does not diminish the magnitude of the human effort spent by a majority of non-citizens.

Beyond the Central Pacific
The Southern Pacific Railroad

Following the "Marriage of the Rails" of the Transcontinental Railroad in May 1869, the economic depression caused by the massive layoff of workers from both the Union Pacific and the Central Pacific railroads, was fueling the already hostile discrimination and prejudice against the Chinese. Hostilities increased continuously for ten years culminating with the passage of the anti-Chinese exclusionary laws of the 1880's.

Fines and special taxes were levied on the working Chinese. Hiring was virtually nonexistent, except for the now experienced rail workers who migrated throughout the United States to lend their expertise to build many of the nation's railroads.

The majority of workers returned to China, but those who stayed continued to contribute to the development of a country that largely rebuked them. They pioneered the canning industry in California; reclaimed the swamps and bogs of the Sacramento Delta by building levees and irrigation canals, and changed hardpan soil into fertile land.

With overdue appreciation and gratitude, various types of commemoratives have been erected and continue to be built that describe the actions which took place at each site, such as Bloomers Cut, Cape Horn and Golden Spike National Historic Site, a site, which is totally dedicated to the preservation and dissemination of this period's history.

More tributes have been placed at Lang Station following the completion of the rail line to Los Angeles, in September 1876.[16] Another plaque location is at the entry of Port Harford Wharf in Avila Beach, near San Luis Obispo, praising the completion of the Pacific Coast Railway in 1882.

**PORT HARFORD WHARF
& PACIFIC COAST RAILWAY
COMMEMORATION: July 19, 1986**

**John Harford Wharf & Horse Drawn/Gravity Railroad 1873
Pacific Coast Steamship Company Organized 1876
Pacific Coast Railway (PCRR, SLO & SMVRR) 1882**

**VISION & ENTERPRISE OF THE NARROW GAUGE RAILROAD
EXPANDED TRADE & SETTLEMENT ON THE CALIFORNIA
CENTRAL COAST BETWEEN AVILA; SAN LUIS OBISPO,
ARROYO GRANDE, NIPOMO, SANTA MARIA, ORCUTT,
LOS ALAMOS & LOS OLIVOS. AH LOUIS, SUPERVISOR OF HIS
CHINESE LABOR CREW, BUILT THE ROADBED AND LAID THE RAIL.**

**PORT SAN LUIS HARBOR DISTRICT
FRIENDS OF THE PACIFIC COAST RAILWAY
SOUTH COUNTY HISTORICAL SOCIETY,
RAILWAY CENTENNIAL COMMITTEE**

Inscription on a plaque posted at the entrance of Avila Beach pier

A life size bronze sculpture depicting two Chinese railroad workers has been erected, with considerable backing from local civic leaders, Caucasians and Chinese, in Railroad Square, San Luis Obispo. Among these supporters is the esteemed Chinese-American citizen of San Luis Obispo, Howard Louis.

A table top bronze mockette, dedicated to the Chinese rail workers, can be seen at the Sacramento State Library and at Union Station Museum in Ogden, Utah. Here one can also see a diorama of trains traversing the Sierra Nevada Mountains and Summit Tunnel #6. In addition, in the grand lobby of this Museum, on the east wall, a mural 40 feet long and 20 feet high depicts the Chinese workers of the Central Pacific. The California State Railroad Museum, besides preserving the timeline and mementos of this period, has added a large exhibit illustrating the Chinese scaling the cliffs of Cape Horn.

Out of the many needs of the transplanted Chinese, a few simple acts of leadership have brought some credit to Chinese individuals.

Lee Chew a sixteen year old from Hong Kong immigrated to America in 1860 on a steamer and worked as a houseboy for a San Francisco family. A few years later he worked for the CPRR for three years and saved enough money to return to China wealthy and help build railroads in China.

Moy Jin Mun came to California in 1860 from a small village in Toishan and worked as a gold miner eking out gold dust from the tailings of abandoned mines.[17] He later organized a volunteer Chinese railroad crew who had agreed to work for free to build a Chinese mining railroad. The project failed for lack of financial backing.

Howard Louis was the youngest of eight children of Ah Louis. In 1873, Capt Harford contracted Ah Louis to build a narrow gage railroad from Avila to his operation at Port Harford. A plaque posted at the entrance of Avila Beach pier recognizes this accomplishment by stating (below):

In 1884 Ah Louis, a labor contractor, was asked by the Pacific Coast Railroad Company to build the Cuesta Ridge roadbed and tunnels connecting the north and south route in California going through San Luis Obispo. His 2,000 Chinese workers completed the job in 1886, creating a land boom in the area. The Cuesta Ridge grade was so steep that the roadbed had to be stretched into a horseshoe shape road making it one of the few tracks where a traveler situated in the front of the train can see the end of the train as it loops around the track.

In 1885 the Central Pacific and Pacific Coast Railroad companies merged to become the Southern Pacific Railroad Company.[18] The Company continued to built links and new lines in Tucson, Yuma, and Casa Grande in the southwest, giving birth to Chinatowns in these areas.

Howard Louis honors his father by continuing the pioneering civic leadership for the development of the City of San Luis Obispo. He spearheaded the successful "Art in Public Places" program, raising donated funds for the first life-size bronze statue depicting two Chinese railroad workers. This sculpture can be seen at the center of Railroad Square in San Louis Obispo.[19]

Another unsung achievement of the Chinese railroad workers is the building of the third longest tunnel in the United States at 6,940 feet, the San Fernando Tunnel in Santa Clarita. A second golden spike was driven at Lang Station in September, 1876, completing the rail line to Los Angeles.

Today, the legacy of our Chinese pioneers is carved in stone. Bloomers Cut, Cape Horn, thirteen tunnels, deep cuts and fills, forty miles of snow sheds, the record laying of ten miles of railroad track in one day, and the completion of 690 miles of the most treacherous roadbed of its time, each standing as a monument to their quiet but invincible spirit.

Our pioneers left a legacy beyond their achievements: their keen ability to adapt and assimilate to a new culture, maintain scrupulous work ethics under duress; establish a reputation for astute observation, and apply constant learning and commitment. These are the traits left by the Chinese pioneers for present and future generations to nurture and uphold.

About the author:

William F. Chew, grandson of a CPRR and SPRR worker, is the author of *Nameless Builders of the Transcontinental Railroad*. He searched the payroll records of the archives of Central Pacific Railroad from 1864 to 1867 to come up with the approximate number of Chinese railroad workers and to reconstruct the progress of the construction. The research, interviews and writing took over five years and the book was published in 2004.

References

1. Ambrose, *Nothing Like it in the World* - pgs 363-366
2. Central Pacific Railroad, *Building the Central Pacific: A Narrative History* - www.learncalifornia.org.
3. California State Railroad Museum (CSRRM), Commemorative Plaque, Sacramento, Calif.
4. Kraus, *High Road to Promontory* - p-151
5. CSRRM Library, Sacramento, Calif.
6. Ambrose, *Nothing Like it in the World* - p. 149
7. Chew, *Nameless Builders of the Transcontinental Railroad* - Trafford Publishing, 2004
8. CSRRM, Sacramento, Calif., pgs. 49-51.
9. Ibid, Payroll Sheet 102
10. Ambrose, *Nothing Like it in the World* - p.148.
11. Ibid, p.157
12. Ibid, pgs. 244-247.
13. Ibid, pgs. 349-351.
14. Chew, *Nameless Builders of the Transcontinental Railroad* - Trafford Publishing, 2004
15. Kraus, *High Road to Promontory* - p-274
16. *History of the Santa Clarita Valley, its roads, and railroads.*
17. Southern Pacific Railroad, en.wikipedia.org/wiki/Southern_Pacific_Railroad
18. Chew, *Nameless Builders of the Transcontinental Railroad* - Trafford Publishing, 2004, pgs. 92-93

Agriculture:

The Role of Chinese Immigrants in California's Farming Infrastructure

By Lucky Owyang and L.P. Leung

Beginning in the 1860s, the 19th century saw vast contributions to California's agricultural infrastructure by Chinese immigrants.

Agricultural workers from China's Pearl River Delta brought great experience and knowledge with them, including innovation in land clearing and centuries of experience in levee construction. Landowners in California's Sacramento-San Joaquin River Delta region hired Chinese crews to carry out the backbreaking work, which the average Anglo worker did not want.

By the 1880s, Chinese workers had become the backbone of farm labor in the American West; the state of California was the wheat capital of the United States; and the Delta was producing almost 90% of the world's asparagus crop.

Studies in 2008 reported California agriculture as a near-$32 billion industry that generated $100 billion in related economic activity. Today, greatly owing to early participation of Chinese labor, agriculture remains a principal component of California's wealth as well as the entire United States.

Immigrants from China played a pivotal role in the infrastructure development of the West Coast in the second half of the nineteenth century. Most of the large development projects undertaken, whether they were railroads or levee construction, irrigation projects, or farming and orchard operations, relied heavily on Chinese laborers. Very little was written about the work of the Chinese immigrants by journalists and historians, who mostly portrayed the Chinese negatively as inferior aliens. The fortitude and courage of the Chinese pioneers deserves to be emphasized and included in the region's history.

Chinese immigrants completed the most difficult section of the transcontinental railroad, facilitating the western migration of thousands of people from the east coast. The Chinese worked to reclaim the fertile farmland from the regular flooding of the Sacramento-San Joaquin River Delta; this area was to become the food basket of the west and beyond.

Land Reclamation-Building Levees and Irrigation Systems; Turning Swampland and Sloughs to Fertile Farmland

In California, the Chinese made major contributions in building California's agricultural infrastructure.

Chinese laborers played a major part in reclaiming the Sacramento-San Joaquin River Delta by building a complex series of levees and irrigation channels, transforming millions of acres of unusable marshland into one of the world's richest agricultural regions.

The delta, one of the largest estuaries on the west coast, acts as the funneling point for a watershed covering millions of acres of California's central valley. Early levees built by Chinese, Hawaiians, Native American Indians were routinely destroyed by floods. Until a well designed system of levees was built to confine water flow to the riverbeds, huge swaths of water flooded regularly with every spring melt.

Realizing the importance of the fertile delta farmland to the nation, the United States government, as part of the Federal Swampland Act in the 1850s, offered millions of acres of delta swampland at very low prices to anyone who would reclaim it. In 1868 a series of California laws were passed that made it profitable to reclaim delta lands for farming. By 1871, most of California's swampland was in private ownership.

Delta landowners hired Chinese crews, who had recently completed the Central Pacific railroad in 1869, to work to reclaim the land, a job Anglo laborers did not want. Building levees was hellish, backbreaking, and dangerous. Malaria took a heavy toll of white laborers. Only Chinese workers, in spite of malaria, were willing to labor waist-deep in water, draining swamps and marshes, digging up hard peat soil by hand to build the levees. The crews constructed a long series of levees, dikes and gates throughout the delta's waterways to reclaim and preserve farmland and control irrigation. The levee workers lived in primitive conditions in tents right at the site of the levees and worked in groups of 8 to 30 men.

Applying their land-clearing knowledge from working around the Pearl River Delta, in southern China, the Chinese brought with them many innovations in levee construction, including developing an oversized horseshoe wired to hooves of horses for packing and leveling dirt. For over twenty years, from the 1860s to the 1880s, they performed these difficult tasks without the aid of drainage machinery, earthmovers, mechanical machine tools, or trucks. Many died from malaria, infections and other diseases. There were no records to disclose the number of Chinese who gave their lives for land reclamation.

One of the largest land developers in the delta was George D. Roberts, president of the Title Land Reclamation Company. Roberts had close political ties with California legislators; these connections helped his company to obtain thousands of swampland acres for two or three dollars per acre. He hired 3,000 to 4,000 Chinese laborers for about a dollar a day. The reclaimed land was sold for up to $75 an acre, making Roberts a very wealthy man.

By the late 1870s, the land developers had begun to realize that manual labor could not maintain the reclaimed delta lands. Bricks made from peat soil would sink and when dry, could develop cracks and fissures throughout the levee system. Steam-powered dredges began to be used to move the large volume of alluvial soils from the river channels to construct the large levees. These dredges were capable of moving the earth much faster at half the cost of manual labor.

Chinese field hands. By permission of The Huntington Library, San Marino, California.

first large group of Chinese farm laborers entered the region in the summer of 1866, they brought with them thousands of years of horticulture heritage. Their skills in planting, cultivating, and harvesting were a godsend to regional farm owners. The Chinese helped to introduce many different varieties of fruits, vegetables and flowers. They contributed the seeds and the sweat to transform the California Central Valley into a pastoral cornucopia. By the 1870s, the Chinese dominated the strawberry-growing industry in California. In the 1880s, the top cash crops of the region included broccoli, strawberries, apples, cut flowers, wine grapes, cauliflower and mushrooms. At one time towards the end of the 1890s, asparagus grown in the Sacramento River Delta supplied ninety-five percent of the world's needs. These were all labor-intensive crops requiring laborers to work with their hands and on their knees from planting to harvesting. "Although never more than a tenth of the California population, they (Chinese immigrants) formed about a quarter of the state's labor force because they were nearly all males of working age." (Harvard Encyclopedia, p. 219)

Farming the Central Valley; Filling the Nation's Food Baskets

In the 1850s and 1860s, a single crop dominated the farming region in California. Wheat fields covered over 3 million acres in California, which produced 1.5 million tons of wheat each year. The reliance on a single crop began to strain the fecundity of even the rich alluvial soils of these coastal valleys.

As levee work became mechanized with dredgers in the mid-1870s, the Chinese moved on to find work in developing Bartlett pear orchards and in other farming. When the

Chinese laborers developed a reputation from the Gold Rush days of being hard working, industrious, and diligent workers. These qualities made them sought after workers and soon Chinese moved from the delta up throughout the central valley. They found their way into Sonoma County planting 4000 grapevines for William McPherson's Glen Ellen Winery. They labored in Napa Valley vineyards and dug huge storage tunnels for wine aging and storage.

With the completion of the transcontinental railroad, many farm products were shipped throughout the country. In fact, farm product sales played a part in alleviating California from the depths of the economic depression of the 1870s that affected the rest of the nation so deeply.

"In 1870, only one in ten California farm laborers was Chinese; by 1884, it was one in two; by 1886, almost nine in ten." *Iris Chang, The Chinese in America, 2003.*

Gathering mulberry leaves. California Historical Society, FN-24209/CHS2010.234.tif

Bartlett Pear "Gold"
For years Rueben Kercheval, a former gold prospector turned farmer, battled the annual surge of water from melting snowfall of the high Sierras. He built and rebuilt one levee after another on Grand Island near Sacramento using Chinese laborers. Other farmers in the area followed. Grand Island reputedly has some of the finest peat soil for growing Bartlett pears. These trees, planted in the late 19th century, are still producing fruit today. Kercheval and other farmers became prosperous from the "gold" of Bartlett pears, nurtured and harvested by Chinese labor.

In the last part of the 19th century, the delta, known as the home of the Bartlett pear, was ranked as the pear

In the 1880s, Chinese formed the backbone of western farm production. They helped California become the wheat capital of the United States. Some farmed as sharecroppers; others raised their own vegetables for sale to the townspeople. By doing this they produced approximately two thirds of the vegetables in California.

When technological improvements in canning made it profitable to can asparagus in the 1880s, the delta eventually accounted for nearly 90% of the world's asparagus crop. Many Chinese farmers grew asparagus in the 1890s. Others grew potatoes or labored on the farm of others.

capital of the world. North of the Sacramento River Delta in the Suisun Valley, Chinese from Loong Doo district were hired to work on the orchards. Wheat was the primary crop then but once the discovery that continuous production of wheat robs the earth of its valuable nutrients, the Chinese began planting fruit trees. These Chinese, from the Pearl River Delta, had a long history of tending orchards. Along with nurturing and growing fruit, the Chinese excelled at drying and preserving fruit which provided additional revenues for the orchard owners.

Today, Sacramento County has about 6,000 acres of pears, mostly along the Sacramento River in the Courtland/Walnut Grove area, but extending from south of Freeport to Isleton. Sacramento County is California's leading pear producing county, with about half the tonnage being produced there. In 2006, 6,482 acres were harvested, with a value of $28 million (77,123 tons were sold for processing; 29,986 tons were sold for fresh consumption and 9,567 tons were sold for juice).

On developing a system to make pear-loading easier: *My father was a WW II veteran and aeronautical engineer. He was also a pear rancher. As the fruit collection was changing from wooden lugs to huge bins, manpower could not handle the increased weight. So ranchers needed to devise a way to get the empty bins into the orchard and back to the loading yard with fruit filled bins. Dad designed and drafted the roller/grill and anchors that fit into the flatbed trucks. Two blacksmith brothers in Walnut Grove worked with the plans. My father would alter the parts where needed and the blacksmiths would rework his modifications. It took many months to accomplish the goal. Now the tractors could pull the rollers/grill on flatbed trailers into the orchard. Other ranchers received my father's permission to copy the design for their use. Dad did not apply for patents on his invention nor received rewards from it financially. He was just happy that others in the industry could benefit from his innovation. The local Rotary and Lions Club acknowledged his contributions.*

-Stephanie Lee, daughter of John Lee.

Market Gardening or Truck Farming

Chinese truck farmers grew fruits and vegetables and were the suppliers to residents of many towns and cities in California. One might surmise these were the early versions of today's popular Farmers' Markets.

Market gardening as a business is based on providing a wide range and steady supply of fresh produce through the local growing season. Many different crops and varieties are grown, as in contrast to large mechanized farms which tend to specialize in high volume production of a single crop - a practice known as monoculture. Market gardening also re-

quires more manual labor and expert gardening techniques. Such a farm is sometimes called a market garden or truck farm.

On truck farming: *I remember my dad had a little truck farm in town, it's where the trailer park is now on Main Street. He grew an assortment of vegetables for our own use and also sold to some of the town's people. Also on the truck farm he grew bitter melon, long beans, squash, chard, which were shipped to Oakland, then to SF. We had to crate up everything, and then take it to Williams train station where it was railed to Oakland and ferried to San Francisco.*

My dad rented his plots of ground from different ranchers around Colusa. He also grew a melon seed crop, and winter melons that required lots more land. Not knowing the language it was amazing how he was able to do this.

Everybody pitched in working on the farm. We lived on two different farms back in those days and all we knew was work. My mother took care of the household chores plus did all the cooking; her spare time was spent working out in the fields. The only time we needed help was while harvesting the seed crop, and the melons. They were then sold to Chinatowns throughout California.

-George Chan, a native of Colusa, California

Rice Crop

The Chinese were active in rice growing for a short time from 1915 through 1926. They first came to Colusa County in 1869, when the Ah Chew and Company leased thirty acres of land. An agreement to clear the land resulted in free rent for a number of years. Chinese were able to lease 150 acres to 1120 acres to grow rice by the turn of the century. "Guey Jones developed a superior variety of rice that led to a prized industry in Glen County, California." *Ruthanne McCunn, An Illustrated History of the Chinese in America.*

What Happened to the Chinese Immigrant Farmers?

As the 1870s recession worsened, white workers who were losing their jobs were told by the likes of Dennis Kearney and the printed media that the problem was Chinese immigrants. The constitution of California was rewritten in 1879 forbidding any man or woman of "Chinese or Mongolian" ancestry from earning a living by working for a white man. Instead of giving credit to the horticultural contributions of the Chinese immigrant farmers, journalists and the print media of the time went out of their way to concentrate on their "Anti-Chinese" attacks.

A wave of racist anti-Chinese riots broke out in the California Central Valley. "From Ukiah to the Napa Valley, to Fresno, to Redlands, Chinese were beaten and shot by white workers and often loaded into trains and shipped out of town." *Ronald Takaki, A Different Mirror, a History of Multicultural America.* "Many of the large ranchers and farmers watched their farms, factories and vineyards go up in flames. Leland Stanford had the largest vineyard in the world at that time. He employed over 300 Chinese workers. Mrs. Stanford said the white workers 'threatened to burn everything in sight'. This commenced, and all the vineyard tools, ploughs, and so forth were destroyed. As a result, the contracts with the Chinese workers were broken, and they were replaced with white men." *Ruthanne McCunn, An Illustrated History of the Chinese in America.*

The Chinese in these farming communities were dispersed. Some laborers left to work in other states; others continued to travel up and down California as seasonal migrant workers wherever it was safe to do so. The vast majority of Chinese immigrants were driven from the land and forced into marginal survival or worked in menial jobs like hand laundry and cooking.

The Chinese Exclusion Act of 1882 prohibited immigration of new Chinese laborers. The number of first generation Chinese farm workers began to dwindle as older farmers returned to China or died. New immigrants from Japan, the Philippines and Mexico replaced many of the Chinese farm laborers. The remaining second generation then third generation Chinese began the process of moving into the cities. The opportunity to seek higher education played an important part of the urban migration.

Chinese Farmers and the Entrepreneurial Spirit

Chinese farm laborers worked hard and preferred to be paid a piece-rate rather than a fixed daily wage. Sharecropping arrangements were desirable, but the most highly prized working arrangements for the capital-poor Chinese were leases under which they reclaimed the marshland in exchange for free rent for four or five years. When Chinese cleared the swamp for planting, the crop of choice was berries.

In the 1880s, a number of Pajaro Valley landowners entered into sharecropping arrangements with Chinese berry farmers. The landowners furnished the land, plants, water and boxes while the Chinese furnished the skilled labor to plant, cultivate, pick and pack the berries north of Watsonville. They cultivated one hundred acres of strawberries and forty acres of raspberries and blackberries. They leased more desirable tracts of land in different parts of the valley, paying cash rent in advance to cultivate blackberries.

At the turn of the century, adventurous and highly

CITY OF
SAN JOSE
CAPITAL OF SILICON VALLEY

THOMAS FOON CHEW
1889 - 1931

Born in 1889, Thomas Foon Chew entered the canning industry at age 17 and soon built Bayside Canning Company into the third largest cannery in the world. He had a reputation for treating his workers fairly and kindly. Workers lived for free on lands around the cannery, pay was usually good, and Thomas personally made sure his workers had enough to eat, even in the canning off seasons. Thomas Foon Chew died in 1931 from pneumonia. His funeral attracted 25,000 people and was said to be the largest funeral in Chinatown. He was remembered as a keen businessman and a caring person.

Courtesy of Timothy C. Chew

motivated Chinese men such as Sai Yin Chew, and later in 1906, with his son Thomas Foon Chew, became involved in food processing in the central California city of Alviso.

Thomas Foon Chew –
Asparagus King

At the age of 16, Chew came to America to help his father. It was young Chew's involvement with growing and canning asparagus which pushed the asparagus production in the Sacramento River Delta to be the leading producer in the world. Chew bought Benjamin Holt (now Caterpillar) farming equipment and made his own tools when necessary. Beginning with the original Alviso cannery, Chew established canneries in Isleton and then Santa Clara. His plants were able to pack 600,000 cases of vegetable and fruit for an annual sale of $3 million. Chew became known as the "Asparagus King". A resolution was made by the California State Assembly on August 7, 2004 to honor Chew by dedicating a street in his name – "Thomas Foon Chew Way."

A bronze plague mounted on a large granite rock was made to commemorate the dedication, and placed on the main street of the city of Alviso, California. It stated:

"Born in 1889, Thomas Foon Chew entered the canning industry at age 17 and soon built Bayside Canning Company into the third largest cannery in the world.

He had a reputation for treating his workers fairly and kindly. Workers lived for free on lands around the cannery, pay was usually good, and Thomas personally made sure his workers had enough to eat, even in the canning off-season. Thomas Foon Chew died in 1931 from pneumonia. His funeral attracted 25,000 people and was said to be the largest funeral in Chinatown. He was remembered as a keen businessman and a caring person."

From Tim Chew, son of Thomas Foon Chew

Chin Lung –
"Chinese Potato King"

Chin was born in Dao-Mun village and came to San Francisco in 1884. He went to work for the Sing Kee Company bagging imported rice, a profitable trade. Using his savings, he invited some friends and clansmen to join with him to buy land in the Delta to grow potatoes. He reinvested his earnings from crops and became known as the "Chinese Potato King" to rival George Shima, the Japanese Potato King of the delta. Chin Lung amassed a fortune and was able to buy mechanized equipment and his own barges to ship crops up the river to San Francisco, Sacramento and Stockton. His was the first Chinese business to acquire and use tractors. Chin Lung knew nothing about potato farming but was able to organize help to do so. In his best year, he earned $90,000.

This Bittersweet Soil: The Chinese in California Agriculture, 1860-1910—Dr. Sucheng Chan

Chinese grape pickers. California Historical Society, FN-23451/CHS2010.233.tif

Lincoln Chan – from preserved plum candy retailer
to Bartlett pear orchard owner

Lincoln was born a U.S. citizen on Abraham Lincoln's birthday in 1919 to Courtland merchant Chong Chan. Chong bought and sold preserved plum candies, a favorite snack of the Chinese, in his store and this gave him the opportunity to make a good profit. He acquired acres of land under his son Lincoln's name and thwarted the Alien Land Law of 1913. Lincoln Chan turned the acreage his father Chong Chan acquired into successful Bartlett pear orchards. He would learn a great deal and became an expert in pear farming.

Lew Hing – canning of fruits and vegetables

By any measure, Lew Hing was one of the first Chinese tycoons in the United States. He built his business empire in Oakland, where he started a cannery that advanced the science of food preservation. Lew also had substantial interests in banking, shipping, and real estate.

Lew came to the United States from southern China as a 13-year old to help his older half-brother at his San Francisco metal shop. A few months later, his brother died in a tragic sea accident. That left young Lew to cope with his brother's business. He experimented with preserving fruits and vegetables in cans. When he was 18, he founded his first cannery at Sacramento and Stockton Streets. That successful venture enabled Lew to retire at age 44, in 1902, and to return to China to start some new businesses.

He returned to California in 1904, this time to move his San Francisco cannery to Oakland, starting up the Pacific Coast Canning Company at 12th and Pine Streets, adjacent to Southern Pacific railroad that shipped his products across America under the "Buckskin" label. By 1911, Pacific Coast Canning was one of Oakland's largest employers. At peak season, it had 1,000 Portuguese, Italian, and Chinese workers. Canned food from Pacific Coast Canning and other processors boosted the troop morale during World War I.

With Pacific Coast Canning's success, he expanded his business empire. He became president of the Bank of Canton in 1907 and chairman of the China Mail Steamship Co. Ltd. in 1915. He developed two San Francisco hotels. And he was part owner of a cotton plantation in Mexicali, Mexico, where his workers established a Chinatown. He considered his proudest legacy to be the swimming pool he had built at the San Francisco Chinese YMCA in 1925.

Gim Wong – Bel Air Super Market

Gim Wong, a truck farmer, was growing and bringing his produce to China Hill in Auburn for sale. He and his sons built the Bel Air supermarket empire in the Sacramento valley. Later, Bel Air was acquired and merged into the Raleys supermarket chain. Gim Wong's fresh vegetables brought by horse and cart to Auburn, personifies one of the main features of the Bel Air stores – selling the freshest and the best produce available.

Shopping at Giant Foods: Chinese American Supermarkets
in Northern California—Dr. Alfred Yee

"Poison Jim" Jack – Mustard-turned-into-gold

The mustard plant was probably introduced to California during the Spanish era as a seasoning. By the 1850's, the Salinas Valley in California was covered with this unwanted plant. Ranchers and farmers considered mustard a nuisance to their farms and livestock because of its aggressive and dense growth nature. One spring, following a wet winter, the wild mustard was crowding out the grain crops. Jim Jack, a Chinese immigrant, who was known as "Poison Jim" for his work in poisoning squirrels, went to the farmers and offered to pull the mustard in exchange for keeping the seeds. Jim hired enough Chinese workers to harvest the seeds and sold them to a French buyer for $35,000 in gold. The story of mustard-turned-into gold story spread quickly through the Monterey Bay Region and mustard seed became a very valuable cash crop.

Chinese Gold—Sandy Lydon

King Kee – Apple drying – "China Dryer"

Excess apple crops and those that were substandard were generally dried and packaged for sale as dehydrated fruit. The dried apple business had not been a steady profit maker for the apple farm owners due to a lack of dependable and low cost workers.

In 1904 F.P. Marinovich, Luke Scurich, and C.W. Adamson built a tray-loaded, kiln-type dryer (Unglish-style) on Walker Street in Watsonville and leased it to a Chinese named King Kee. Operating under the company name Quong Sang Lung, King Kee hired fellow Chinese to work in the dryer. By the end of the 1904 season, the success of the Chinese-operated apple dryer made it the prototype of the Pajaro Valley apple-drying industry for the next twenty years. The Chinese so dominated Pajaro Valley apple drying that the Unglish-style apple dryer became known as the "China Dryer." As with mustard, slough lands and squid, Chinese muscle and ingenuity transformed a discarded commodity into a valuable product.

Chinese Gold—Sandy Lydon

Chinese Immigrant Farmers' Legacies; Horticulture Skills

Following are some of the people that garnered admiration for their horticultural talents:

Lue Gim Gong – the "Citrus Wizard"

Lue came to San Francisco with his uncle when he was 12 years old. His Sunday school teacher Fannie Burlingame learned of his skill with plants and asked him to tend to

Rear view of Miller and Chong Brothers asparagus plow. California. 1927

her greenhouse. He was converted to Christianity and became a U. S. Citizen. Due to his health situation, he was advised to live in a warmer climate. The Burlingame sisters owned land in Deland, Florida and offered Lue the opportunity to move there to work in the orange groves. Lue noticed that oranges in Florida were very susceptible to cold weather. After a number of experiments in cross-pollination, he developed a new orange in 1888 that was both sweet and hardy to cold weather. The species that he developed is called the "Lue Gim Gong Orange". The American Pomological Society awarded the Silver Wilder Medal to Lue in 1911, the first time such an award was made for citrus.

Other plants he developed included a perfumed grapefruit that grew individually on the tree rather than in clusters. He also propagated seven varieties of roses and other flowers and fruits.

The West Volusia Historical Society in Deland, Florida, erected a bust, displayed in a Gazebo, in his memory. It was inscribed with a proverb Lue lived by:

NO ONE SHOULD LIVE IN THIS WORLD FOR HIMSELF ALONE BUT TO DO GOOD FOR THOSE WHO COME AFTER HIM.

Ah Bing – Bing cherry

Today, there are over 1000 different varieties of sweet

cherries. The Bing, as the supreme eating cherry, tops the list for both flavor and popularity. The flesh is sweet, firm and juicy; the color is dark red, inside and out. It sets the standard by which all other cherries are compared. In 1875, the Bing cherry was developed in Henderson Lewelling's orchard in Oregon from a Black Republican cherry. The Bing cherry was named for Lewelling's Chinese foreman, Ah Bing. Little else is known about the life of Ah Bing.

Miller & Chong Asparagus Plow

"As asparagus plants became old and unproductive, farmers have to uproot the plants and start other crops. But unless the roots could be thoroughly ridden, the asparagus plants and spears would continue to grow among the new crops. Prior attempts at developing mechanized plows to chop up the old asparagus roots were not successful. Jue Chong started a partnership with a friend, Tony Miller, and approached the Bank of Isleton for a loan to develop an asparagus plow. They were rejected, as the venture was deemed to be too risky. But they persevered, and developed the first "Miller and Chong" asparagus plow in 1926. The plow soon gained local notoriety for its success. Jue involved his brothers Sam, Bing, and Look in the development and maintenance of the plows they manufactured, and used to plow old asparagus fields for other farmers. Miller and the Chong brothers were awarded seven U.S. Patents for design of the blades and the plow machinery. They manufactured more than ninety asparagus plows, each unit numbered and improving upon the prior design.

Tony Miller and the Chong brothers made money by subcontracting plowing of asparagus fields, digging up roots of old asparagus plants no longer productive. "The business was highly profitable and competitive."

From Ron Chong, grandson of Lee Chong.

References

1. Chinese Gold – The Chinese in the Monterey Region – Sandy Lydon. 1985
2. The Chinese in America – Iris Chang 2003
3. An Illustrated History of the Chinese in America – Ruthanne McCunn 1979
4. The Story of the Chinese in America – B. L. Sung 1971
5. A Different Mirror, a History of Multicultural America – Ronald Takaki 1993

Fishing:
Pioneers of California's Fishing Industry

~

A Story of Hardship, Fortitude, Resourcefulness, and Success in Commercial Fishing

By Linda Bentz

"Today (2007), the role of Chinese Americans in the state's commercial fishing industry is practically non-existent. Yet it should not be forgotten that it was the immigrants from China who founded this enormous industry in our state. They were, indeed, the pioneers of California's fishing industry."

~Oakland Museum of California, Suitcase Exhibits

Life of a Lonely Chinese Fisherman

Norma Engel's family were lighthouse keepers at Ballast Point from 1914-1931. In her book, Beams of Light: Chronicles of a Lighthouse Keeper's Family, Norma described a relationship with a Chinese fisherman whose junk was anchored near the lighthouse for many years.

Our Chinaman, as we affectionately called him . . . spoke no English so we never learned his name. Whenever we met ashore we never spoke and communicated primarily by gesturing. His was a gentle nature and his tanned leathery face was always creased in a shy smile. No one ever came to visit him on the junk, and he lived a very solitary existence... What about his family and friends? . . . My mother . . . sent me out with some of her baked goods. The short row from the pier to the junk gave me time to wonder where he had come from, why he was here, and how old he was . . . [as a reciprocal gesture] in the next day or two, Dad would come into the kitchen carrying a choice piece of carefully cleaned fish.

On rare occasions, the junk was pulled up on the beach for scraping and painting. Norma, her siblings, her father and other fishermen helped with painting and repairs. "His life followed such a simple routine that it was easy to anticipate his activities each day." In his heavy skiff, probably a sampan, the Chinese man would go out to check his traps or go ashore for water. One day, when the skiff was still attached to the stern of the junk, the Engel family knew that something was wrong. Upon boarding the junk, Mr. Engel found that the Chinese fisherman had passed away. "Within a week, the junk disappeared during the nighttime. Its leaving left a big void. I had lost a dear friend."

The Chinese fishermen were pioneers in an industry that is essential to California's economy. In the 1850s, they were harvesting the seas in junks and sampans built locally of traditional designs. Their knowledge of the preservation methods by salting, sun drying and soaking in oil made it possible to ship seafood to the inland regions and overseas. Indirectly, they played a key role in the infrastructure development of California and the Pacific Coast by supplying the inexpensive stable diet of preserved fish and seafood needed by Chinese laborers who worked on the railroads and reclaimed fertile farmlands from swamps.

The Chinese fishing camps and villages were found along the coast from Oregon, California, along the Sacramento delta and south to Baja. Chinese fishermen experienced short-term prosperity; and the tide turned against them. At the time when the nation was enthralled in anti-Chinese sentiment, the fishers were accused of depleting the fisheries. Laws were passed to limit their fishing seasons and their tools (nets) were outlawed. In 1882, a ban was placed on the use of junks in American waters, declaring them to be foreign vessels. By the late 1880's, repressive California laws and the steep decline of Chinese-American population due to the enactment of the 1882 Chinese Exclusion Act put them out of business.

Chinese fishermen were among the first to recognize and harvest the vast marine resources in California waters. Through their efforts they brought delicacies, such as bay shrimp, abalone and calamari to the western table. Junks and sampans were the workhorses of the fisheries, and provide unique silhouettes in Pacific Coast maritime heritage. During their tenure, the fishers were confronted by hostility from Anglo-Americans who viewed the Chinese as unskilled, servile and greedy. Yet, Chinese fishermen dispel this myth as they were hardworking, innovative, entrepreneurial with the tenacity to succeed.

This is the story of the Chinese fishing industry in California, with some personal accounts of life in fishing settlements in the San Francisco Bay area, Monterey, and San Diego

After the nets were emptied . . . the crew took large bamboo baskets from a hold [of the ship], and shoveled the contents onto the pier. [The baskets were] wheeled to a large platform used as a processing table for separating the shrimp from the miscellaneous sea life mixed in with the catch . . . . This particular phase of separating shrimp was somewhat of a treasure hunt – as anything tasty like an occasional squid, crab, or choice fish, would end up in the camp's kitchen to be shared by the workers and family at dinner time. [1]

Bill Jong's Family at Hunter's Point circa 1923.

Courtesy Bill Jong collection

Chinese fishermen worked the waters of California for over one hundred years. These pioneers came to California just after the state achieved statehood and were among the first non-native fishermen to exploit the natural resources found along the Pacific Coast. Chinese fishermen helped initiate the commercial fishing industry in California.

The fishers who came from China hailed from regions where fishing was a livelihood. They came with the knowledge of shipbuilding; junks and sampans were built in the San Francisco Bay area, Santa Barbara and San Diego.[2] These beautiful vessels are a part of Pacific Coast maritime history, and their unique silhouette captured the ire or the imagination of those who saw them. Designed for a specific purpose, these workhorses were vital for success in the fisheries.

These tenacious men were successful, yet success had its price. Chinese fishers were faced with hostility from other fishermen and were forced to pursue alternative prey in Monterey and other regions. They were accused of depleting the fisheries along the California coast. Laws were passed to limit the season when certain species could be taken, fine mesh nets were outlawed, and ultimately the fishermen were classified as laborers, a class excluded by the federal government for migration. Chinese fishermen fought the unjust laws and legislation in the courts with little success. They were denied of their livelihood and forced to leave the industry to return to China or move on to farming work.

Chinese Fishermen in California

The first mention of Chinese fishermen in California, found to date, comes from the San Francisco *Daily Alta California* dated March 5, 1853. The article describes a settlement of Chinese fishermen, presumably catching sturgeon, on the shore of Rincon Point, located on the South San Francisco Bay. During the next few decades, Chinese fishing camps and villages were established from the Oregon border to Baja California, on offshore islands and along the Sacramento River Delta.

Shrimp camps dominated the San Francisco Bay area; Monterey specialized in squid and market fisheries; and San Diego was primarily concerned with abalone and fresh market fish. The marine resources from these areas were dried and shipped to China, Chinese communities, as well as sold fresh locally.

A vast number of the Chinese fishermen who settled in California displayed great skill in their ability to obtain and process marine products. They seldom rejected any food products from the sea. While the fishermen living in the Monterey Bay region were known for harvesting abalone and catching squid, they also caught and dried rockfish, cod, halibut, flounders, red fish and blue fish, yellow tail, mackerel, sardines, shark, seaweed, and shellfish.[3]

It appears their skills were developed in regions in China where fishing was a livelihood. 1880 census data provides evidence that fishermen, who worked the fisheries at Point San Pedro on San Pablo Bay in Marin County, hailed from areas of the Guangdong province where shrimp fishing was practiced. Approximately sixty-eight percent of the fishermen at Point San Pedro came from the Toishan district in China located in the Pearl River Delta and bordered by the South China Sea. Thirteen percent of the residents came from the Heungshan district that is bordered by the Tam Kong Delta and the Pearl River estuary.[4]

Chinese fishermen in California maintained traditional fishing methods, and their adherence to these practices is best displayed by their use of traditional watercraft. Junks in China have traditionally been used for many purposes such as fishing, transportation of cargo and ferrying. In his classic work *The Junks and Sampans of the Yangtze*, G.R.G. Worcester claims that sea-going junks from North China were among the oldest known ships and date back perhaps thousands of years.[5]

Chinese shipwrights in California built traditional watercraft at several locations including San Diego, Roseville, Santa Barbara, San Mateo, San Pablo, Point San Pedro, San Bruno, and Hunters Point. The use of California redwood was a departure from traditional junk building materials. It was a good choice of wood for California junks because it was amply available during the nineteenth and early twentieth centuries. Some of the advantages of this wood material were that it could be easily obtained in

wide and long dimensions, it was cost efficient, and it was resistant to rot.[6]

The business of fishing was extremely dangerous. Since Chinese fishermen harvested the sea for fish and mammals, they carried firearms as part of their fishing gear. The Santa Barbara *Daily Independent* reported, "One of the hunters on the Chinese junk had the misfortune to shoot himself. The ball entering the arm at the elbow and coming out at the shoulder"[7] Chinese junks were known to strand. Such was the case in 1884, when a junk sailing from San Diego was anchored near San Nicolas Island and drifted upon a reef at high tide. The vessel was pounded on the rocks and the crew feared for their lives. Fortunately, the sloop *Ocean King* from Santa Barbara was sailing in the vicinity and rescued the crew of eight Chinese fishermen.[8]

Fisheries in the San Francisco Area

The shrimp fisheries located in the San Francisco Bay region provided jobs for hundreds of Chinese fishermen. Chinese fishing operations could be found at San Pablo in Contra Costa County; Point San Pedro and Point San Quentin in Marin County; Redwood City and Burlingame in San Mateo County; Newark in Alameda County; and Hunters Point in San Francisco County.[9]

One of the largest Chinese shrimp-fishing villages was Point San Pedro. In 1880, the census recorded 347 fishermen along with cooks, boardinghouse keepers, servants, gardeners, a junk dealer, a barber and school teacher who worked to support fishing activities and the fishermen. The total population for Point San Pedro for this year was 469 residents.[10] The fishing village spanned ten to fifteen acres and consisted of 32 houses, boat building and shipping facilities. The side of a nearby hill was used for drying marine products.[11] Today, a part of this settlement still exists and is known as China Camp State Park.

Hunters Point, located on the extreme southeastern part of San Francisco, was also the home to Chinese fishermen and their families. The earliest mention of shrimp camps at Hunters Point is found in 1880 census. At that time one hundred and fifty-one fishermen lived in the area. By 1910, there were five camps on the north side of the point and two on the south side. The shrimp business expanded, and twelve camps with sixteen vessels and fifty-three men were established at Hunters Point in 1930.[12]

Two former residents of Hunters Point reminisced about their childhoods in the shrimp camp. Bill Jong was born at the camp in 1922 and resided here until 1932. Angela Lee Soo Hoo resided there with her family from 1933 to approximately 1940. Bill's father was the tugboat captain and chief mechanic for the Bay City Shrimp Company.[13] Bill describes the camp:

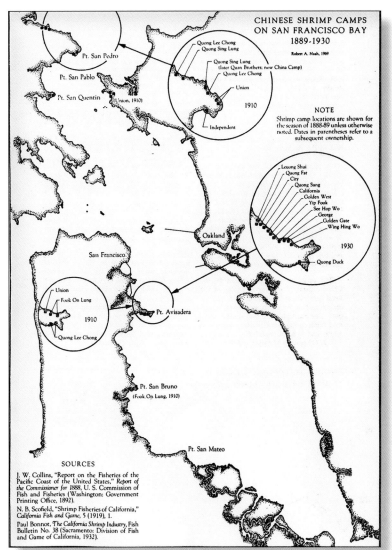

San Francisco Bay. Courtesy of Robert A. Nash

was remarkable how well this basic architectural substructure held up in the many severe wind and rainstorms common to the area.[14]

Bill recalls that the fishermen at Bay City Shrimp Company were young to middle age, and for the most part seemed to have no particular skills just a lot of brute strength and stamina, which was a definite requirement.[15] During the shrimp-fishing season about half-a-dozen unmarried fishermen worked for Bill's father, Jong Kwong Yin, and they all spoke Cantonese.

It appears that Bill's and Angela Lee Soo Hoo's fathers worked in different camps at Hunters Point. Coming to the industry without any fishing experience, Angela's father, Mr. Lee, paid $1.00- $1.50 per acre for the land at Hunters Point. He was an entrepreneur and invested in many businesses. At the camp, Angela remembered "a whole bunch of single people living in a dormitory, and about ten or twenty people worked for my dad."[16]

Approaching the camp on foot, one followed a long dirt road that cut through an empty expanse of field. In the distance, one building stood out, a two-story barn-like structure, put together with unpainted weathered wood and accented with a hand painted sign – Bay City Shrimp Company . . . The camp was situated on a bluff overlooking the Bay, about ten feet above the shoreline. Our house faced the shrimp camp . . . about a third of the houses actually extended over the edge, supported by strategically placed creosoted pilings. It

Shrimp Fishing

The choice of fishing ground was very important, and an experienced fisherman, one who understood the currents, would dictate the exact location where the net stakes would be placed. Once the net stakes were driven into the bay floor, they would remain in place for the entire season. Sup

Quok, an extremely experienced fisherman who worked at Hunters Point, "Knew exactly how to throw something on the water to tell how the tide flowed." He also showed the fishermen how to test the area where the shrimp could be found and helped to set the nets.[17]

Fishing territory was respected by other Chinese fishermen. "At Hunters Point, because of the expensive investment there, some one can't go in and use your equipment. Because you put the posts [stakes] in there, and that is part of the major investment, there was sort of an understanding among the fishermen that they didn't interfere with one another."[18] While the Chinese recognized ownership of the fishing grounds, it was not legally sanctioned.

The shrimp fishing companies of the Bay area reflected at least three organizational patterns: the owner-operator, the owner-lessor/the lessee-operator, and the owner-employer. The definition of ownership was based on the assets of the company such as camp structures, vessels and gear, and

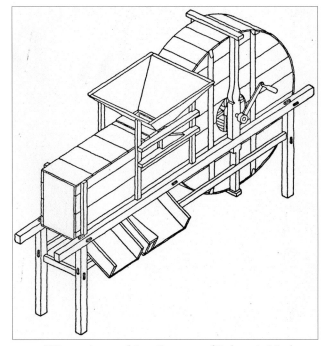

Winnowing machine. Courtesy of Robert A. Nash

processing equipment. Since the land was leased, the camp property was not considered an asset.

The owner-operator was perhaps the most common pattern in the early shrimp fishery. In this organization the men required to perform the various jobs formed a partnership. They found a fishing area, built the camp and vessels, obtained the gear, and began their fishing and processing activities. One partner may own the vessel, while other partners could own the capital materials. Profits would be split by giving the owner of the vessel a share, and then expenses would be deducted. The remainder would be split equally between the rest of the partners.

The most common patterns in the later years were the owner-lessor and lessee-operator patterns. These two forms worked together. The camps and vessels were owned by companies in Chinatown, which were basically marketing enterprises. The entire catch would be sold to the owner at a fixed price. Under this agreement the partners worked on shares. In the final organization, the owner-employer pattern, the owner would find the crews and pay wages.[19]

The process of harvesting shrimp was arduous. The fishermen's day could start as early as 1:00 o'clock in the morning, and their success was dependent on the ebb and flow of the tide. Upon arrival at their designated fishing ground, as the tide was outgoing, large fine meshed conical nets would be attached to the stakes on the floor of the bay with their mouths facing the current. Up to forty-two nets would be placed. The crew would rest and nap as the incoming tides swept the shrimp into their nets.

One young fisherman who stayed awake as the others slept recalled, "We had permission from Fish and Game to keep the sea lions away from our nets . . . while the men were sleeping I'd sit on the deck with a .22. I never hit many, just scared them mostly."[20] If sea lions ripped at the nets, the catch could be lost and the gear was expensive to repair or replace.

The nets were pulled in with the help of a windlass and the contents shoveled into the ship's hold and bamboo baskets. The fishermen could remain in their vessel for about six hours laying and hauling their nets. The daily catch of a single junk ranged from 1,000 to 2,000 pounds depending on the number of nets used.[21] Shrimp was not the only sea life found in the nets; lamprey eels, string rays, skates, angel fish, and jelly fish were caught in the nets as well. Sharks and rays caught in the net were dangerous while still alive, and a hook was used to remove them from the catch. If touched by hand the electric ray would give a powerful shock.[22]

The handling of the shrimp once it reached the shore was described in a United States Commission of Fish and Fisheries Report from 1880.

The shrimp are, when caught, put into live-baskets made of basket ware, with a covering of netting, also home-made . . . These live shrimp are taken to Vallejo-street market and sold at 5 cents per pound. Those unsold are brought back and put into boiling brine. They are then taken out and put on the ground to dry, being spread out and turned over with a sort of broom . . . The ground is denuded of grass, and made bare and smooth, . . . for the purpose of drying the shrimp. When dry they are taken and crushed under large wooden pestles, and then put through a fanning mill, which separates the meat from the shells . . . The fanning-mill is constructed on precisely the same principle as the kind used for winnowing grain . . . The pulverized meats are shipped to China or consumed in Chinatown . . . The shells are used for manure, most of them being shipped to China.[23]

Dried shrimp, the largest percentage of the catch, was exported to China via steamship. The product is called *ha mai* or shrimp rice because it is small like gains of rice. It was, and still is, used in vegetable dishes, mixed in rice, used as a condiment for soup, sautéed with cucumbers, put in eggs, and cooked in radish cake.

Memories of Life in Shrimp Fishing Camps

The children who lived at Hunters Point have fond memories of life in a shrimp camp. Angela Lee Soo Hoo remembered that the camp had a whole pack of dogs; about 20-40. Her father used to feed the dogs, and they were allowed to run around so that people would not take the shrimp. Both Angela and Bill Jong attended school while living at the shrimp camp, and their form of transportation was thrilling and unique. Bill remembered:

My second elementary school was a considerable distance from Hunters Point . . . there was no direct transportation, the school board determined some kind of service needed to be supplied, and miraculously arrangements were made with the Yellow Cab Company to do just that. We were picked up every morning and returned home in the afternoon. This kind of luxury was a real treat for all of us. When we weren't awed into silence by the trip – we were laughing and joking all the way, which we did in English.[24]

Angela attended Brett Harte School, in San Francisco, which later burned down. She spoke fondly about her rides to school in a taxi. The car came right to her front door at Hunters Point. Two other children from Angela's family rode to school in the taxi, along with two more children from across the street. Angela thinks that the taxi service was for grammar school students only, since her older sister and brother never came along. Another girl came from around the bend to ride the taxi, but she was not Chinese.

Public opinion turned against Chinese fishermen in the Bay area, and they faced discrimination and regulation. During the 1880s, fear arose that the Pacific Coast fisheries were becoming depleted. The California State Board of Fish Commissioners launched a study of the Bay Area shrimp industry. "In a series of reports laced with the virulent anti-Chinese rhetoric that was common currency in late nineteenth-century California . . . [the reports] insisted that up to half of the shrimper's catch consisted of smelt and other small fish."[25] Consequently in 1901, legislation was passed that established a closed season for shrimp fishing between the months of May and October. These months coincided with prime shrimp fishing season. The Chinese challenged the constitutionality of the law and the legislature abolished the closed season in 1905. Around the same time, in another attempt to end the Chinese fishing industry, the legislature enacted a much more damaging law by prohibiting the exportation of dried shrimp and shells from the state. This law stayed in place until 1919. Additional legislation prohibiting the use of the bag net was enacted in 1910 and remained in place until 1915.[26] After the laws were rescinded, shrimp fishing rebounded. As World War II approached, the fishery declined and the last of the shrimp camps, Hunters Point Shrimp Company, went out of business in 1959.[27]

Fisheries in Monterey

The Monterey Bay region was home to the some of the first Chinese fishermen who came to California. There is a legend among early Chinese settlers in the Monterey region that in the 1850s, seven 30-foot-long Chinese junks left the Guangdong Province in China and traveled to North America. According to the story, at least one vessel landed near Monterey and another in Mendocino.[28] Further evidence is required to substantiate this account.

The earliest Chinese fishing village in the area was established at Point Lobos, probably around 1851. By 1876, fourteen buildings could be found in the Chinese village at Carmel Bay.[29] One building remains and is known as the Whalers Cabin. Built around 1851, this structure provides physical evidence of Chinese fishing activities in the Monterey Bay region and "is believed to be the oldest remaining wooden frame residence of Chinese origin in California."[30] Portuguese fishermen began to share the cove with the Chinese fishermen, and the two groups remained at Point Lobos until the late 1870s.

Another fishing community was established at Point Alones, located in Pacific Grove, one and a half miles

northwest of Monterey. It was described as "a large Chinese fishing village, composed of rude shanties . . . and appears to be one of the most thriving settlements of its kind on the west coast."[31]   The exact date that Chinese fishermen established the village is unclear. It is possible that fishers were there as early as 1853, as Sandy Lydon suggests in his book Chinese Gold: the Chinese in the Monterey Bay Region.

Pescadero, a third fishing community, was established in 1868. By 1879, the village had a resident population of approximately 40 Chinese inhabitants living in eight houses.[32] The village remained at that location until 1912.

Chinese Fishing Activities

Chinese fishermen exploited a wide variety of marine life in the Monterey Bay region, such as, rock fish, cod, halibut, flounders, red and blue fish, yellow tail, mackerel, sardines, shell fish, shark, seaweed, sea urchins, skate, sea trout, and sea slugs. Most of the products were dried and shipped to China and Chinese communities in the United States. A portion of the products was sold in fresh condition. A twelve-ton junk plied the waters between Pescadero and Point Alones and transported their marine products to San Francisco, for export and distribution.[33]

During the 1850s and 1860s, the Chinese in the Monterey Bay region harvested abalone. The meat was dried and the shells were shipped to China to be used for cabinet inlays and jewelry. Exported shells were also made into buttons and curios in France and Germany. Ambitious Chinese entrepreneurs sold abalone, urchin shells and other items from the sea to local tourists.

There was competition in the Monterey Bay fisheries between ethnic groups. Portuguese whalers established a settlement in Monterey in 1855 and additional fishermen from Portugal arrived in the area in 1860. Italian fishermen arrived in Monterey County from San Francisco in 1873.[34] Yet, more than half of the fishermen in the area were Chinese. These men, using methods learned from their respective homeland, frequently came into conflict. At Point Alones, Chinese fishermen were accused of ignoring established fishing territories by using trawl lines, which were prohibited. Portuguese whalers engaged in malicious acts of running their ships into Chinese nets and cutting them with their knives.

Chinese fishermen decided to set a net for the whalers. In March 1880 the Chinese took a white American out with them, and while this potential witness hid in the bottom of the boat, the Chinese spread their nets and began to fish. Right on cue the Portuguese whalers sailed up and began cutting the fishing gear; the witness then stood and formally observed the entire incident. The Chinese sued the Portuguese whaling company, and when the suit came to trial the witness testified that he saw the Portuguese cut the nets. The attorney for the whalers was able to argue successfully that the witness was biased, and the suit was thrown out of court.[35]

Without protection from the law, Chinese fishermen in the Monterey Bay area feared that they would be driven from their livelihood. They were alarmed by the hostile treatment at the hands of competing fishermen, and adding to their strife was anti-Chinese sentiment that was sweeping the nation at the time. Consequently, Chinese fishermen decided to seek different marine species and relieve the hostility directed at their fishing practices. Squid fishing, conducted at night by the light of the lantern, was the answer.

To catch squid, a blazing lantern or torch was attached to the boats to attract the squid to the surface of the water, while purse seines were used to capture the prey. The technique is still being used today in squid fishing around the world.

Crew eagerly and anxiously watching for the signal that announces a school of squid has been "raised" and is hovering just beneath the surface, in the glow of the light that flares and sparkles in the wind. Instantly, when the signal is given, the seine is thrown out, the fishermen guiding their craft so that the net makes a complete circle around the boat with the light. The seine is quickly pursed up, and its contents are taken into the boats, which return to the shore and land their catch.[36]

A description of Chinese fishing activities and export practices at Monterey elicited a newspaper account from as far away as Chicago; "The squids are dried and shipped to China to be used as food and also as fertilizer. The duty on fertilizer in China is low, the duty on salt high. By mixing a little dried squid with a great deal of salt and calling it fertilizer, a considerable amount of salt finds its way into the celestial kingdom at a low duty rate."[37]

Point Alones Fishing Village

A visitor to Point Alones would find a fishing village situated on a lovely secluded cove where wooden buildings were built in rows with some structures elevated on stilts, jetting out over the water. During the day sampans were pulled up on the sand while fishermen prepared for another outing at sea. This self-contained community provided its residents with a general store, an employment agency, a cemetery, an outdoor shrine and an association hall. A council of elders adjudicated disputes and mediated political and economic issues that arose in the village. Known in the region as a cultural center, Chinese residents from nearby towns would gather and share in traditional celebrations such as the Ring Game parade, held in honor of the God of Wealth, and Lunar New Year festivities.

Fishing was a family endeavor at Point Alones, and these pioneers came to the California to work the sea. This unique community was started and settled by families who shared fishing responsibilities. A surprisingly large percentage of women lived at the village. The 1870 census reported that 43% of the 47 Chinese living there were female, while nationwide only 7% of the Chinese population was women.[38]

California-born Chinese children played a large role in the village. Working together with their families, they helped process marine products. When they were not working they attended a school established by the Methodist Episcopal church in 1883. The school educated an average of twenty or more students until 1894.[39] Although educational opportunities were limited, some of the second-generation residents took a leadership role in the village. Among the leaders were Tuck Lee, Tom Yuen and Tom Wong.

Descendants of Point Alones residents shared their family histories and provide a view of life in a Chinese fishing village. On August 13, 1859, Quock Mui was born to Quock Bo and Loy So May at Point Lobos. The Quock family was reportedly among the early settlers who sailed from China to the Monterey Peninsula via ocean-going junks in the 1850s. Quock Mui was the first documented Chinese female born in the region. Quock Tuck Lee, community leader, was her brother. The Quock family moved from Point Lobos to Pescadero and ultimately settled at Point Alones. Quock Mui married Jeung Yow Hoy and together they had six children.[40]

Quock Mui is remembered as a woman of strength and intelligence. She was surrounded by a population of diverse people who spoke many languages, and consequently she became multilingual. She became known as Spanish Mary, and her abilities as a linguist gave her the opportunity to act as a translator among the different ethnic groups in Monterey.[41] Today the home where she lived, located on Wave Street in Monterey and called Quock Mui Tea House

Bancroft junk, Point Alones

Courtesy of the Bancroft Library. University of California, Berkeley. Alice I. Hare #839.

stands as an enduring memorial to this pioneer of one of the earliest Chinese fishing villages in California.

Munson Kwok's family reportedly left Macau and arrived in Monterey via an ocean-going junk in the early 1860s. Munson's father, Kwok Loy, caught squid in the Bay in 1912. After over fifty years of Chinese fishing activities on the Monterey Peninsula, Kwok Loy said that the marine life in the region was abundant, and the fishing boats were heavily laden upon their return to the beach. Moreover, he described the sampans used in the squid fishery as large boats; larger than those found in other Chinese fisheries in California.[42]

The Decline of Chinese Fishermen in Monterey

Point Alones village remained in the same location for over 50 years. While the village was picturesque, by 1900, it was seen as a mess of old buildings without a sewer system, or enough water pressure available to extinguish a fire. Moreover, the process of Chinese fish drying became unnecessary when canneries began to be built in Monterey; the first built in 1896 and was located between Monterey and Point Alones.

Just after the turn of the century, changes were taking place in Monterey and Pacific Grove. These communities were actively modernizing, and local residents complained about the smell of the fish products drying in the sun. Consequently by 1905, the landowner, the Pacific Improvement Company, responding to public opinion, was in the process of evicting the Chinese residents at Point Alones.[43]

Residents of the fishing village were incensed by the eviction; after all they occupied the land for decades. Chinese fishing activities were declining in the state, and the fishermen at Point Alones feared that they could not find a new location to build a new fishing village. Quock Tuck Lee, a California-born Chinese leader of the community, negotiated with their landlords.[44] The Pacific Improvement Company did not agree with the leaders' reasoning and accused the Chinese of stalling.

Tragedy struck on May 16, 1906, when the fire broke out at Point Alones and two thirds of the Chinese settlement burned to the ground. The residents lost practically everything, while Euro American spectators cheered as the fire reduced the village to ashes. Vandals looted stores, homes and personal possessions. All but sixteen of the one hundred buildings were destroyed. The Pacific Improvement Company moved in to protect their land. The *Los Angeles Times* takes the story from here.

Officials of the Pacific Improvement Company have for months desired to eject Chinese from their picturesque village . . . The conflagration seemed to furnish an opportunity, and Saturday the company fenced across the road used by the public for twenty years, by which access to the place is obtained . . . Meanwhile, the Chinese commenced the reconstruction of dwellings, with canvas and such material as was at hand. M. Prior, land agent for the company and his guards proceeded to demolish these dwellings . . . . The Chinese, determined to maintain their rights, expect the arrival tonight of the Chinese Consul and the Chinese Minister from Washington, who has been staying in Oakland.[45]

By 1920, the effects of the Chinese Exclusion Act were apparent in the thinning of the fishermen population in the Bay. Local resistance to rebuilding the fishing village at Point Alones continued. A lengthy lawsuit ensued between the Chinese and the Pacific Improvement Company. Ultimately the Chinese leased land at McAbee Beach on the north side of the Monterey Peninsula. The population at the new location did not exceed 100 people, and the fishing activities diminished.

Fisheries of San Diego

Chinese fishermen dominated the industry in San Diego from the early 1850s until the 1890s. The earliest fishing village in the area was established on Point Loma most likely at Ballast Point. In 1869, there were at least two fishing settlements; the second at Roseville, also known as La Playa, where ten shanties were constructed along with large racks for drying fish. Each shanty had a chicken coop, and scraps of fish were used to feed the birds.[46] Another fishing village was located on the waterfront adjacent to the Stingaree district and Chinatown.

Ten to twelve unpainted shacks positioned in two rows at right angles to each other; racks for drying fish, outhouses, and piles of rotten fish . . . give the colony an extremely unsavory odor. The headman of the colony furnishes the greater part of the fishing capital, and the fishermen repay him out of the proceeds of their catches . . . Some of the Chinamen live entirely on their boats, visiting their houses on land perhaps once a month.[47]

Many species of marine life was captured by the fishermen, such as red fish, barracuda, shark, smelt, and mullet. Chinese fishermen extended their activities to Baja California, yet maintained San Diego as their base of operations for shipping and fresh market sales. Abalone was their main target and it was abundant in Baja California, or Lower California. Chinese fishermen would sail their junks up to 400 miles from San Diego to gather the mollusk. Chinese fishermen from both San Diego and Santa Barbara worked and lived periodically on several of the Channel Islands. Fishing camps were established on San Clemente, San Miguel, Santa Cruz, Santa Rosa, San Nicolas, Santa Catalina, Anacapa and Santa Barbara Islands. Practically every island in the Channel Island chain has recognized Chinese fishermen by naming a bay, camp, or harbor after their presence. For example, China Camp is located on Santa Rosa Island and Chinese Harbor is noted on maps of Santa Cruz Island.

Abalone Harvesting

Before the Chinese arrived in California, abalone was enjoyed by native people who ate the meat and used the shells for trade and ornamentation. Abalone was the perfect resource for Chinese fishermen to pursue. Dried abalone was considered a delicacy in China and the shells could be exported to be used as raw material for buttons, combs, jewelry and curios. Chinese fishermen could harvest the mollusk with very little competition.

By the time Chinese fishermen arrived in San Diego, the abalone population had exploded. Sea otters are native to California, and their fur was highly desired. Due to over hunting, the animal was driven to near extinction. An element of their diet is abalone; consequently, abalone flourished and multiplied once the sea otters were removed.

Abalone was harvested between San Francisco and Turtle Bay, Baja California; however, the main center for abalone harvesting in the nineteenth century was San Diego. Abalone could be obtained on foot by gathering at low tide, or rowing among the rocks just off shore in a sampan. To remove the creature from the rocks, a trowel, spade or long pole with a wedge tip was used to pry the abalone from the rocks. A gaff was used to recover the abalone.

Once the abalone was gathered it was prepared on site. Meat preparation was done by scooping the meat from its shell and placing it into a large kettle of boiling water. It was then spread out in the sun to dry. The amount of abalone procured by Chinese fishermen in San Diego can be found in *United States Commission of Fish and Fisheries Reports*. "The catch of the Chinese junks in 1888 amounted to 75,000 of salted fish, 646,344 pounds of abalone shells, and 204,771 pounds of abalone meat."[48]

Chinese Fishermen in San Diego

To get a glimpse of Chinese individuals who made their living in the fishing industry in San Diego, one must consult several sources. Census data from 1870 show nine Chinese men who listed their occupation as fishermen. In 1880, twenty-eight Chinese men were listed as fishermen, and three of these men had families present. The population in the fishing communities grew, and reports from the Untied States Fish Commission from 1888, listed 52 Chinese fishermen in San Diego.[49] Finally, according to the 1900 census, Chinese men engaged in fishing in San Diego declined dramatically with only five men from China who claimed to work as fishermen.

An individual who appears on census enumerations and in newspaper accounts is Ah Ti. His name is listed on both the 1870 and 1880 censuses. In 1870, he was 26 years old; he was single; he lived alone; and he claimed personal property that totaled $150. A newspaper account from Christmas day 1872 titled, 'Champion Clam Chowder and a Chinaman' describes how Ah Ti organized and was in charge of activities for a chowder party at La Playa.[50] He appears again on the 1880 census, and he lived with six other men.

A San Diego County Coroner's Inquest Report, dated November 2, 1878, provided details of the death of a Chinese fisherman. Ah Sing and his wife "Mrs." Pat were fishing in their boat when it capsized in a patch of kelp, throwing both into the water. Speaking through an interpreter, Mrs. Pat stated that she was able to right the boat and she tied her husband to the side; however, the rough seas injured Ah Sing's head and he died. She specifically noted that they had "no fight". H.S. Leland, captain of steamer *Santa Cruz*, upon hearing the cries of Mrs. Pat, rescued the couple three miles southwest of Point Loma.

Mrs. Pat stated in the Coroner's Report that she lived at La Playa with her husband who came to America around

1874, and he was 45 years old at the time of his death. Lum Fook, another Chinese fisherman who lived at La Playa, testified that he knew Ah Sing and Mrs. Pat, and they had 200 to 300 pounds of salt fish at La Playa worth 2 ½ cents per pound at the time of Ah Sing's death.

Sun Yun Lee, San Diego junk.   Courtesy of CHSSC

the "wealthiest Chinese merchants with an estate worth over one-half million dollars." He owned the *Sun Yun Lee,* a three-masted junk.

Wo Sing was another man who was involved in the fishing industry. He was a merchant, labor contractor and medi-

In addition, Fook stated that Ah Sing owned only a boat; he had no money, but the couple "agreed well together."[51]

By matching the Coroner's Inquest Report with census data, aspects of Mrs. Pat's life emerge. Two years later, the 1880 census lists a woman named Ah Pat who was married to John Silva, a Portuguese fisherman. Two children lived in their residence: Yin Hay, age ten and Lum Tye, age eight; both listed as stepchildren. Their neighbors were Chinese fishermen. Is it likely that Mrs. Pat remained at La Playa and married a Portuguese fisherman? Ah Pat and John Silva do not appear on the 1900 census.

Quong Sow Kee (sometimes Quong Sun Kee) was a merchant in San Diego's Chinese community and carried on a lucrative business. His store was located at Second and J Streets in New Town. His death notice, posted in the San Diego Union of September 1, 1887, stated that he was one of

cal practitioner. It appears that he was very successful in his business endeavors because in 1888, he was described by the San Diego *Union* as "one of the wealthiest Chinese in San Diego."[52] In the City Directory for 1889-1890, his business, Quong Wo Sing, was listed as dealers in abalone shells.[53] He owned two junks, as the *Acme* and the *Sung Wo On* which were sold by Wo Sing to Euro Americans in 1892. Another San Diego local notable, Ah Quin, the legendary mayor of Chinatown, was reported to have been involved in the abalone trade.[54]

Chinese Shipbuilding

A Chinese shipbuilding yard was established near Roseville, and the ships in the Chinese fleet in San Diego grew as the fishing industry prospered. From 1880 to 1888, there were 13 junks at San Diego and the total value of the junks was $5,200, which means they were worth $400 per vessel.[55] The junks in San Diego began to vanish from the bay;

in 1890 only six vessels could be found, and by 1893 one lone Chinese vessel remained.[56]

Decline of Chinese Fishing Activities in San Diego

Several factors contributed to Chinese withdrawing from fishing activities in San Diego. Concerned citizens, noticing the shortage of fresh market fish, became concerned about the decimation of the bay's fisheries by Chinese fishing practices, particularly their use of fine-nets. Consequently, local officials began to monitor Chinese fishing activities very closely.

Federal legislation contributed to the decline of the fisheries. The passage of the Scott Act in 1888, invalidated Return Certificates, documentation required for Chinese laborers to leave the country and return. At first this legislation did not concern Chinese fishermen, however upon the passage of the Geary Act in 1892, fishermen were classified as laborers stating, "Anyone taking, drying, or otherwise preserving shell or other fish for exportation; as such they fall under terms of Chinese Exclusion Act."[57] Therefore, Chinese fishermen traveling from San Diego to Baja California could not return. Junks were sold, and after decades of success in the fisheries, Chinese fishermen left the industry.

References

1. Bill Jong describing shrimp processing at Hunter Point, San Francisco in a letter to the author July 7, 2001.
2. It is possible that junks were built in additional cities in California.
3. Sandy Lydon, *Chinese Gold: The Chinese in the Monterey Bay Region* (Capitola: Capitola Book Company, 1985), 36.
4. Robert A. Nash, "The Chinese Shrimp Fishery in California" (PhD dissertation, University of California Los Angeles, 1973), 184-186.
5. G.R.G Worcester, *The Junks & Sampans of the Yangtze* (Annapolis: Naval Institute Press, 1971): 7.
6. The distinction between the junk and the sampan is that the sampan was a smaller craft, constructed without decks and was propelled by sail, oar or poles. The average length of a sampan was twenty-one feet and it rarely exceeded ten net tons.
7. Santa Barbara *Daily Independent* June 25, 1885.
8. Ibid, July 31, 1884.
9. William A. Wilcox, "Fisheries of the Pacific Coast in 1899", *United States Commission of Fish and Fisheries. Report of the Commissioner for the Year Ending June 30, 1901* (Washington D.C.: Government Printing Office, 1902), 550.
10. Nash, "The Chinese Shrimp Fishery," 185-186.
11. History of Marin County, California: Including its Geography, Geology, Topography and Climatography (Alley, Bowen & Co. Publishers, 1880), 346-347.
12. Paul Bonnot, "The California Shrimp Industry," *Fish Bulletin* 38 (1932): 6.
13. The types of vessels used by the Chinese in the shrimp fishery changed over time. Modified junks, tow boats and small fishing boats operated out of Hunters Point. Nash, "The Chinese Shrimp Fishery," 285-286.
14. Bill Jong letter.
15. Some scholars have written that once the fishing settlements were established, new arrivals would learn the fishing trade from experienced fishermen. See Eve L.

Armentrout-Ma, "The Chinese in California's Fishing Industry, 1850-1941," *California History LX*, no 2 (Summer 1981):151.

16. Interview with Angela Lee Soo Hoo by Linda Bentz, September 11, 2007.

17. Interview with Jennie Quok Limm and Robert A. Nash, August 23, 1970. On file, Nash Collection, box 4, folder titled Shrimp Fishery, Technology, Process, and Equipment. Chinese Historical Society of Southern California, Los Angeles.

18. Interview with David Chan by Robert A. Nash, January 23, 1970. On file, Nash Collection, box 4, folder titled Shrimp Fishery, Technology, Process, and Equipment. Chinese Historical Society of Southern California, Los Angeles.

19. Ibid, 158-160.

20. Interview with Don Lim by Robert A. Nash. n.d. On file, Nash Collection, box 4, folder titled Shrimp Fishery, Technology, Process, and Equipment. Chinese Historical Society of Southern California, Los Angeles.

21. Nash, "The Chinese Shrimp Fishery," 143.

22. Ibid, 289.

23. George Brown Goode, "Fisheries of the Pacific Coast," *United States Commission of Fish and Fisheries. The Fisheries and Fishery Industries of the United States, Section II, A Geographical Review of the Fisheries Industries and Fishing Communities for the Year 1880* (Washington: Government Printing Office, 1887), 612.

24. Bill Jong letter.

25. Arthur McEvoy, *The Fisherman's Problem* (Cambridge: Cambridge University Press, 1986), 103.

26. Bonnot, "The California Shrimp Industry," 5.

27. Nash, "The Chinese Shrimp Fisheries," 135-139.

28. Hee and Quock (Kwok) families' legends states that there were two trans-Pacific voyages in ocean going junks. The first in the 1850s and another junk voyage occurred in the early 1860s, when two junks reportedly landed at Monterey.

29. Lydon, *Chinese Gold*, 140.

30. Personal Communication with Kris N. Quist, District Museum Curator, Monterey District, California State Parks, November 8, 2007

31. J.W. Collins, "Fisheries of the Pacific Coast," 57-58.

32. George Brown Goode, "The Fisheries of the Pacific Coast," 603.

33. Lydon, *Chinese Gold*, 36-40; J.W. Collins "Fisheries of the Pacific Coast," 57.

34. David S. Jordan, "The Chinese Fishermen of the Pacific Coast," 30, 33.

35. Lydon, *Chinese Gold*, 54.

36. J.W. Collins, "Fisheries of the Pacific Coast," 60.

37. Chicago *Daily Tribune*, October 11, 1899.

38. Lydon, *Chinese Gold*, 155

39. Ibid, 156.

40. Interview with Gerry Low- Sabado by Linda Bentz, September 16, 2007.

41. Ibid.

42. Kwok Loy's name is presented in traditional form; surname first with given name second. Interview with Dr. Munson Kwok by Linda Bentz, September 22, 2007.

43. The Pacific Improvement Company was the land development arm of the Southern Pacific Railroad.

44. Lydon, *Chinese Gold*, 373.

45. Los Angeles *Times*, May 23, 1906.

46. Robert A. Nash, "The Chinese Fishing Industry in Baja California." Paper presented at the Baja California Symposium IX, Santa Ana, California, May 1971: 2.

47. David S. Jordan, "The Chinese Fishermen of the Pacific Coast," 37.

48. J.W. Collins, "Fisheries of the Pacific Coast," 33.

49. Ibid, 28.

50. San Diego *Daily World*, December 25, 1872.

51. Mark Allen, "Death of Chinese Fishermen Reveal Their Lives; Tuberculosis Claims A Chinese Fisherman," *Mains'l Haul* 35, no. 2 & 3 (Summer 1999): 8-9.

52. Arthur McEvoy, "In Places Men Reject: Chinese Fishermen at San Diego, 1870-1893," *Journal of San Diego History* 23, (1977):19-20.

53. Personal communication with Murray Lee, December 7, 2007.

54. Information regarding Chinese activities in San Diego can be found in Ah Quin's diary which spans twenty-five years: 1877-1902. The diary is on file at the San Diego Historical Society.

55. J.W. Collins, "Fisheries of the Pacific Coast," 32.

56. William A. Wilcox, "The Fisheries of the Pacific Coast," *United States Commission of Fish and Fisheries. Report of the Commissioner for the Year Ending June 30, 1893* (Washington, D.C.:Government Printing Office, 1895), 189.

57. Murray K. Lee, "The Chinese Fishing Industry of San Diego," *Mains'l Haul* 35, no. 2 & 3 (Summer 1999):13.

58. Norma Engel, *Beams of Light Chronicles of a Lighthouse Keeper's Family.* (San Diego: Tecolote Publications, 1986), 239.

59. Ibid, 240-241.

Technology:
Engineers and Scientists

By L.P. Leung

• Based on the U.S. Census of 2000, only 1% of the total U. S. population is Chinese-American. There were, however, more than 150,000 Chinese-American engineers and scientists working in industry, government and academia, including some 15,000 in the national defense sector.

• Among national defense industry contractors, 10% to 15% of the technical staff are Chinese Americans involved with critical project details. In many instances, their innovations have allowed the United States to retain prominence in high technology defense systems, space exploration, and other scientific fields.

• Among recent PhD recipients in science and engineering from U.S. universities, about 25% are ethnic Chinese.

"We [the U.S.] have been skimming the best and the brightest minds from across the globe, and prospering because of it; we need these new Americans more now as other countries become more technologically capable."

~Dr. William Wulf, President, National Academy of Engineering,
speaking before the U. S. House of Representatives in September, 2005

President Clinton, on June 7, 1999, remarked to Dr. Charles Sie, Vice Chairman of the Committee of 100 that he knew the Chinese Americans had made major contributions to U.S. prowess in science and technology. He has no idea of what they really have done? We would like to provide him with some answers.

Beginning with Dr. H. S. Tsien's work in the 1940s in aeronautics, rocketry and co-founding Jet Propulsion Laboratory (JPL), Chinese-Americans engineers and high technology scientists have had a long history of participating and playing leading roles in the design, development, and deployment of tactical and strategic defense systems, space explorations, as well as many innovative discoveries in high technology industries. Most of them worked as journeymen scientists and engineers whose individual contributions would not be celebrated or acknowledged. Without their contributions, the United States would neither be as prosperous nor as secure as it is today.

The *Chinese Historical Society of Southern California* would like to pay tribute to the successes of this very large group of known and unknown engineers and scientists who made tremendous contributions to our nation.

Why So Many Chinese Americans in the Engineering Profession?

Throughout the history of China, education was the vehicle for young people to advance their careers. The annual government examination determined the choice of appointment to government posts. Scholars were rated as the top profession.

The last years of the declining Qing Dynasty suffered repeated invasions and demands by western colonial nations and Japan. They forced the importation of opium to China and opening of seaports for foreign trade and cessation of its territories. China's outdated military was defeated and humiliated time and again.

Realizing the importance of modernization of their nation, the education system began to look to western curriculum of modern sciences. Mathematics and engineering took on new importance as a chosen profession to help modernize their nation.

In Hong Kong, students were educated under the British system of modern western curriculum; mathematics, biology, chemistry and physics were required core courses to graduate from the British Colony's best high schools.

In Taiwan, university students were taught under outstanding professors who escaped from China's communist regime. They received excellent basic scientific and engineering background and were readied for advanced studies.

Thus the large number of immigrant students from Hong Kong since the middle of 1960s was mostly young men coming to the U. S. to study engineering and science. Taiwan students came later for their advanced degrees. Many of them completed their education and sought employment here because the cold war created the need for engineers and scientists. The opportunities to participate in exciting technological advancement were another inducement that neither Hong Kong nor Taiwan could provide. Going to China was not an option then as many of their families were refugees from the Communist regime.

The First Generation of Engineers Before World War II - The Pioneers

Between 1930 and 1950, some of China's brightest students in science were doing advanced studies and research at the best U. S. universities. Many came under the Boxer Rebellion Scholarship Grants set aside by the United States from its share of China's indemnities for losing the war against the western nations and Japan. Among them, two of the brightest, Dr. H.S. Tsien and Dr. Chung-Yao Chao made significant contributions to America's rocketry and nuclear sciences.

Dr. Tsien was the leading aerodynamic scientist in America. The United States sent him to Germany before the end of World War II to collect Germany's rocket research document from which he compiled the 800-page "Bible" on Jet Propulsion. He devoted twenty years of his life doing breakout research and teaching on pioneering aerodynamic technology for the California Institute of Technology and United States. He received numerous merit citations from the U. S. Armed Forces and was given the rank of Lieutenant Colonel in the U. S. Air Force. He applied for U. S. citizenship in 1949.

Dr. Chao, who earned a Ph.D. degree in physics from Cal Tech, was a top-notch nuclear physicist who was once an official observer at the U. S. atomic bomb test site at the Bikini Atoll. He spent over 20 years doing fundamental nuclear research in the United States.

tific research in America, and their work was prominent to our national defense. However, the McCarthy era Communist witch-hunt made these scientists at risk without cause or proof of wrong doing, placing them in a very tenuous position to continue with their classified research for the United States.

By 1955, under the cloud of fear and suspicions, most of the brightest Chinese scientists working in national defense research had their security clearance revoked and could no longer apply their expertise in their work. They were forced to leave America either by deportation, escape, or just move on. No one from this group was found guilty of transmitting secret U. S. weapons data to Communist China even with the targeted effort of the FBI.

The "Great Dome" at Massachusetts Institute of Technology

Dr. Tsien, Dr. Chao and many other outstanding Chinese scientists came to the U. S. years before the Communist regime came to power in China. They were not known for voicing their political beliefs or having Communist affiliations. They thrived on the intellectual challenges of scientific research in America, and their work was prominent to

These scientists returned to China and helped transform China from a basically agrarian society in the 1950s to a modern military power in less than two decades by the ultimate joining of the nuclear warhead to the inter-continental ballistic missile.

The Second Generation of Engineers
After World War II

During this period, there were no more Boxer Rebellion Scholarships for financial support. Restrictive immigration laws and lack of funds limited the number of students from China, Hong Kong and Taiwan to attend American Universities.

Many Chinese Americans served in the military services during Would War II. After the war, the G.I. bill provided them the financial resources and admittance into universities previously unattainable to them. They made good use of this opportunity to study in their chosen fields: medicine, law, engineering and others.

This generation of Chinese Americans were coined the "Model Minority". Despite legal discrimination and social marginalisation, they achieved a degree of success in America. This was the slow beginning of gradual integration of U. S. citizen of Chinese descent into the fabric of American society as opposed to the perception of being viewed as "perpetual foreigners." The 1965 Immigration Reform removed some of the legislated obstacles under the Chinese Exclusion Act passed by the U. S. Congress in 1882.

This is the generation that TV anchorman Tom Brokaw wrote in his best seller "*The Greatest Generation*." Please read the stories of some of this group's struggles and successes in our first *Portraits of Pride* book.

The Third Generation – New Arrivals
The Cold War and Thereafter

In the 1960s, many post WW II babies in Hong Kong and refugees from China completed their high school education. Hong Kong had only two universities with limited admittance opportunity. To continue their education, these students needed to look outside of Hong Kong. With China being a Communist country and Taiwan under the threat of war at that time, the viable option was to go overseas.

The 1965 Immigration Reform Act was the impetus. Aided by their English language skills learned under the competitive British education system, most students moved directly into universities in the United States with some going to England, Australia, Canada and Taiwan. They were, in fact, some of the best and brightest minds of graduating high school students of that era, and represented the first wave of "brain-drain" from Hong Kong.

They became the largest group of the first three generations of engineers working in the United States. And their contributions are huge, working to keep America strong and powerful during the cold war era against communism.

Many who came to the U. S. chose the engineering profession and remained in the U. S. because of a number of factors:

1. Good basic skills in mathematics and science from their high school curriculum. Engineering was a preferred profession.
2. Good speaking skills in English were not critical in learning engineering skills.
3. Demand for engineers under the threat of the cold war created many job opportunities for engineering graduates.
4. The new skills acquired had little use in their technologically backward home country.
5. Immigration laws provided avenues to acquire permanent resident status and eventually citizenship from student visas with employer sponsorship.
6. Generally well paid and prestigious careers.

A decade or so later, graduates from Taiwan's best universities began to come to the U. S. for advanced degrees. They generally did not have good English language skills, but were armed with excellent engineering and scientific backgrounds. They represented the wave of "brain-drain" from Taiwan.

Since the advent of the Cold War with the USSR, Chinese-American engineers were important components in the work force of science and technology, both in industries and military classified research. By recent accounts, they make up about 8% of the American workforce in science and technology, even though Chinese Americans make up of only 1% of total population. Most of them work in systems research and design. They have contributed much to the advancement of American high technology, and to the development of American national defense and weaponry systems.

All top major defense contractors and aerospace companies in this era employed a disproportional large percentage of Chinese-American engineers compared to other ethnic groups. These companies included: Boeing, McDonald Douglas, TRW, Lockheed Martin, Hughes, JPL, Loral, Aerojet General, Northrop Grumman, General Dynamics, General Electric, United Technologies, Lawrence Livermore Lab, Los Alamos Lab, U.S. Government Department of Defense, Department of Energy, etc.

phenomenon; the "glass ceiling" and the "model minority" Its combined effect denied many Chinese American engineers, with few exceptions, the opportunities for professional, economic and personal advancement.

The "Glass Ceiling" is the unseen, yet unbreachable barrier that keeps minorities from rising to the upper echelons of the management ladder, regardless of their qualification and achievements. It is normally an unwritten and unoffcial policy.

The general perception of the Chinese American engineer as "model minority" is as follows:

1. He is quiet but personable with his peers and superiors.
2. He is devoted to his job, works hard long hours and keeps his nose to the grindstone; he is a team player.
3. He believes his hard work will get him a well-deserved promotion with appropriate remuneration.

However, the factors that attracted Chinese Americans to the engineering sector also contributed to the limitations and restriction in the much-deserved upward movement of their careers. It can best be described by two known

Courtesy of Don Loo

Royce Hall, University of California, Los Angeles

It worked up to a point until he hit the glass ceiling when a "white peer" with equal or less qualification or experience was promoted above him.

In addition, the continued perception of Chinese

American as "perpetual foreigners" put them in an unfair disadvantage in securing "security clearance," without which he would be denied of much-preferred management positions, critical job assignments and deserving promotions.

Statistics from the U. S. Equal Opportunity Commission show 18% of white Americans had managerial or executive-level position in 2000 compared with only 8% of all Asian Americans.

The fallout from the Wen Ho Lee investigation of weapons espionage in the 1990s brought home the realization that if one Chinese American became a suspect, all Chinese Americans working in the classified defense projects were maligned as prime targets by the FBI. Journalists Dan Stober and Ian Hoffman spelled out this "racial profiling" many times in their 375-page book "A Convenient Spy – Wen Ho Lee and the Politics of Nuclear Espionage". McCarthyism seems to be alive and well in the 1990s.

What are the contributions of Chinese-American engineers to the progress of high technology? Below are a few of the notable individual accomplishments:

Dr. Tung-Yen Lin – Known as "Father of Pre-stressed Concrete" was a world-renowned structural engineer. He did not invent pre-stressed concrete, but he developed its practical use to its fullness. Professor Lin initiated new and innovative courses at the University of California Berkeley, including the design of long-span bridges and large arenas.

He visited the USSR and China in technical exchange sessions in "pre-stressed concrete" prior to the commencement of cultural exchanges, using the power of technology to transform world relations. He gave many lectures around the world to engineering and architectural groups.

He conceived many brilliant structures, among them the Moscone Convention Center in San Francisco, the Kuan Du Bridge in Taiwan and the roof of the National racetrack in Caracas, Venezuela. His design is often ahead of the state-of-the-art of its time, one of which was the proposed International Peace Bridge across the Bering Strait, which joined the Soviet Union and Alaska. He presented his 16-page plan to President Reagan in 1986 upon his receiving of the National Medal of Science.

Dr. Chang-Lin Tien - He made history by being named the first Chinese American to head a major U. S. research university, U.C. Berkeley. A mechanical engineer, he helped to solve the heat shield problems on board a space shuttle and contributed to the design of the Saturn booster rocket. The Japanese used his formulas for super insulation in their fast-moving levitation trains.

Dr. Shao-Chi Lin of AVCO Research Lab and Prof. H. K. Cheng of University of Southern California – they established the physics of hypersonic flow, which enables the successful re-entry of the ICBM's and spacecraft into the atmosphere.

Dr. Steve Chen - He is best known as the principal designer of the Cray multiprocessor supercomputer. He was considered as one of our nation's most brilliant supercomputer designers in the 1980s.

Professor Theodore Y. Wu of Cal Tech – Prof. Wu's work in stratified flow in hydraulics has contributed critically to our underwater warfare program.

Ted Wong, President of the Missile System Group, Hughes Aircraft Company – A letter from the U. S. Air Combat Command stated "….. your career has advanced aerial warfare by an order of magnitude. We're the world's best combat air force, because of the contribution of Ted Wong and I can see and measure these contributions eventually in the air and on the flight line of Air Combat Command around the world."

Dr. Yuan-Cheng "Bert" Fung - He is regarded as the "Father of Bioengineering" and the "Founder of Biomechanics." Dr. Fung contributed directly to the development of artificial skin, used to treat burn and other severe tissue injuries such as diabetic foot ulcers.

"Dr. Fung was one of the first visionaries to recognize that quantitative and analytical engineering principles and technologies could be used to develop innovative ways to diagnose, treat, and prevent human diseases," said U.C. San Diego President Richard Atkinson. "Today, medical researchers, physicians and government leaders agree that major medical advances in the 21st century will only be possible through the active involvement of the engineers."

His research is the basis for the entire field of automobile safety design – automobile crash tests today rely on his fundamental studies about tissue response. Since the 1980s, Americans have experience about a 30% reduction in motor vehicle fatalities.

Kerchoff Biological Laboratory at Caltech. Courtesy of the Archives, California Institute of Technology

In year 2000, President Clinton awarded Dr. Fung the prestigious President's National Medal of Science, the nation's highest scientific honor. He received the Fritz J. and Delores H. Russ prize in 2007, one of the top three engineering prizes in the world.

The New High Tech Generation
New Era of Technology

Since the 1980s, a new generation evolved with the children of immigrants and new immigrants. Instead of looking back at the connection to their old world, they adapted to their role as citizens and full participation in the more tolerable American society. With the end of the Cold War toward the end of the twentieth century, the need for engineers in space and weaponry was reduced, but many still choose to do research work for defense industries and in academic institutions. Other native-born as well as immigrants from Taiwan and China are using their engineering and scientific innovations to start new high technology businesses and generate jobs and wealth just at the same pace as their U.S. counterparts.

This generation of Chinese Americans is less restricted by the prejudices of the past and has more freedom and choices in their careers and business partners. They now form the backbone of American high technology alongside of their non-Chinese American associates. Chinese-American entrepreneurs started about 20% of the companies in Silicon Valley alone; accounting for approximately one third of the technological personnel there. They are innovators in the high technology industry of the 21st century.

With their cross-Pacific networks, they have a substantial advantage over their competitors who lack the language skills, cultural background and contacts to build business relationships in Asia.

Add to it the two-way nature of high technology business in the labor market, trade and investment; the most successful business in Silicon Valley is a glowing example of "globalization" of the 21st century.

231

This technological revolution has made our nation's industry stronger, more diversified and richer. At the same time, their innovations have helped to upgrade both the hardware and software of military applications.

Below are a few of the notable individual accomplishments:

Prof. Chih-Ming Ho of UCLA – he is a pioneer in applying MEMS (Micro Electromechanical System) technology to the development of the "smart wing" for our future fighter aircraft design. MEMS can be applied to develop a smart-bat reconnaissance purposes.

Dr. Ho believes that "the biomedical application will dominate the progress of MEMS, The application of using MEMS for medical diagnosis, drug synthesizing, drug testing, and drug screening will all be interesting development." In life science, "we're applying MEMS systems to understanding how cells work and how we can control the development path of cells."

Jerry Yang – Co-founder of the popular search engine and internet portal Yahoo!, acknowledged industry pioneers. Yahoo! is a very successful global media company.

Steve Chen – Co-founder of YouTube.com., a popular free video sharing website. YouTube is an exciting and powerful media platform to organize video information and make it easily accessible and useful. Selected by TIME as the best invention in 2006, "It created a new way for millions of people to entertain, educate, shock, rock and grok one another on a scale we've never seen before." Google acquired the company for $1.65 billion in stock.

Ming Hsieh – A product of the Chinese Cultural Revolution, he somehow found his way to a U. S. university with the help of his uncle. The idea of storing thousands of fingerprints on a computer chip led him to establish Cogent Inc., which makes the fingerprint identification system, with his schoolmate in USC, Archie Yew. The company

has contracts with numerous Police Departments, Welfare Departments, and Federal Agencies for identity verification and welfare fraud prevention. He made a $30 million donation in 2007 to USC because it "definitely helped me reach the American Dream."

Please see *Appendix A: Engineering and Engineers* in the pages following for more Chinese-American engineers/ scientists and brief descriptions of their accomplishments. The author sincerely apologizes for any possible omissions.

Appendix A
Engineering and Engineers

by Edgar Wong and Frank Bupp

Engineering

The history of "engineering" began in the earliest times when man started making clever devices to ease his burden of work; e.g., the wheel, pulley, lever, etc. Since then, engineering has become a well-respected and trusted profession, affecting virtually every aspect of our lives: buildings, transportation, energy, chemistry, electronics, (indeed, computers), space etc. And perhaps most importantly, but in a subtle way, the safety and security in all we do.

And who has not marveled at such engineering feats as the Empire State Building, the Golden Gate Bridge, the Space Shuttle, Hoover Dam, the Panama Canal…and the list goes on and on. On the other hand, we take for granted those "engineering marvels" that are a part of our everyday life: the car, the microwave oven, the refrigerator, the computer, the cell phone…and that list goes on and on, too.

The scope of engineering – the number of engineering professions – has become so large that the National Academy of Sciences (NAS) and the National Academy of Engineering (NAE) categorize engineering according to professions, ranging from Aerospace to Earth Resources. More information on the academies is found at the end of this Appendix.

Chinese-American Engineers

With the technology explosion in the mid to late 20th century, engineers went from being commonly known as a "nerd" to a highly respected stature in our society. For the Chinese-American engineers before this golden era though, they faced the double disadvantage of being a nerd and a male minority; and for women the triple disadvantage of being a nerd, a minority, and a female.

Notwithstanding these disadvantages over the past four decades, Chinese-American engineers have been accorded national recognition--by their election into the academies and by their award of "Engineering Oscars." These engineers come from all geographic locations, all engineering disciplines, and from all work sectors. Therefore, it is with great pride that we present a representative listing of over a hundred engineers, along with a one-sentence resume showing their work affiliation, membership citation, and academy election year.

NAS Section 31: Engineering Science

Ping King Tien of Bell Laboratories, Lucent Technologies, for his research/expertise: device physics, microwave technology, optics, material science, wave phenomena, communication industries (NAS 1978).

Alfred Y. Cho of Bell Laboratories, Lucent Technologies, is the co-inventor and the principal developer of the molecular beam epitaxy (MBE) technique for growing single crystal semiconductors. Through his accomplishments, it is now possible to grow a single crystal as few two atomic layers thick. MBE is making possible singular advances in fundamental solid-state physics as well as in novel devices (NAS 1985).

Yuan-Cheng B. Fung of the University of California, San Diego, for his pioneering contributions to the mechanics of muscle and of biological tissues; for greater understanding of how the functioning of the cardiovascular, respiratory and urinary systems are governed by mechanics and fluid mechanics; for landmark text/monographs; and for nurturing the profession of bioengineering from infancy to maturity (NAS 1992).

Shu Chien of the University of California, San Diego, for contributions to the study of blood rheology, microcirculatory dynamics, and cell membrane behavior. He discovered the cellular pathway via which macromolecules cross-vascular endothelium and enhanced our understanding of how mechanical forces effect gene expression and signal transduction (NAS 2005).

NAE Section 1: Aerospace Engineering

James W. Mar of the Massachusetts Institute of Technology for his leadership in research and education in aerospace structures and composite materials, and for service to his country (NAE 1981).

Hsien K. Cheng of the University of Southern California for original contributions to hypersonic flow theory and to the aerodynamics of three-dimensional wings in subsonic and transonic flows (NAE 1988).

Theodore H. H. Pian of the Massachusetts Institute of Technology for pioneering research and continued development of hybrid finite element methods for the analysis of structures (NAE 1988).

Henry T. Y. Yang of the University of California, Santa Barbara, for contributions in the integration of finite element methods into structural computations, and for effective leadership in education (NAE 1991).

Stephen Wei-Lun Tsai of Stanford University for contributions to the theory and design of composite structures (NAE 1995).

Chih-Ming Ho of the University of California, Los Angeles, for contributions to the understanding and control of turbulent flows (NAE 1997).

Chung K. Law of Princeton University for outstanding contributions to the understanding of the fundamentals

of combustion processes and theory and the application in propulsion systems (NAE 2002).

Sau-Hai Lam of Princeton University for contributions to aerospace engineering in the areas of plasma flows, combustion, turbulence, and adaptive controls (NAE 2006).

Lee-Lueng Fu, senior project scientist, Jet Propulsion Laboratory, Pasadena, Calif. For contributions to the development of satellite altimetry and applications in oceanography, geodesy, and climatology (NAE 2008).

NAE Section 2: Bioengineering

Van C. Mow of Columbia University for major contributions toward orthopedic engineering, particularly understanding the physical behavior of cartilage and the arthritic process (NAE 1991).

Yuan-Cheng B. Fung of the University of California, San Diego, for Contributions to the theory of elasticity and aeroelasticity, and applications to bioengineering (NAE 1979).

Daniel I. C. Wang of the Massachusetts Institute of Technology for basic contributions to the field of biotechnology resulting in improved control of bioprocesses and recovery of biomaterials (NAE 1986).

Savio L-Y. Woo of the University of Pittsburgh for contributions to orthopedic biomechanics and tissue engineering and understanding of sports injury, repair, and remodeling (NAE 1994).

Shu Chien of the University of California, San Diego, for research in blood rheology, microcirculation, cell mechanics, atherogenesis, and tissue engineering (NAE 1997).

Edmund Y. S. Chao of Johns Hopkins University for development of rigorous biomechanical models for functional analysis of human limbs and limb-salvage procedures in cancer patients (NAE 1998).

Albert I. King of Wayne State University for advances in understanding the mechanism, response, and tolerance of the human body to normal and traumatic loading (NAE 2000).

Miranda G.S. Yap of Bioprocessing Technology Institute for her outstanding achievements in education, research, and management in the field of mammalian cell culture (NAE 2006).

Ann L. Lee of Genentech, Inc., for innovation and development of large-scale, cost-effective production of vaccines that have saved lives worldwide (NAE 2007).

NAE Section 3: Chemical Engineering

Morgan C. Sze, an Independent Consultant, for contributions to the technology of petroleum refining and petrochemical process design and manufacture (NAE 1976).

James Wei of Princeton University for advancement of chemical engineering by mathematical analysis of complex reaction of such analysis to commercial processes (NAE 1978).

Edwin A. Gee of the International Paper Company for Contributions to metallurgical engineering, practical water quality standards, and national materials policies (NAE 1979).

Nai Y. Chen of the Mobil Research & Development for discovery of commercially important shape selective catalytic processes for producing premium fuels and lubricants (NAE 1990).

Norman N. Li of NL Chemical Technology for leadership in separation science and the development of liquid membrane separation technology (NAE 1990).

Liang-Shih Fan of the Ohio State University for leadership and contributions to research and education in the field of fluidization and particle technology (NAE 2001).

W. S. Winston Ho of Ohio State University for leadership and contributions to research and education in the field of fluidization and particle technology (NAE 2002).

Chau-Chyun Chen of Aspen Technology for contributions to molecular thermodynamics and process-modeling technology for designing industrial processes with complex chemical systems (NAE 2005).

Ralph T. Yang of the University of Michigan for the development of the theory, methods, and materials for the removal of environmentally hazardous compounds from transportation fuels and other difficult separations (NAE 2005).

Xianghong Cao, chief techology officer, China Petroleum and Chemical Corp. (SINOPEC), Beijing. For innovations and leadership in petroleum refining and petrochemical production technologies, and for leadership in international collaboration (NAE 2009).

NAE Section 4: Civil Engineering

Alfredo H-S. Ang of the University of California, Irvine, for developing practical and effective methods of risk and reliability approaches to engineering safety-and-design structural criteria formulation (NAE 1976).

Alfred A. Yee of the Applied Technology Corporation for pioneering the development of precast prestressed concrete construction for various types of land and sea structures (NAE 1976).

Paul Zia of the North Carolina State University for making significant contributions to the advancement of structural concrete design practice (NAE 1983).

Hsieh W. Shen of the University of California, Berkeley, for the development of flow control and release plans of reservoirs to restore and enhance the ecological environment of rivers (NAE 1993).

Wai-Fah Chen of the University of Hawaii for contributions to the theories of structural stability and plasticity and their application to structural design (NAE 1995).

Man-Chung Tang of T.Y. Lin International for the design and construction of long-span, cable-stayed bridges (NAE 1995).

Yu-Kweng M. Lin of the Florida Atlantic University for research contributions to the theory of stochastic dynamics and its applications to engineering structures (NAE 2000).

Cecil Lue-Hing of Cecil Lue-Hing & Associates for contributions to the practice of water pollution control engineering, particularly biosolids management (NAE 2000).

William W-G. Yeh, distinguished professor and chair, department of civil and environmental engineering, University of California, Los Angeles. For the development of methodologies for optimizing the management of water resources, and for inverse methods of estimating subsurface parameters (NAE 2008).

NAE Section 5: Computer Science & Engineering

Steve S. Chen of Galactic Computing (Shenzhen) for leadership in the development of super-computer architectures and their realization (NAE 1991).

H. T. Kung of Harvard University for introducing the idea of systolic computation, contributions to parallel computing, and applying complexity analysis to very-large-scale integrated (VLSI) computation (NAE 1993).

Victor W. Zue of the Massachusetts Institute of Technology for advances in the understanding of acoustic phonetics and systems for understanding spoken language (NAE 2004).

Simon S. Lam of the University of Texas for contributions to computer network protocols and network security services (NAE 2007).

Teresa H. Meng of Stanford University for pioneering the development of distributed wireless network technology (NAE 2007).

NAE Sections 6 & 7: Electrical & Electronics Engineering

Ping King Tien of Bell Laboratories, Lucent Technologies, for invention and engineering contributions to microwave amplifiers and integrated optical circuits and devices (NAE 1975).

Tingye Li of the AT&T Labs Research for co-discovering the existence of low-loss electromagnetic-wave modes in open structures with application to laser resonators (NAE 1980).

Alfred Y. Cho of Bell Laboratories, Lucent Technologies, for his pioneering development of a molecular beam epitaxy technique leading to unique semiconductor layer device structures (NAE 1985).

Chung L. Tang of Cornell University for contributions in the field of quantum electronics, which include traveling-wave laser resonators and electro-optic modulators (NAE 1986).

Yu-Chi Ho of Harvard University for pioneering and sustained contributions to applied optimization, control, and systems engineering theory and application (NAE 1987).

Eugene Wong of the University of California, Berkeley, for outstanding contributions to relational models of data, design of data base management systems, and the theory and applications of stochastic processes (NAE 1987).

Leroy L. Chang of Hong Kong University of Science & Technology for pioneering achievements in superlattice heterostructures (NAE 1988).

Frank F. Fang of the IBM Thomas J. Watson Research Center for pioneering work in two-dimensional quantum transport in semiconductor inversion layers and for related contributions to device physics (NAE 1989).

Charles K. Kao of the Chinese University of Hong Kong for pioneering and sustained accomplishments towards the theoretical and practical realization of optical fiber communication systems (NAE 1990).

Tak H. Ning of the IBM Thomas J. Watson Research Center for contributions to advanced bipolar device technology and theory and to the understanding of hot-electrol effects in metal-oxide semiconductor devices (NAE 1993).

Simon M. Sze of the National Chiao Tung University for technical and educational contributions to semiconductor devices (NAE 1995).

C. Denis Mee, an Independent Consultant for contributions to magnetic storage and the development of thin-film heads (NAE 1996).

Chenming Hu of the University of California, Berkeley, for contributions to the modeling integration-circuit devices and to the reliability and performance of VLSI systems (NAE 1997).

Nicky C. Lu of Etron Technology for contributions to high-speed dynamic memory chip design and cell array technology, and sustained technical leadership in the VSLI/memory industry (NAE 1999).

Chun-Yen Chang of the National Chiao Tung University for contributions to Taiwanese electronics industry, education, and materials technology (NAE 2000).

Shung-Wu Lee of the University of Illinois for contributions to the understanding of radar scattering from complex objects and stealth aircraft technology (NAE 2000).

Jian Song of the Chinese Academy of Engineering for contributions to aerospace engineering, environmental protection, science and technology administration and fostering international technical cooperation (NAE 2000).

Thomas S. Huang of the University of Illinois for contributions to the theory and practice of image compression, retrieval, and analysis (NAE 2001).

Morris Chang of the Taiwan Semiconductor Manufacturing for contributions to the integrated circuit industry, the creation of the pure-foundry business model, and the enabling of the fabless semiconductor industry (NAE 2002).

Evelyn L. Hu of the University of California, Santa Barbara, for contributions to the processing of semiconductor structures and devices (NAE 2002).

Bede Liu of Princeton University for contributions to the analysis and implementation of digital signal processing algorithms (NAE 2002).

Tso-Ping Ma of Yale University for contributions to the development of CMOS gate dielectric technology (NAE 2003).

Young-Kai Chen of the Electronics Research Bell Laboratories for contributions to the development of high-speed compound semiconductor electronics and optoelectronics for telecommunications (NAE 2004).

Sunlin Chou of the Intel Corporation for pioneering work on silicon processes resulting in 35 years of improvements in accordance with Moore's law (NAE 2004).

Daniel C. Tsui of Princeton University for contributions to the understanding of quantum physics of two-dimensional electron systems at semiconductor interfaces (NAE 2004).

Ching Wan Tang of the University of Rochester for the invention of the organic light-emitting device and organic bilayer solar cell, the bases of modern organic electronics (NAE 2006).

Mau-Chung Frank Chang, professor, electrical engineering department, University of California, Los Angeles. For the development and commercialization of GaAs power amplifiers and integrated circuits (NAE 2008).

Burn-Jeng Lin, senior director, Nanopatterning Technology, Taiwan Semiconductor Manufacturing Co., Ltd., Taiwan, Republic of China. For technical innovations and leadership in the development of lithography for semiconductor manufacturing (NAE 2008).

NAE Section 8: Industrial, Manufacturing & Operational Systems

Kuo K. Wang of Cornell University for outstanding interdisciplinary research, teaching, and writing, contributing to a broad spectrum of processing technologies, benefiting the manufacturing industry worldwide (NAE 1989).

Way Kuo of the University of Tennessee for contributions to reliability design for microelectronics products and systems (NAE 2000).

James M. Tien of the Rensselaer Polytechnic Institute for contributions to reliability design for microelectronics products and systems (NAE 2001).

Chien-Fu Jeff Wu of the Georgia Institute of Technology for conceiving and building modern systems of experimental design based on contemporary methods for parameter estimating to provide quality improvements (NAE 2004).

Josephine Cheng of the IBM Corporation for sustained leadership and contributions to relational database technology and its pervasive applications to a wide range of digital operational systems (NAE 2006).

Hau L. Lee of Stanford University, Stanford, Calif for contributions demonstrating the impact of information-sharing on supply chain design and management (NAE 2010).

NAE Section 9: Material Engineering

Y. Austin Chang of the University of Wisconsin for applications of thermodynamics, phase diagrams, and kinetics to the understanding of modern materials of technological significance (NAE 1996).

Jennie S. Hwang of Asahi America for entrepreneurship in electronic assembly technology (NAE 1998).

Sungho Jin of the University of California, San Diego, for research on new magnetic materials and high-temperature superconductors (NAE 1999).

C. P. Wong of the Georgia Institute of Technology for contributions to materials development leading to plastic packaging of electronics (NAE 2000).

Chain T. Liu of Oak Ridge National Laboratory for advancing ordered metallic compounds from the laboratory to practice (NAE 2004).

James C.M. Li of the University of Rochester for contributions to micromechanics and mesoscopic mechanisms in materials and to the commercialization of amorphous metals (NAE 2006).

Kuangdi Xu of the Chinese Academy of Engineering for contributions to the efficient manufacturing of quality steels with minimal environmental impact (NAE 2006).

Stephen Z.D. Cheng, dean, College of Polymer Science and Polymer Engineering, University of Akron, Akron, Ohio. For the development of materials for liquid crystal displays and the elucidation of structure-property relationships in polymeric materials (NAE 2008).

Zhigang Suo, Allen E. and Marilyn M. Puckett Professor of Mechanics and Materials, School of Engineering and Applied Sciences, Harvard University, Cambridge, Mass. For fundamental and applied contributions to the thermomechanical performance of electronic material systems, actuator materials, and composites (NAE 2008).

Yet-Ming Chiang, Kyocera Professor, department of materials science and engineering, Massachusetts Institute of Technology, Cambridge. For contributions to understanding of new energy storage materials and their commercialization (NAE 2009).

NAE Section 10: Mechanical Engineering

Frederick F. Ling of the University of Texas for contributions to the understanding of friction and wear, metal cutting and forming, and the dysfunction in human joints (NAE 1977).

Bei Tse Chao of the University of Illinois for pioneering contributions to heat transfer research and leadership in engineering education (NAE 1981).

Shih-Ying Lee of Massachusetts Institute of Technology for original research on control valve stability, for innovative

dynamic measurement instrumentation, and for successful entrepreneurial commercialization of his inventions (NAE 1985).

Yih-Hsing Pao of Zhejiang University for contributions of basic significance and for stimulating innovative applications in the field of wave propagation in elastic solids (NAE 1985).

Shan-Fu Shen of Cornell University for fundamental contributions to aerodynamics and non-Newtonian fluid mechanics (NAE 1985).

Herbert S. Cheng of Northwestern University for pioneering contributions to the tribology of gas, elastohydrodynamic, plastohydrodynamic, and mixed lubrication, and for leadership in developing collaborative university and industrial research in tribology (NAE 1987).

Richard C. Chu of IBM Corporation for path-finding contributions and creative technical leadership in the development of cooling technology and thermal systems for electronic equipment (NAE 1987).

Yao Tzu Li of Massachusetts Institute of Technology for contributions to innovation in instrumentation, control, and to engineering education (NAE 1987).

Benjamin Y.H. Liu of the MSP Corporation for pioneering research on the design of novel aerosol instrumentation, and for contributions to the understanding of fine particle behavior and to the prediction of availability of solar radiation (NAE 1987).

Chieh-Su Hsu for the University of California, Berkeley, for the development of innovative techniques, especially cell-to-cell mapping, and for the analysis of the dynamics of nonlinear systems (NAE 1988).

Tung H. Lin of the University of California, Los Angeles, for pioneering development of micromechanical theories of plasticity, creep, and fatigue crack initiation and major contributions to inelastic structure analysis (NAE 1990).

Zhemin Zheng of the Institute of Mechanics, Chinese Academy of Science, for contributions to the theory and application of explosion mechanics (NAE 1993).

David H. Pai of the Foster Wheeler Development Corporation for contributions to the development of design standards for high-temperature nuclear components (NAE 1994).

Francis C. Moon of Cornell University for experimental research in chaotic and nonlinear dynamics and development of superconducting levitation devices (NAE 1996).

Yih-Ho Michael Pao of the ecoPower LLC for research, development, and commercialization of water-jet technology for machining, trenchless boring, and surface preparation (NAE 2000).

Choon Fong Shih of the National University of Singapore for the development of innovative computational methods in nonlinear fracture mechanics and for international leadership in engineering (NAE 2004).

Gang Chen of the Massachusetts Institute of Technology, Cambridge for contributions to heat transfer at the nanoscale and to thermoelectric energy conversion technology (NAE 2010).

Xiang Zhang of the University of California, Berkeley for the pioneering contributions in metamaterials and creation of the first optical superlens with resolutions beyond the fundamental diffraction limit (NAE 2010).

NAE Section 11: Earth Resources Engineering

A. Tobey Yu of the ORBA Corporation for pioneering contributions to materials handling, transportation, and processing (NAE 1989).

Dianzuo Wang of the Chinese Academy of Engineering for pioneering contributions in flotation theory for mineral processing (NAE 1990).

W. John Lee of Texas A&M University for contributions to the theory and practice of formation evaluation of low-permeability gas reservoirs (NAE 1993).

Rong-Yu Wan an Independent Consultant for accomplishments in metallurgical research and industrial practice, and for teaching, supervising, and inspiring students, researchers, and industrial colleagues (NAE 2000).

NAE Section 12: Special Fields & Interdisciplinary Engineering

Theodore Y. Wu of California Institute of Technology for milestone contributions to hydrodynamics, and its application to the motions of vehicles and to the propulsion of animals through fluids (NAE 1982).

Chiang C. Mei of Massachusetts Institute of Technology for application of the theories of wave hydrodynamics and elasticity to problems in coastal and ocean engineering (NAE 1986).

Jaw-Kai Wang of the University of Hawaii for research, development, and design of commercial aquaculture systems used in the United States and China and for leadership in interdisciplinary biology and engineering projects addressing improved production systems (NAE 1995).

Jin Wu of Cheng Kung University for advancing knowledge of the air-sea interface through experiments with applications to remote sensing and the environment (NAE 1995).

Kuo-Nan Liou of the University of California, Los Angeles, for contributions in the theories of radiation transfer and light scattering, with applications to remote sensing technology and climate modeling (NAE 1999).

Norden E. Huang of NASA Goddard Space Flight Center for contributions to the analysis of nonlinear stochastic signals and related mathematical applications in engineering, biology, and other sciences (NAE 2000).

The United States National Academies

The National Academies comprises four organizations: the United States National Academy of Sciences (NAS in 1863), the United States National Academy of Engineering (NAE in 1964), the Institute of Medicine (IOM in 1970), and the United States National Research Council (NRC in 1916).

"Academies" members are "advisers to the nation on science, engineering, and medicine," and perform an unparalleled public service by enlisting the nation's foremost experts to address the scientific and technical aspects of some of society's most pressing problems. Each year, more than 6,000 of these experts serve on hundreds of study committees to answer specific sets of questions. All serve without pay.

Recent studies--and their reports--cover such topics as: the obesity epidemic, the use of forensics in the courtroom, invasive plants, underage drinking, the Hubble Telescope, vaccine safety, the hydrogen economy, transportation safety, climate change, and homeland security.

The National Academies Press (NAP) is the publisher for the National Academies and makes its publications available for online reading since 1994. Hundreds of these books can be downloaded for free by the chapter or the entire book, while others are available for purchase.

For more information on the National Academies:
National Academy of Science (NAS):
 http://www.nasonline.org/site/PageServer
National Academy of Engineering (NAE):
 http://www.nae.edu/nae/naehome.nsf
Institute of Medicine (IOM):
 http://www.iom.edu/
National Research Council (NRC):
 http://www.nationalacademies.org/nrc/
National Academies Press (NAP):
 http://www.nap.edu/about.html

Education:
Inconspicuous Prominence in Academia

By Yong Chen

For much of the 20th Century, Chinese Americans were viewed as laundry-men and restaurant workers. Today, that image is no longer a valid reflection of their socioeconomic status. Vast increases of Chinese-American scholars in the halls of academia remind us of their changing role of being mentors to the youth of today and tomorrow.

From Hand Laundries,
Chop Suey Restaurants to Ivy Towers

Beginning in the 1960s, immigrant Chinese achieved noticeable achievements as students. Now, there are at least 30,000 Chinese Americans in academia as full time faculty, mostly in the nation's elite institutions. Their growing presence on university campuses is part of the gradual transformation that has taken place in the demographic characteristics and socioeconomic status of the Chinese-American community. Such a transformation mirrors their remarkable contributions to American education, scientific research and high technology advancements.

Excellence in university education is a major factor in the rise of Chinese Americans in their journey to the Ivy Tower; they have come a long way in a relatively short time. It is not simply a journey of a few talented individuals but one that reflects generally the heritage of the Chinese-American community's emphasis on the value of education.

Since 1970, institutions of higher education became an important conduit for immigration, through which tens of thousands of Chinese students arrived annually, many pursuing graduate degrees. Higher education plays an important social role in Chinese America, as becoming an educator and researcher is regarded as a direct path to respectability and social mobility.

Education: the agent of change for
Advancement Demographics

The early Chinese immigrants encountered enormous racial discrimination and physical violence. By the end of the 1880s, as Jean Pfaelzer notes, "close to two hundred towns . . . had driven out their Chinese residents."[1] Partly as a result of such attacks, the Chinese population tended to gravitate from rural areas to larger cities. The urban concentration was accompanied by an occupational concentration in the service industry. By 1940, the laundry business and restaurant work had become the two principal occupations of the Chinese in or near the remaining 28 Chinatowns in the United States. World War II opened some employment opportunities for Chinese Americans, including women, as Judy Yung has shown.[2] But the overall occupational pattern of Chinese Americans did not change until the 1970s, and successes in higher education were central to the change.

It is important to note that many of new immigrants after 1965 came with what sociologists called "middle-class resources," with a high school diploma or better. American universities became an important channel not only for Chinese to immigrate to America but also an effective path to achieve upward social mobility and into more professional fields than previously possible.

How University Education Affected the Socioeconomic
Status of Chinese Americans

Here is a brief look at the growing socioeconomic significance of higher education in the American economy and society:

- Higher education became an equalizer for some socially disadvantaged groups. In the post-1965 years, more and more Chinese Americans and other minority groups sought to achieve social mobility through higher education.
- In 2005 53% of Chinese Americans had at least a 4-year college degree, which is much higher than the figure for Anglos (39%)[3]. Meanwhile, other Asian American and Pacific Islander groups seriously lagged behind. For example, only 25% of Vietnamese, 17% of native Hawaiian and other Pacific Islanders, and 13% of Cambodian, Laotian, and Hmong have at least a 4-year college degree.
- Higher education leads to a better income. In 2005 the average income for Chinese Americans with at least a college degree was $72,755 and $30,515 for those without. The comparable numbers for Anglos are $74,760 and $39,554, respectively.[4] Facing persistent inequality, many Chinese Americans see excel-

lence in education as the preferred means for advancement, and their hard work earned them the dubious honor of the "model minority."[5]

Quantifying Chinese Americans in Institutions of Higher Learning

The elevation of Chinese-American professors in higher education as a social group is a relatively new phenomenon. Therefore, it is extremely challenging to research systematic data, including statistical information, about them. Government agencies, colleges and universities tend to lump Chinese Americans, both students and faculty, together with other Asian groups under the category "Asian American." Such an inclusive classification or "racial lumping" has been widely practiced and unfairly targeted. (Asian Americans are generally excluded from the so-called "under-represented minority" that receive special quotas for admissions and other benefits). More specific identification of ethnicity is needed and desired.[6] Adding to the difficulty of data collecting is the fact that Chinese-American scholars are scattered in different physical locations and disciplines, making them a socially *diffuse* group. For many, their disciplinary and institutional affiliation is more important than their ethnic affiliation in their professional life. Academic work tends to be quite solitary, further reducing the social *cohesiveness* among them.

This essay is not focused on individual achievements, which are far too many to enumerate. Rather, it represents an attempt to quantify the extent of the growing visibility of Chinese American faculty in American colleges and universities.

In all, this study covers 50 colleges and universities, which include public and private institutions, located in different geographical regions of the country and ranging from what the Carnegie Classification calls "very high research activity" universities to community colleges.[7] Information was also obtained from oral interviews of individual Chinese Americans.

While the focus was on full-time university and college professors, my data and analysis do occasionally include part-time instructors. I have consulted and used a wide range of data, including statistics compiled by different organizations, such as professional societies, higher-education institutions, and government agencies. Because of the practice of "racial lumping" that was noted earlier, much of the information was obtained by visiting the websites of individuals and their affiliated departments.

Nonetheless, the statistical profile of Chinese American faculty in higher education that is being presented here has limitations. Certain kinds of institutions are not included in

Sather Gate, University of California, Berkeley

Courtesy of UC Berkeley

245

the sample, such as stand-alone professional schools, faith-related institutions, art and music institutions, and tribal colleges. Moreover, miscounting undoubtedly could take place. For example, a Chinese person, who has acquired the name of "Jane Smith" and does not have a picture or detailed biography on the website, is likely to be missed in the counting. Besides, I did not make a conscious effort to count those whose parents are of mixed ethnic backgrounds. For all these reasons, the actual number of Chinese American scholars in higher education could be higher than my estimate. It is almost impossible to provide a thorough head-count of all Chinese-American scholars in all of America's more than 4,000 institutions of higher learning. Based on a substantial sample, my estimate is designed to provide a critical reference point through which to offer a glimpse of their relative numerical importance in their respective institutions and disciplines.

Chinese Americans and
Other Asian Americans in Higher Education

The discussion of Chinese Americans in this section is juxtaposed with an analysis of the collective profile of Asian Americans. It is necessary to do so because Chinese Americans are a substantial part of the Asian presence on the university and college faculty. Systematic data are far more readily available on Asian Americans than on Chinese Americans as "racial lumping" comes into play.

The strong education tradition and background of Chinese Americans and others such as Asian Indians have allowed them to take advantage of the opportunities provided by U.S. university education. Asian Americans have become the second largest racial group among the instructional faculty and staff in American higher education – an impressive accomplishment for a numerically small racial minority.

Asian Americans account for a disproportionally high percentage among the faculty in colleges and universities. In 2005 the 14.4 million Asian Americans represented 4.7% of the national population.[8] But they have a higher percent-

age in faculty members. Estimates on the precise number of Asian American faculty members vary by the method of counting:

- A report issued by the American Council on Education in 2004, of all the 590,553 full-time instructional faculty in American institutions of general higher education in 2001, 499,557 or nearly 85% were white; Asians and Pacific Islanders were the next largest group, with 38,026 or more than 6%.[9] *The Chronicle of Higher Education* also has a similar estimate.
- However, estimates from others sources such as the National Center for Education Statistics and *Education Statistics Quarterly*,[10] are much higher, consistently putting the percentage at 9%.

The count by the American Council of Education is based only on full-time faculty. The *Chronicle of Higher Education* excludes groups like non-resident aliens, who possess enormous numerical importance among the predominantly immigrant populations such as Chinese Americans and Asian Indians. The data from the authoritative National Science Foundation puts the percentage of Asian Americans and Pacific Islanders at 9.1% among full-time instructional faculty and staff in degree-granting institutions in 2003. The numbers for African Americans and Hispanics are 5.6% and 3.5%, respectively.[11]

The "Marginal Men"?

To be an ethnic Chinese faculty at an American university entailed many challenges. A 1994 study of China-born professors calls them "marginal men,"[12] a notion that Paul Siu had used to characterize Chinese laundrymen in Chicago and their social isolation.[13] "Marginal men" reminds us of the ordeals that many have gone through working as faculty in American universities. It is also a reminder that when we talk about the achievements of Chinese American academics, we often do not sufficiently recognize the extra effort that they had to make. A Chinese American member of the National Academy of Engineering noted in the 1990s that in order to get to the same positions of their Anglo colleagues, the Chinese had to be twice as outstanding and excellent.[14]

Meanwhile, more and more Chinese Americans continue to aspire to professorial positions. In the early twenty-first century, there are at least 30,000 Chinese American professors on American university campuses, representing 1% of the total Chinese American population and more than 4% of all university professors.[15] In areas such as mathematics, sciences, and engineering, their vigorous and fruitful research is of critical importance for the advancement of modern science and technology. Of eight Chinese-American Nobel Prize winners, six are in physics and two in chemistry. In engineering, one of the highest honors is election to the National Academy of Engineering. Eighty-six or more than 4.4% of the 2003 active U.S. members are Chinese.[16] Most of them are university professors. In mathematics, the Chinese also have assembled a critical mass. In 2003 and 2004 the American Mathematical Society had 54,437 members, and 2,886 or 5.3% of them were Chinese

Americans. Most of them have direct or indirect affiliations with higher education.

Concentration in Elite Research Institutions: Prestige or Constraint?

The presence of Asian American professors represents not merely a success story to be celebrated but a complex historical and sociological phenomenon that calls for further analysis of some of its characteristics.

+ One characteristic is that most Asian Americans are concentrated at the nation's prestigious research institutions, as Alison Schneider has pointed out in a recent report in *The Chronicle of Higher Education*.[17] Schneider regards this as a "success" on the part of Asian Americans.

+ Schneider also notes that a relatively high proportion of them (around 43%) work in the physical/biomedical sciences, mathematics, engineering, and other technical fields. This is much higher than the percentage for Anglos (20%) and African American (9%) professors

Courtesy of Don Loo

Powell Library, University of California, Los Angeles

working in those areas. She appears to be uncertain about how to explain this concentration of Asian Americans in such areas, commenting vaguely that this may be connected to "their areas of expertise."

Asian Americans' "areas of expertise" describe where they landed in their academic career but do not explain how they got there as a result of critical choices they made. For many, the choice is between a comfortable career with an undergraduate degree, or to invest more years to pursue advanced "expertise". Their concentration in elite research institutions and in science/technical areas reveals the constraints they face in making their choices. Such constraints reflect lingering racial prejudice in society. Equally important, these constraints have to do with Asian Americans' own limitations in a number of areas, including social and language skills.

Career Constraint: Academics vs. Corporate

Many Chinese Americans choose an academic career in part because they feel, consciously or subconsciously, the racial prejudice that still prevails in corporate America.

- In the corporate world, for example, there has existed a largely invisible "glass ceiling," which severely limits the career advancement of Chinese-American professionals. My formal and informal interviews with more than 60 Chinese Americans up to November 2007 confirmed a widely shared concern over the glass ceiling facing them.
- Academic work is highly autonomous, and the meritocracy that prevails in institutions of higher education rewards people on the basis of their individual accomplishments, giving talented Chinese Americans and others a sense of control over their career. This helps to explain the highly concentrated presence of Chinese-American professors in elite research institutions, where individual merits are especially emphasized.

Reasons for Concentration in "Hard Science" Fields

Asian American academics also tend to concentrate in certain fields. According to a study published in Education Statistics Quarterly, a significant portion of them are found in such areas as engineering (21%), natural sciences (15.7%), business (13.9%), and health sciences (11.7%), while fine arts, humanities and social sciences were among the least attractive areas.[18]

- This is consistent with the general employment trend of Asian Americans, who have a tendency to go to sciences and engineering, which offer more job opportunities and a better pay scale than other fields.[19]
- Compensation appears to be one of the major factors. In "hard science" fields, such as engineering, medical and physical sciences, mathematics and business, faculty salaries are generally higher than in the humanities and social sciences.
- Cultural factors appear to be more important. Most of my interviewees, especially those born outside the United States, consider academic jobs in the humanities and social sciences to be extremely difficult. Part of this concerns verbal language skills. For most foreign-born individuals, working in a science or technical lab is much preferred to confronting the daunting reality of having to publish lengthy articles and books in English. Faculty generally has greater teaching responsibilities in the humanities than they do in the technical fields.
- Science and engineering professors, especially those in elite research institutions, can devote more time and effort to research than teaching. This allows foreign-born professors to maximize their strengths while minimizing their disadvantages. Statistical data from the National Science Foundation for 1999 shows that of those with a doctorate in sciences and engineering, Asian Americans demonstrated a preference to work for 4-year colleges and universities over "other educational institutions" by a ratio of 20:1.[20]

Prominence of Chinese Americans in the "Hard Science" Fields

High technology has been the reason the United States dominated the world in space, military and high tech industries since before the second half of the 20th century. The presence of Chinese Americans in mathematics, sciences, and engineering was created by a growing need in the United States to support the academic and high technology markets. That need stemmed from a combination of two factors: the increasing demand for world-class intellectual talent created by global competition on the one hand, and the decreasing number of Caucasian students on the other. Graduate enrollment of white students declined for 6 consecutive years from 1993 to 1999.[21] In their place, Chinese and Asian-American students became highly competitive, enabling them to secure higher numbers of graduate admissions. In other words, in sciences and engineering as well as areas like medicine and business, Asian-American faculty are performing an important service to U.S. high technology and higher education by doing the kind of work that fewer native born Anglos choose to do.

The outstanding career of Hsue-shen (H.S.) Tsien, a prominent figure in the space and missiles programs in both the United States and China, and the 2007 Person of the Year by the journal *Aviation Week & Space Technology*, is covered in another chapter of this volume.[22]

(Please refer to Appendix A following the Group Portrait on Scientists and Engineers for an impressive and long list

Courtesy of Yale University

Harkness Tower, Yale University

of Chinese-American scientists and engineers with brief descriptions of their major accomplishments. They were elected to various prestigious professional society memberships.)

Beyond the Hard Sciences

Besides earning an inconspicuous prominence in the "hard science" fields, a smaller number of Chinese-American scholars and educators have distinguished themselves across a spectrum of disciplines in the arts and social sciences.

The Chinese presence in American universities began with Yung Wing, who graduated from Yale in 1854, as the first Chinese to graduate from an American college. In 1870, a man named C.H. Wing was reportedly teaching at Cornell University as its first Chinese teacher.[23] A few years later, in 1879, Ko Kun-hua arrived at Harvard University with his wife and six children. He was hired by Harvard, as its first Chinese teacher, to teach the Chinese language. His presence started one of the most important and largest China studies programs in the world. But such nineteenth-century cases are extremely rare.

Yuen Ren Chao settled in the United States in the pre-war years and worked outside the usual technical areas as a renowned linguist and musician. He would eventually master 33 different dialects and several languages. He taught at Yale, Harvard, Michigan, and UC Berkeley. He was an intellectual giant in his areas of study and was elected President of the Linguistics Society of America (1945) and the American Oriental Society.

Rose Hum Lee was born in Butte, Montana, in 1904 and trained in the Chicago School of Sociology in the 1940s. In 1956 she became the chairperson of the sociology department at Roosevelt University – the first Chinese to chair a sociology department in America. Keenly aware of the obstacles that she faced, she told the *Chicago Sun-Times*: "I was a woman, I was in a man's field, and I was Chinese. That meant three strikes against me." She noted, "The fact that I was able to overcome these barriers is a tremendous encouragement to others, particularly women who belong to minority groups."[24] Lee is known for her 1960 book entitled *The Chinese in the United States of America*.

Maxine Hong Kingston became a professor of creative writing at UC Berkeley.[i] Her first book, *The Woman Warrior*, won the prestigious National Book Critics Circle Award for best non-fiction published in 1976.[ii] For *China Men*, she was awarded the National Book Award in 1980. She won the National Humanities Medal, presented by President Bill Clinton, in 1997. Her novel, *Veterans of War, Veterans of Peace*, published in 2006, was awarded the Northern California Book Award, Special Award in Publishing.

Dr. Albert H. Yee, a fourth-generation Chinese American, is an educational psychologist, and the author and editor of numerous books and articles in academic and professional journals.[iii] Dr. Yee's teaching of advanced research methods of educational psychology at the University of Wisconsin in 1970 led him to continue his transnational career with a Senior Fulbright Lectureship at Tokyo University and several other Asian universities. He was considered China's first "foreign expert" in psychology. His book, *East Asian Higher Education*, was published in 1995, and *Yee-Hah!: Remembrance and Longing*, in 2005.

Prof. Beverly Shue—a Southern California Chinese American woman—achieved success by surmounting obstacles of race and gender institutionalized in the world of academia. She distinguished herself by drafting language reflective of revised curriculum standards at Los Angeles Harbor College, thus bringing curricula into compliance with the mandates of California Assembly Bill 1725 (1988). Over her 43-year career, her laudable teaching skills were demonstrated through her microbiology students' consistently outstanding scores on statewide qualifying exams. Professor Shue's peers elected her both statewide chairperson of faculty governance and curriculum, and vice president of the Los Angeles Community College District Academic Senate.

Two pioneers in Chinese American Studies, *Philip P. Choy* and *Him Mark Lai*, cannot be overlooked in the scope of academia.[iv] Both attended the University of California at Berkeley where Lai received an Engineering degree and Choy received his degree in Architecture. Both pursued careers in their respective fields, but were moved to action by the Civil Rights Movement of 1967 when a sense of activism and ethnic awareness in Chinese Americans was awakened. In 1969, Choy and Lai established and co-taught the nation's first Chinese American Studies course at San Francisco State University. The two highly respected historians have devoted many decades to studying and writing Chinese American history, including transnational history, historic preservation, and ethnic studies.

Cracking the "Glass Ceiling"?

Because of their increasing presence, higher education has become an increasingly important stage, where Chinese Americans demonstrate and nurture their scholarly and leadership talent. A small but growing number of them have been able to penetrate the glass ceiling and hold notable administrative roles. The Taiwan-born former chancellor of UC Berkeley (1990-1997), *Chang-Lin Tien*, an engineer by training and now a household name among Chinese Americans and people in China, is a pioneer in this area. So is the current chancellor of UC Santa Barbara, *Henry T. Yang* (1994-present), who was born in Taiwan where he studied in college with an engineering major. Besides high-profile individuals like Tien and Yang, other scholars who have ventured into the area of administration in higher education have remained less visible.

Frank H. Wu, JD, was appointed dean of the Wayne State University Law School in his hometown of Detroit, in 2004.[v] Prior to that appointment, from 1995 to 2004, he served on the Howard University Law School faculty; as an adjunct professor at Columbia University; as a visiting professor at University of Michigan; and as a teaching fellow at Stanford University.

Dr. James Wei, Emeritus Dean of Engineering and Applied Science at Princeton University, found success in both business and academia. He shares his formula to achieve success in an article *"Making it in America"* elsewhere in this book.

It is their scholarly achievements that led these educators to administrative leadership positions, as we can see from *Frederic Yui-Ming Wan's* career story. His experience helps us appreciate the transnational trajectory in the scholarly and personal life of many Chinese-American faculty. He was born in Shanghai, and migrated and settled in Vietnam before coming to California in the late 1940s. Trained in applied mathematics at MIT in the 1960s, he went on to achieve notable career accomplishments, including election to the membership of American Association for the Advancement of Science (1994) and the Russian Academy of Natural Sciences (1999). He was one of the first Asians to hold an administrative position at the National Science Foundation, as the director of its Division of Mathematical Sciences (1993-1994). From 1995 to 2000 he served as the Vice Chancellor for Research and Dean of Graduate Studies at UC Irvine.

Foreign born vs. American born

Reflecting an important characteristic of the general Chinese-American population, a large number of Chinese-American university faculty members were born outside the United States. The data set I obtained from the restricted data sets of the National Academy of Engineering helps shed some light on this. Of the 86 members identified as Chinese, only 3 were born in the United States. The aca-demic excellence of Chinese-Americans reveals the role of university education in facilitating Chinese immigration to the United States in the post-war, especially post-1965, era. For hundreds of thousands of aspiring Chinese immigrants without access to the extremely limited immigrant quotas, studying at an American university was the only viable way to pursue their dream. After obtaining their degree, many have stayed and settled in the United States, which explains the high educational level of the Chinese American population. American universities attracted some of China's best-educated and most talented people. College enrollment of foreign-born Chinese students (including those from mainland China, Taiwan and Hong Kong) grew from 23,000 in 1976 to 104,539 in 2006.[25]

America's ability to attract the best and most talented from China and other parts of the world is a most important reason why it has maintained a leadership position in science and technology. According to the National Science Foundation's Scientists and Engineers Statistical Data System, among those who work in post-secondary institutions with at least a science or engineering degree, 54,000 were born in China, Hong Kong or Macao.[26] The number does not include those born in Taiwan or Chinese settlements elsewhere.

Chinese-American Scholars
Transnational and International

In part because of the preponderance of the foreign-born among them, Chinese American professors have played an active role in facilitating international interaction, especially between the United States and China. The international arena allows them to make contributions beyond academic research, and it gives them a level of visibility and influence they cannot dream of in the U.S. setting alone. They travel across the Pacific Ocean frequently, participating in various educational and research projects. Those in sciences, mathematics, and engineering have had a particularly effective and far-reaching impact. A case in point is the China-U.S. Physics Examination and Application, envisioned by the Nobel laureate *Tsung-Dao Lee* at the beginning of China's reform era. This program brought nearly a thousand talented Chinese physics students to American campuses. Many have subsequently become academic leaders in a diverse range of research areas, and fields such as physics, biology, and finance. Mathematics is one of the areas of accelerating international collaboration between Chinese-American professors and their Chinese colleagues. Many of them have simultaneous, transnational joint appointments in Chinese and American institutions. One important figure is *Shing-Tung Yau*, born in 1949 in Shantou, Guangdong Province, a professor at Harvard since 1987. He is one of the world's most accomplished mathematicians, winning numerous prestigious awards, including the Fields Medal in 1982 (often dubbed as the Nobel Prize in mathematics), a MacArthur Fellowship in 1984, the Crafoord Prize in 1994, and the (U.S.) National Medal of Science in 1997. He founded the Morningside Center of Mathematics in Beijing and the Center of Mathematical Science in Zhejiang University and organized several international conferences, bringing together mathematicians from China, the U.S. and other parts of the world. Growing international activities have broadened and extended the professional and personal stage for Chinese American professors like Yau.

Some have chosen to return to Asia permanently. Among those who have returned, a few have assumed prominent leadership roles. In 1994, after 32 years of academic work in the U.S., *Yuan Tseh Lee*, for instance, left UC Berkeley to return to Taiwan as President of Academia Sinica. He was also named Honorary Professor by China's Chinese University of Science and Technology in Hofei in 1986. Another Chinese American professor who has returned to Asia is *Paul Chu* (also known as *Ching-Wu Chu*), a native of Taiwan, a member of the U.S. National Academy of Sciences, and a world-renowned expert on superconductivity. He has received the U.S. National Medal of Science and the International Prize for New Materials, was selected the Best Researcher in the U.S. by *U.S. News and World Report*

in 1990, and assumed the presidency of the Hong Kong University of Science and Technology in 2001.

References

1. Jean Pfaelzer, *Driven Out: The Forgotten War Against Chinese Americans* (New York, 2007), p. 253.
2. Judy Yung, *Unbound Feet: A Social History of Chinese Women in San Francisco* (Berkeley: University of California Press, 1995). Also see Jade Snow Wong, *Fifth Chinese Daughter* (New York, 1950).
3. United States Government Accountability Office, *Higher Education: Information Sharing Could Help Institutions Identify and Address Challenges Some Asian Americans and Pacific Islander Students Face* (Washington, D.C., 2007), pp. 15-18.
4. Ibid., pp 16 and 18
5. The following is a list of selected articles in mainstream new media that depicts Asians, including Chinese, as America's model minority:
William Petersen, "Success Story, Japanese American Style," *New York Times Magazine*. January 9, 1966.
"Success Story of One Minority Group in the United States," *U.S. News and World Report*. Dec. 26, 1966.
"Asian Americans: A Model Minority," *Newsweek*. December 6, 1982.
"Confucian Work Ethic," *Time*. March 28, 1983.
Suzana McBee, "Asian Americans, Are they Making the Grade?" *U.S. News and World Report*, April 1984.
David Bell, "The Triumph of Asian Americans," *New Republic*. July 1985.
Jay Mathew, "Asian-American Students Creating New Mainstream," *Washington Post*. November 14, 1985.
Lynn Smith and Bill Billiter, "Asian Americans: Emphasis on Education Is Paying Off," *Los Angeles Times*. December 19, 1985.
Fox Butterfield, "Why Asians Are Going to the Head of the Class," *New York Times Magazine*, August 3, 1986.
Robert Oxnam, "Why Asians Succeed Here," *New York*

Times Magazine. November 30, 1986.

Malcolm W. Browne, "A look at Success of Young Asians," *New York Times.* March 25, 1986.

Anthony Ramirez, "America's Super Minority," *Fortune Magazine.* November 24, 1986.

Stephen G. Graubard, "Why Do Asian Pupils Win These Prizes?" *New York Times.* January 29, 1988.

6. Anna Gorman, "More Specific Listing of Ethnicity at UC Urged: Pacific Islanders and Asians at UCLA Say Some Student Groups' Numbers Are Not Recognized," *Los Angeles Times*, July 22, 2007.

7. First developed in 1970, the Carnegie Classification is highly regarded and widely used. For more information on it, see the 2005 article by Alexander C. McCormick and Chun-Mei Zhao, "Rethinking and Reframing the Carnegie Classification" (http://www.carnegiefoundation.org/dynamic/publications/elibrary_pdf_634.pdf) and the Carnegie Foundation website: http://www.carnegiefoundation.org/classifications/index.asp.

8. Source: Census Bureau, "Annual Estimates of the Population for the United States, Regions, States, and Puerto Rico: April 1, 2000 to July 1, 2007"; and "U.S. Census Bureau News: Asian/Pacific American Heritage Month," issued on March 1, 2007.

9. American Council on Education, "Full-time Instructional Faculty, by Gender, Institution, Academic Rank, and Race: 2001," 2004.

10. National Center for Education Statistics, "Full-time and Part-time Instructional Faculty and Staff in Degree-granting Institutions, by Field and Faculty Characteristics: Fall 1992, Fall 1998, and Fall 2003," http://nces.ed.gov/programs/digest/d05/tables/dt05_232.asp; Emily Forrest Cataldi, Mansour Fahimi, and Ellen M. Bradburn, "2004 National Study of Postsecondary Faculty: Report on Faculty and Instructional Staff in Fall 2003," *Education Statistics Quarterly*, Vol 7, Issues 1 & 2.

11. http://nces.ed.gov/programs/digest/d05/tables/dt05_232.asp

12. Paper presented at an annual meeting of the Association for the Study of Higher Education in 1994, by Alan T. Seagren and Han Hua Wang.

13. Paul Siu, *Chinese Laundrymen: A Study of Social Isolation* (New York, 1987). Completed in 1953 based on research performed a decade earlier.

14. Zong Ying, "How to Maintain 'Cultural Roots' Overseas"? Renmin Ribao, February 20, 2008.

15. This is a conservative estimate. It is based on data on full-time regular faculty from seven disciplines (mathematics, physics, chemistry, biological sciences, political science, history, and sociology) in 23 4-year public and private universities across the nation. My choice to concentrate on 4-year institutions is based on the predominant preference of Chinese and other Asian Americans for such institutions. The sample does not include California institutions, which, especially the University of California, tend to have large numbers of Chinese faculty. The total number of Asian Americans from the sample account for 6.2%, which is consistent with national figures compiled by various agencies. And Chinese represent 65% of the Asian American faculty. This is quite consistent with data from elsewhere. At the University of California, Santa Barbara, for example, Chinese represent nearly 4.3% of the entire faculty. At the University of California, Irvine, Chinese represent more than 6% of all teaching faculty and 66.8% of all Asian American faculty. The 30,000 figure is based on the assumption that Chinese are 50% of all Asian American faculties in higher education.

16. This is based on data I directly obtained from the National Academy of Engineering in 2007.

17. Alison Schneider, "Proportion of Minority Professors Inches Up to About 10%." The article is based on a 1995-1996 survey that generated 34,000 faculty respondents.

18. Emily Forrest Cataldi, Mansour Fahimi, and Ellen M. Bradburn, "2004 National Study of Postsecondary Faculty (NSOPF:04) Report on Faculty and Instructional Staff in Fall 2003," *Education Statistics Quarterly*, Vol 7, Issues 1 & 2.

19. http://www.nsf.gov/statistics/seind06/c3/c3h.htm.

20. National Science Foundation, "Employed U.S. scientists and engineers, by highest degree attained, occupation, race/ethnicity, and employment sector: 1999."

21. http://www.nsf.gov/sbe/srs/databrf/db.htm.

22. Iris Chang's *Thread of the Silkworm* (New York, 1996) captures the drama in Qian's life.

23. "First Asians in Ithaca," http://ithacaaaa.org/node/8.

24. Helen Zia and Susan B. Gall, eds., *Notable Asian Americans* (New York, c1995), p. 201.

25. Institute of International Education, New York, NY: "Foreign (Nonimmigrant) Student Enrollment in College: 1976 to 2005." Institute of International Education, New York, NY: "Open Doors 2007 Report on International Educational Exchange."

26. Restricted data set. Correspondence with Nirmala Kannankutty, NSF, summer 2007.

i. *Maxine Hong Kingston*, Wikipedia.

ii. *Maxine Hong Kingston*, Contributing Editor, Amy Ling

iii. *Biography of Albert H. Yee*, Internet

iv. *Making History: Our Grand Historians Phillip P. Choy and Him Mark Lai*, Chinese Historical Society of America, Bulletin, September/October, 2005

v. *Frank H. Wu, J.D.*, Who's Who of Asian Americans (asianamerican.net)

Reflections

Making it in America

By James Wei

- Asian American Engineer of the year 2007.

- Emeritus Dean of Engineering and Applied Science, Princeton University.

When I first came to the US in 1949, my goal was to get a good engineering education and return to China to work, according to the tradition of that time. I received a bachelor degree in chemical engineering at Georgia Tech in three years, followed by a masters and a doctors degrees at MIT in three more years. There was little pressure on me to learn how to make it in America. I found lots of time to build theatrical sets for the student theater and did my minor in Fine Arts at Harvard. But my plan to return in 1955 ran into a roadblock when the State Department informed me I could not leave the U.S. since the Korean War was on, and my knowledge of engineering could be of use to the enemy. It never occurred to me that this rule could be challenged, so I got an entry research job at the Mobil Oil Company, and waited for the rules to change. In the mean time, my research in reaction kinetics and catalysis was going very well, and I was winning awards and recognition. But I still had very low expectations of what I could achieve in the US, as I have heard the expression often "this guy does not have a Chinaman's chance", so I was content to do a good job in the lab and get a good pay check.

It was unexpected that I attracted mentors who changed my life, as they promoted my research as valuable and useful, and they also thought I should be groomed for higher positions. They made me rehearse my oral communications, and made critical changes in my method of delivery; they made heavy corrections on my writing and made me polish my papers. They said "how come you do not yell and scream at people when they did something wrong, so how else can they know what you want them to do?" So after a dozen years in research, they said that they are sending me to Harvard Business School to learn about management. I protested that I already have a doctorate in engineering from MIT, and am happily doing research, and what is the use of a business degree for a research engineer? They said that they are preparing me for management, and I needed to learn how to relate to important people. So I went off dutifully to school again, and it appeared that I am further away from my goal of returning to China to work for my career.

However, it turned out that my mentors were too optimistic about the rate of change to equal opportunity for Asians in management, and some top management still have doubts. I remembered the old Chinese hierarchy of Si-Nong-Gong-Shang, (Scholar-Farmer-Worker-Merchant) - where a scholar outranks a farmer, and a farmer outranks a worker, etc. So I resigned from Mobil Oil after 15 years and became a professor at the University of Delaware. My sponsor at Mobil was Rawleigh Warner who later became CEO of Mobil Oil, and he regarded my departure as an investment that did not pay off. But oil people are used to the idea that you need to drill ten holes, and find only one hole that would produce oil and the other nine would be dry holes.

Life is full of strange twists and unexpected turns, so after 6 years of being a professor, I received a call to return to MIT as Head of the Department of Chemical Engineering. To make a move like this, you know that MIT must be in distress and ready for drastic actions. I went to see my doctor for the last checkup in Delaware, and told him that I am leaving to be Department Head at MIT He said "that is impossible, as MIT will never come to Delaware to look for a department head in engineering". It turned out that a powerful trustee Ralph Landau asked the MIT Administration why is the Chemical Engineering Department ranked 9th in the country, instead of the rightful Number One position, and it is time to go outside to find fresh leadership. So I made another career change from teaching and research to managing a complex mix of people, programs, ideas and assets. I changed many of the hallowed Departmental rules to avoid inbreeding, as the problem was excessive inbreeding and not enough looking outward for ideas and talents. Henceforth, a bachelor graduate would not be permitted to remain as a doctorate candidate, and a doctorate graduate would not be retained as assistant professor. We scoured the world for new talent, and new money to support their needs of innovations in teaching and research. Happily with the help of many well-placed alumni in industry, the strategy worked and MIT Chemical Engineering became recognized as Number One again.

After 15 years, President Harold Shapiro of Princeton University called to offer me the Deanship of Engineering and Applied Sciences. Of course mentors and friends were pulling the strings again, and one of them turn out to be Rawleigh Warner who is a Princeton trustee, and called me to say that his investment in me would pay off if I go to Princeton, and he would be willing to make more investments. Princeton University is a very different place than MIT, and a dean has to manage at an even greater scale and complexity than a department head. I became an expert in raising money for programs, faculty, buildings, and students, and I exceeded one hundred million dollars. When I put together a Deans Council, I had from the aerospace industry alone such heavy lifting alumni as Norman Augustine of Lockheed Martin, Phil Condit of Boeing, and John McDonnell from you know where. I discovered that at MIT, fund raising consists of putting together a new research program and visiting corporations and foundations to say that we have the best program in the world, and you can tap our research results, faculty and student resources by putting up so many million dollars. But at Princeton, fund raising consists of visiting an old alumnus and saying you had a great time at Princeton 20-30 years ago, and we want you to make a benefit for the eager and bright young students. Both approaches work, and you use the method that suits the place you are.

So when Asian students and graduates come to ask how to make it in America, what does a dean tell them? I tell them that there are really two main keys to success: what do you know and who do you know. You go to MIT because you want to become very smart, learn about quantum mechanics, solve partial differential equations, and manipulate material and energy with great skill. Being a well-rounded person is not high on the agenda; you go to Princeton because you have another agenda in mind, how to meet and network with many important people, who would be your friends and mentors and would help you in the future. The culture of MIT frowns on too many extra-curricular activities as distractions on the main agenda, but

Princeton encourages sports, clubs, debates, theater, social services, etc. A semester at MIT is 15 weeks of lecture, but a semester at Princeton is 12 weeks. So when I moved from MIT to Princeton, I had the option of talking 20% faster or to cut out 20% of the course material. Do the deans at Stanford or Caltech prefer MIT to Princeton graduates? They are on my Advisory Council, and they told me that they are equally adorable in similar but slightly different ways. The middle management from industry tend to be more comfortable with MIT engineers, who are more likely to hit the ground running, but the upper management tend to prefer Princeton engineers as they are regarded as having more management potential. They are paid the same starting salary, despite the difference in the length of the semester.

America welcomes foreigners to entry level jobs willingly, and no other nation on earth is more welcoming. However there are many organizations where the top positions have never been given to an Asian. We Asian Americans often have to do much more to achieve the same level of rank and salary. America has improved tremendously in the last few decades, but it is not a pure meritocracy where the only thing that counts is what you know, as it is still important who you know. There are so many success stories among Asian Americans. The chancellorships of the University of California at Berkeley and at Santa Barbara have been occupied by Chinese.

The dean of the Yale Law School is a Korean. The CEO of Rohm and Haas is an Indian. There may still be a "Bamboo Ceiling" for Asians in many places, but it is porous and often yields for exceptions. Where is a place that is as open as America to foreigners? The professors of Princeton Engineering School is more than 50% foreign born. If we look at the professors in Tokyo, Munich, Paris, and Cambridge, how many foreigners would you find?

Asian-American engineers tend to be nerds and make more effort to learn things than to be well-rounded and network with people—more like MIT than Princeton. John Reed used to be CEO at Citicorp, and he told me that there are two types of jobs in a bank, which he calls the "back office" and the "front office". He said that he himself is an MIT graduate, who tends to work in the back office writing software, and solving investment problems. Other people live in the front office, and tend to talk to customers, play golf with stock analysts, and attend parties with stockholders and other businessmen. At an entry level job, the work tends to be more about technical knowledge; but if you have any ambition to move into management, life should not be all spent in libraries, laboratories and computers. You will get out of the back office, and circulate with people from the front office. Besides counting the number of publications and patents that you wrote, you should also count and treasure the number of interesting people that you know and can call on for advice and help. Actually, being well-rounded is a good Confucian virtue where a scholar is valued for his skill in Shu-Qi-Qing-Hua or books, chess, music and painting.

An Asian engineer in America should act as if there is no barrier to advancement—to knowing things and knowing people—when he or she learns to walk on both legs.

Quotes:

When Asian students and graduates come to ask how to make it in America, what does a dean tell them? I tell them that there are really two main keys to success: what do you know and who do you know

We Asian Americans often have to do much more to achieve the same level of rank and salary. America has improved tremendously in the last few decades, but it is not a pure meritocracy where the only thing that counts is what you know, as it is still important who you know.

Appendix B
Historical Material

Compiled by Edgar Wong

Knowledge of American history and Chinese culture is helpful in understanding the individuals profiled in this book. While searching the Internet for information on profilees is relatively simple, finding the general socioeconomic environment of an individual—or a group—can be more challenging. As a starting search roadmap, below is an historical timeline of events of significance to all the Chinese in America of then and today.

The scope and content of the Appendix is self-explanatory. The descriptive text is followed by a referenced website for supplemental reading. For readers with access to a computer, why not pop the enclosed CD into the tray and enjoy the surfing? You might be surprised to discover your own family history listed in the National Archives Records Administration website (see Part 2).

Cultural Topics Part 1. "Documented Aliens"
Part 2. General Reading

Historical Periods
Part 3. Open Immigration (Pre-1924) – ten decades
Part 4. Closed Immigration (1924-1965) – five decades
Part 5. Preferential Quota System (1965-Present) – five decades

Historical Documents
Part 6. Text of the Chinese Exclusion Act (1882)
Part 7. Text of California Constitution, Article XIX (1879)

A note on the CD version of this book: the referenced websites (underlined text) are hyperlinks to sites of interest. The websites were recompiled in 2010 for this second book of the PoP series, however, some sites might be unavailable today. If so, please use your search engine to find comparable websites for the topic of interest.

Part 1. "Documented" Aliens
(False papers – forerunners of the "gray" Green Cards)

Paper Children (False citizenship claims after the lost-documents in the 1906 earthquake fires)
http://www.english.uiuc.edu/maps/poets/a_f/angel/natale.htm

Part 2. General Reading
(Cultural topics – relevant to the Chinese experience)

Bound Feet (In China, the "ideal" length, called the "Golden Lotus," was three inches long)
http://www.anomalies-unlimited.com/OddPics/Bound.html

Flying Tiger (Famed American Volunteer Group and on their fighter planes with the Tiger Shark Mouth) http://www.flightpath.us/index.htm (permanent exhibition includes Flying Tigers memorabilia and history).

Immigrant Records Search (Helpful hints on immigrant "Case File" search by UC Berkeley) http://casefiles.berkeley.edu/

National Archives Records Administration (NARA's Pacific Region – immigration records repository) http://www.archives.gov/facilities/ca/san_francisco.html http://www.archives.gov/pacific/laguna/ (Laguna Niguel—retired records) http://www.archives.gov/pacific/riverside/ (Riverside—temporary storage)

Shee: The Name (Married women may use their maiden names and add "Shee")

Women in Aviation (Two Chinese-American women served as pilots in World War II)

Yin Yang (Characterized by some as the foundation of Chinese philosophy) http://www.friesian.com/yinyang.htm

Part 3. Open Immigration (Pre-1924)

1839-1844
Trading conflicts between China and Britain started the Unequal Treaties. These conflicts became known as the first Opium War (1839-1842). The conflicts stopped in 1842 with the Treaty of Nanking, which stated that China would pay the British an indemnity, gave British control over Hong Kong, and to establish a fair tariff. Then in 1844, China signed the Treaty of Wanghia with the United States and the Treaty of Whampoa with France. Both of these treaties expanded the extraterritorial rights and allowed these nations to maintain a separate legal, judicial, police, and tax system in the treaty ports. http://www.historycentral.com/Ant/wanghia.html

1845-2006
The University of Michigan and China: 1845-2006

1848
Gold discovered in Sutter's sawmill in Coloma (50 miles northeast of Sacramento), California. Chinese begin to arrive. The Chinese who found their gold and wanted to return home knew they were popular targets of thieves. They solved the problem by melting the gold and forming it into ugly cooking utensils. When they got home, they melted the utensils and had their gold.

1850
California imposes Foreign Miner's Tax and enforces it mainly against Chinese miners, who often had to pay more than once. This tax required a payment of three dollars each month at a time when Chinese miners were making approximately six dollars a month. Chinese American population in U.S. was about 4,000 out of a population of 23.2 million. [See the year 2000 census

for today's population data]
http://www.museumca.org/goldrush/curriculum/gamsaan/foreigntax2.html

1854

People v. Hall rules that Chinese cannot give testimony in court. The California Supreme Court decided that a state law prohibiting "Blacks, Mulattos, or Indians" from testifying for or against a white criminal defendant should be interpreted to include Chinese. In the court's view, an opposite conclusion would produce an "anomalous spectacle." After all, the court reasoned, Chinese were "a race of people whom nature has marked as inferior, and who are incapable of progress or intellectual development beyond a certain point ... between whom and ourselves nature has placed an impassable difference."
http://www.cetel.org/1854_hall.html

1858

California passes a law to bar further immigration of Chinese and "Mongolians."
http://www.chiamonline.com/Laws/state.html

1862

California passes a "police tax" of $2.50 a month on every Chinese. An act to protect free white labor against competition with Chinese coolie labor and to discourage the immigration of the Chinese into the State of California.
http://www.cetel.org/1862_tax.html
http://academic.udayton.edu/race/02rights/statute1862.htm (An Act to protect free, white labor against competition with Chinese Coolie labor and to discourage the immigration of the Chinese into the State of California)

1863-1865

Chinese men served and many died in the armies and navies during Civil War (Union and the Confederate army), along with German, Irish, French and African American soldiers. Ironically enough, they even served under the "Color Troops" division of the armies.

1864-1869

Central Pacific Railroad Company recruits Chinese workers from Kwantung (now Guangdong) Province for the first transcontinental railroad. 10,000 workers were hired, of which 9,000 were Chinese—1,000 workers died on the job. Leland Stanford, president of the Central Pacific Railroad, reported that not less than 15,000 Chinese laborers could be procured the next year—enabling the push on the work so as not only to complete it far within the time required by the Acts of Congress, but so as to meet the public impatience.
http://cprr.org/
http://www.nps.gov/gosp/
http://cprr.org/Museum/Chinese.html
http://us_asians.tripod.com/timeline-1600.html

1868

China and U.S. sign Burlingame-Seward Treaty: United States and China agreed to trade, travel, and residence rights for each

other's citizens; still prohibited naturalization.
http://academic.udayton.edu/race/02rights/treaty1868.htm

1870
California passes a law against the kidnapping and importation of Mongolian, Chinese and Japanese females, for criminal or demoralizing purposes.
http://www.sanfranciscochinatown.com/history/1870antiprostitutionact.html

1872
California's Civil Procedure Code drops 1854 law barring Chinese court testimony.
http://us_asians.tripod.com/timeline-1600.html

1875
U.S. Congress passed first law—The Page Law—excluding certain categories of aliens (e.g., convicts and prostitutes); declared all earlier state laws regarding immigration unconstitutional.
http://www.cetel.org/1875_page.html

1878
In re Ah Yup: rules Chinese not eligible for naturalized citizenship. A federal judge in California ruled that naturalization laws that were limited to aliens of African descent and "free white persons" should not be interpreted to include persons of the "Mongolian race." So, Ah Yup, the first Chinese immigrant who applied to be a citizen, should be denied. In so ruling, the judge relied heavily on the hysteria raised by one U.S. Senator who warned against changing the citizenship laws to include Chinese: "This amendment involves the whole Chinese problem ... the country has just awakened to the question and to the enormous magnitude of the question, involving a possible immigration of many millions, involving another civilization; involving labor problems that no intellect can solve without study and time. Are you now prepared to settle the Chinese problem, thus in advance inviting that immigration?
http://www.chiamonline.com/Chronology/1850.htm

1879
Californians led the way in anti-Chinese nativism. Numerous state and local laws were passed to limit Chinese economic activity. Denis Kearney organized his Workingmen's party to make anti-Chinese sentiment a partisan political issue. The Workingmen succeeded in including numerous anti-Chinese articles into a revision of the California State Constitution in 1878. California's second constitution prevents municipalities and corporations from employing Chinese. California state legislature passes law requiring all incorporated towns and cities to remove Chinese outside of city limits, but U.S. circuit court declares the law unconstitutional. Repealed in 1952. [See text of the California Constitution of 1879 in Part 7 below.]
http://www.chiamonline.com/Laws/state.html

1880
China and U.S. sign treaty giving the U.S. the right to limit but "not absolutely prohibit" Chinese immigration. Section 69 of California's Civil Code prohibits issuing of licenses for marriages between whites and "Mongolians, Negroes, mulattoes and

persons of mixed blood."
http://www.kqed.org/w/baywindow/othercolors/changingtimes/ (1880 marriage law)

1882

Chinese Exclusion Law suspends immigration of laborers for ten years; subsequently renewed; prohibited naturalization. The Chinese Exclusion Act was subsequently repealed in 1943. [See complete text of the Chinese Exclusion Act of 1882 at the end of this Appendix A—after the year 2000 entry.]
http://www.cetel.org/1882_exclusion.html.

1882

The original Chinese Consolidated Benevolent Association in San Francisco was already operating as a separate entity with some degree of mutual coordination before the first Chinese Consolidated Benevolent Association (CCBA) was formally established in 1882. New York's CCBA was founded a year later in 1883. These CCBAs were founded to serve and protect the interests of the Chinese people in early America. Historically CCBA has performed a quasi-government role in the Chinese community, so that the President of the CCBA is sometimes referred to as the "Mayor of Chinatown." (See 1889 for the beginning of the CCBALA in Los Angeles).
http://en.wikipedia.org/wiki/Chinese_Consolidated_Benevolent_Association#cite_note-2 http://ccbanyc.org/

1884

The 1882 Chinese Exclusion Law amended to require a certificate as the only permissible evidence for reentry; wives barred; anti-miscegenation laws.
http://academic.udayton.edu/race/02rights/immigr05.htm

1886

Chinese laundrymen win case in Yick Wo v. Hopkins, which declares that a law with unequal impact on different groups is discriminatory.
http://www.cetel.org/1886_yickwo.html

1888

Scott Act renders 20,000 Chinese reentry certificates null and void; prohibited immigration of virtually all Chinese, including those who had gone back to China to visit.
http://immigrants.harpweek.com/ChineseAmericans/2KeyIssues/ScottAct.htm

1889

Chinese exclusion case Chae Chan Ping v. United States: Supreme Court ruled that an entire race that the government deemed difficult to assimilate might be barred from entry regardless of prior treaty; upholds constitutionality of Chinese exclusion laws. The court upheld a law that cancelled the validity of return certificates for Chinese laborers who had left the United States for visits to China, and also upheld the racist Chinese Exclusion Act. In the process, the language of the court reveals the acceptance of stereotypical views of Chinese at the time. Chinese were "industrious and frugal." Without families, "their expenses were small; and they were content with the simplest fare, such as would not suffice for our laborers and artisans." Chinese "remained

strangers in the land, residing apart by themselves, and adhering to the customs and usages of their own country. It seemed impossible for them to assimilate with our people, or to make any change in their habits or modes of living. As they grew in numbers, each year the people of the coast saw, or believed they saw, in the facility of immigration, and in the crowded millions of China, where population presses upon the means of subsistence, great danger that at no distant day that portion of our country would be overrun by them unless prompt action was taken to restrict their immigration."
http://www.augustana.edu/Users/Podehnel/cases/CHINEXCL.htm.

1889
The Good Health Civic Unit association began in 1889 and became the Chinese Consolidated Benevolent Association, Los Angeles (CCBALA) in 1910. (See 1882 for the beginning of the CCBA in the U.S.).
http://www.ccba.la/
http://www.ccbala.org/

1892
The Geary Act required Chinese living in the United States to carry a certificate of residence, without which they were subject to deportation or imprisonment and a year of hard labor. It denied bail to Chinese and prohibited them from appearing as witnesses in court.
http://www.geary.com/The_Geary_Act_of_1892

1893
Fong Yue Ting v. United States: Supreme Court declared Congress had the right to legislate expulsion through executive orders; Chinese community had raised money to bring this before the Court to test the Geary Act. Congress amended the Geary Act to make it more difficult for Chinese businessmen to enter this country.
http://caselaw.lp.findlaw.com/scripts/getcase.pl?navby=case&court=us&vol=149&invol=698

1894
Gresham–Yang Treaty: China accepted total prohibition of immigration to the United States in return for readmission of those back in China on a visit; did away with Scott Act of 1888.
http://query.nytimes.com/gst/abstract.html?res=9503E2DF1630E033A25750C2A9659C94659ED7CF

1898
United States v. Wong Kim Ark: Supreme Court rules person born in the United States of Chinese parents is of American nationality by birth—that Chinese born in the U.S. can't be stripped of their citizenship.
http://www.cetel.org/1898_wongkim.html

1900
United States v. Mrs. Cue Lim: Supreme Court ruled wives and children of treaty merchants were entitled to come to the United States. Bubonic plague scare in San Francisco—Chinatown cordoned and quarantined.
http://academic.udayton.edu/race/03justice/aspilaws.htm

1902

Chinese Exclusion Act extended for another ten years. An act to prohibit the coming into and to regulate the residence within the United States, its Territories, and all territory under its jurisdiction, and the District of Columbia, of Chinese and persons of Chinese descent.

http://www.sanfranciscochinatown.com/history/1902exclusionactextension.html

1902

Interracial marriage laws of 1902 in Oregon prohibits marriage between a Caucasian and a Chinese.

1904

Chinese exclusion made indefinite. All Chinese excluded from the United States, Washington, D.C., and all U.S. territories.

http://www.cetel.org/1904_extension.html

1905

Section 60 of California's Civil Code amended to forbid marriage between whites and "Mongolians."

http://www.asianweek.com/2001_02_23/feature_timeline.html

1906

The 1906 San Francisco Earthquake devastated Chinatown, and many of the survivors fled to other parts of the San Francisco Bay Area, but about 500 out of 5,000 remained. A handful of city planners and local politicians considered the earthquake both an opportunity and a great blessing to be rid of the Chinese in a prime real estate area, and move them to Hunters Point.

http://www.pandanet.co.jp/English/art/sfchinatown/sfchinatown.html

1908 & 1911

Upon the suppression of the Boxer Rebellion (1899-1901), the foreign forces consisting of eight countries demanded an indemnity of $333 million from the Chinese government over a period of forty years. President Theodore Roosevelt pushed the U.S. government to return the Boxer Indemnity to China for the establishment of a scholarship program that would allow Chinese students to come to the United States for education. In 1908, the U.S. Senate passed a resolution remitting to China much of the U.S. share of the Boxer indemnity, to establish the China Foundation for the Promotion of Education and Culture. On April 29, 1911, Tsinghua Xuetang, predecessor of the now prestigious Tsinghua University in Beijing, was founded with part of the returned indemnity. It was the first preparatory school for those students sent by the Chinese government to study in U.S.

http://en.wikipedia.org/wiki/Tsinghua_University
http://www.ugcs.caltech.edu/~tjou/words/Tsinghua.pdf

1910

Angel Island opens as an official immigration station.
http://www.cetel.org/angel_poetry.html

1911

On October 10, the Manchu rule was overthrown in China. Sun Yat-sen was declared president of the new Republic of China in 1911. His leadership of the Nationalist Party, or Kuomintang, lasted only 2 years. In 1913, he stepped down and retreated from the political spotlight under pressure from the military leader Yuan Shi-kai. Yuan's death in 1916 plunged China into the warlord era, which was to last until 1927. Sun Yat-sen returned to politics during this time to form a southern Kuomintang government, which exercised nominal control over parts of the south in the 1920s.
http://www.thecorner.org/hist/china/chin-revo.htm
http://www-chaos.umd.edu/history/republican.html

1913

California passes alien land law prohibiting "aliens ineligible to citizenship" from buying land or leasing it for longer than three years.
http://query.nytimes.com/gst/abstract.html?res=9E01E4DD1138E633A2575AC0A96E9C946496D6CF

1918

Servicemen of Asian ancestry who had served in World War I receive right of naturalization. Prior to and during WWI, the US Navy allowed Filipino enlistees to serve under a range of military occupational rating such as petty officer, band master, musician, coxswains' mates, seamen, machinist, fireman, water tender, commissary stewards, officer's stewards, and mess attendants. After World War I, the United States Navy issued new rulings restricting Filipinos, even those with college education, to the rating of officer stewards and mess attendants. These military occupational discrimination practices were stopped in the 1970s when there was a senatorial investigation of the use of stewards in the military due to pressure from the civil rights movement. During World War I (1917-1918) 2,666,867 men were drafted, about 1,300,000 actually were deployed in Europe. All males between the ages of 21 and 30 were required to register for military service. Asian Indians form the Hindustani Welfare Reform Association in the Imperial and Coachella valleys in southern California.
http://us_asians.tripod.com/timeline-1910.html#servicemen-naturalized

1920

Initiative in California ballot plugs up loopholes in the 1913 alien land law. Repealed in 1956.
http://www.pbs.org/race/000_About/002_03_d-godeeper.htm

1921

National Origin System—Immigration Act (Johnson Act): used the country of birth to determine whether an individual could enter as legal alien, the number of previous immigrants and their descendants used to set the quota of how many from a country could enter annually—basis of immigration system until 1965. Washington and Louisiana pass alien land laws.
http://www.maltamigration.com/history/exodus/chapter4-3.shtml

1922

Cable Act declares that any American female citizen who marries "an alien ineligible to citizenship" would lose her citizenship.
http://college.hmco.com/history/readerscomp/gahff/html/ff_029900_cableact.htm

1923

Chinese student immigration ended because of strict requirements for having the funds necessary to return to China.
http://academic.udayton.edu/race/02rights/immigr05.htm

Part 4. Closed Immigration (1924-1965)

1924

Immigration Act (Johnson–Reed Act) restricted all Asians from coming into the United States.
http://www.state.gov/r/pa/ho/time/id/87718.htm

1925

Chang Chan et al. v. John D. Nagle: Supreme Court ruled Chinese wives of American citizens not entitled to enter the United States.
http://academic.udayton.edu/race/02rights/immigr05.htm

1927

Weedin v. Chin Bow: Supreme Court ruled persons born to American parents(s) who never resided in the United States are not of American nationality, thus not eligible for entry.
http://caselaw.lp.findlaw.com/scripts/getcase.pl?navby=case&court=us&vol=274&invol=657

1928

Lam Mow v. Nagle: Supreme Court ruled that a child born of Chinese parents on American vessels on high seas was not born in the United States, therefore not a citizen.
http://www.chiamonline.org/Chronology/1920.htm

1931

Amendment to Cable Act declares that no American-born woman who loses her citizenship by marrying an alien ineligible to citizenship can be denied the right of naturalization at a later date.
http://www.state.gov/documents/organization/104346.pdf

1938

150 Chinese women garment workers strike for three months against the National Dollar Stores (owned by a Chinese).
http://womhist.alexanderstreet.com/sfchina/abstract.htm
http://www.library.sfsu.edu/about/depts/larc/pdfs/newsletter-21-v1.pdf

1942

Executive Order 9066, signed by President Roosevelt on February 19, 1942, was the instrument that allowed military commanders to designate areas "from which any or all persons may be excluded." Under this order all Japanese and Americans of Japanese ancestry were removed from Western coastal regions to guarded camps in the interior.
http://www.cetel.org/1942_9066.html

1943

The Chinese Exclusion Repeal Act of 1943 repealed the Chinese Exclusion Act of 1882; token 105 Chinese immigrants allowed to enter the United States annually, selected by U.S. government. War Brides Act: Admission to the United States for spouses and children of U.S. armed forces members included 722 Chinese.
http://www.cetel.org/1943_repeal.html

1944

GI BILL Act of June 22, 1944: The Servicemen's Readjustment Act of 1944 put higher education within the reach of millions of veterans of World War II and later military conflicts.
http://fcis.oise.utoronto.ca/~daniel_schugurensky/assignment1/1944gibill.html

1946

The number of Chinese women in Los Angeles begins to increase largely because of the passage of the 1945 War Brides Act, the 1946 Fiancées Act, and the enactment of Public Law 713 in 1946, as well as by immigration from other U.S. Chinatowns.
http://www.museumoffamilyhistory.com/erc-ntz-wnl.htm

1947

Amendment to 1945 War Brides Act allows Chinese American veterans to bring brides into the U.S.
http://www.cetel.org/timeline.html

1948

The Displaced Persons Act allowed for admission of many refugees displaced by the war and unable to come to the United States under regular immigration procedures. This act gave permanent resident status to 3,465 Chinese students, visitors and seaman who didn't want to go back to China.
http://www.sanfranciscochinatown.com/history/1948displacedpersonsact.htm

1949

U.S. breaks off diplomatic ties with newly formed People's Republic of China—5,000 highly educated Chinese in the U.S. granted refugee status after China establishes a Communist government.
http://www.personal.psu.edu/ach13/Asia/Diaspora/DiasporaTime.htm

1950

Second Displaced Persons Act further helped Chinese in the United States to change their status (due to communist takeover in China).
http://academic.udayton.edu/race/02rights/immigr05.htm

1952

Immigration and Nationality Act (McCarran–Walter Act) removed total ban of Chinese immigrants but upheld national origins quotas. It somewhat liberalized immigration from Asia, but increased the power of the government to deport aliens suspected of Communist sympathies.

http://modelminority.com/modules.php?name=News&file=article&sid=73

1952

Repeals Article XIX of California Constitution, as adopted in 1879, which directs Legislature to prescribe laws imposing conditions on residence of certain aliens and to provide for their removal from the State; which prohibits Chinese employment by corporations and on public works; which directs passage of laws providing for removal of Chinese from cities or their restriction to certain portions of cities, and adoption of laws to prohibit Chinese from entering State.
http://en.wikisource.org/wiki/Page:California_State_Constitution_of_1879.djvu/19

1953

Refugee Relief Act: 2,800 places allotted to Chinese out of total 205,000 people to be admitted; law expired in 1956. Included for the first time, refugees of Chinese origin, as long as the Nationalist Chinese government vouched for them.
http://www.ed.uiuc.edu/courses/eps300/Asianimmigration.html
http://tucnak.fsv.cuni.cz/~calda/Documents/1950s/Refugee_53.html

1956

Repeals inoperative law of 1920 that formerly denied aliens ineligible to citizenship the right to hold real estate in California.
http://www.pbs.org/race/000_About/002_03_d-godeeper.htm

Part 5. Preferential Quota System (1965-Present)

1962-1965

Attorney General allowed 15,000 Chinese to enter as parolees due to refugee situation in Hong Kong.
http://academic.udayton.edu/race/02rights/immigr05.htm

1965

President Lyndon Johnson signed a bill that has dramatically changed the method by which immigrants are admitted to America. This bill is the Immigration Act of 1965. This act, also known as the Hart-Cellar Act [1], not only allows more individuals from third world countries to enter the US (including Asians, who have traditionally been hindered from entering America), but also entails a separate quota for refugees. [2] Under the Act, 170,000 immigrants from the Eastern Hemisphere are granted residency, with no more than 20,000 per country. One hundred twenty thousand immigrants from the Western Hemisphere, with no "national limitations," are also to be admitted. [3] The significance of this bill was that future immigrants were to be welcomed because of their skills/professions, and not for their countries of origin.
http://www.thenagain.info/webchron/usa/ImmigrationAct.html

1972

President Richard M. Nixon traveled to China. Nixon: "…we simply cannot afford to leave China forever outside the family of nations …"
http://www.pbs.org/wgbh/amex/china/peopleevents/pande01.html

1975

Operation Frequent Wind—US government evacuated U.S. and Vietnamese people from Saigon. More than 130,000 refugees enter the U.S. from Vietnam, Kampuchea, and Laos as Communist governments are established there.
http://ships.bouwman.com/Navy/SubicBay/FREQUENT-WIND.html

1975

The Chinese Historical Society of Southern California (CHSSC) is founded. The Society is the publisher of this book and the Portraits of Pride (PoP) series. See below websites for ongoing CHSSC monthly activities and the Library of Congress online catalog listing of the PoP book.
http://www.chssc.org
http://openlibrary.org/b/OL3296175M/Portraits_of_pride

1976

President Gerald Ford rescinds Executive Order 9066—the Internment of 110,000 Japanese Americans in 1942.
http://www.ford.utexas.edu/LIBRARY/SPEECHES/760111p.htm

1979

Resumption of diplomatic relations between the People's Republic of China and the United States of America reunites members of long-separated Chinese American families.
http://usinfo.org/docs/basic/prc_e.htm

1981

Taiwan and Mainland China each allowed 20,000 immigrants.
http://academic.udayton.edu/race/02rights/immigr05.htm

1982

Vincent Chin, a Chinese-American draftsman, is clubbed to death with a baseball bat by two Euro-American men. The jobless automobile workers reportedly mistook him for a Japanese and blame him for their plight. In 1984 Ronald Ebens was convicted on one count of civil rights violations and sentenced to 25 years in prison; Stepson Michael Nitz was acquitted. Ebens was instructed to undergo treatment for alcoholism but was freed after posting a $20,000 bond. Neither he nor his stepson ever spent a day in jail. And, soon afterwards, the conviction was overturned due to a legal technicality, and a retrial was ordered. In 1987 a jury in Cincinnati cleared Ebens, stating the attack was not racially motivated. Later that year a civil suit against Ebens was settled by a court-approved agreement whereby Ebens agreed to pay, over time, $1.5 million to Chin's estate. But the laid-off 47-year-old does not have a steady job, and the chance that he will ever pay the maximum amount seems extremely unlikely.
http://www.asian-nation.org/racism.shtml
http://asianweek.com/061397/feature.html
http://www.youtube.com/watch?v=m7cyZ9gUpcY
http://us_asians.tripod.com/articles-vincentchin.html

1986

Immigration Reform and Control Act imposes civil and criminal penalties on employers who knowingly hire undocumented aliens.

https://www.oig.lsc.gov/legis/irca86.htm

http://www.lectlaw.com/files/emp34.htm

1990

Immigration Act increased number of immigrants admitted because of skill level; Immigration Act continued priority for skilled workers and family reunification.

http://www.numbersusa.com/text?ID=210

http://findarticles.com/p/articles/mi_m1154/is_n9_v79/ai_11205316/

1996

Illegal Immigration and Responsibility Act of 1996, Pub. L. No. 104-208, 110 Stat. 3009; People who have been in the United States longer than six months after their visas expired can be deported. They will also be barred from returning to the United States for three years. And those who have been in the United States illegally for more than a year will have to wait 10 years before they will be allowed to return legally.

http://www.americanlaw.com/1996law.html

http://www.visalaw.com/96nov/3nov96.html

http://www.takatalaw.com/us/iract96.html

2000

According to the U.S. 2000 Census (see page 212) , there were 2,432,585 Chinese Americans under One Race Category in the United States. They constituted 0.9% of total population. That is, in every 100 Americans, there is a Chinese American. If Chinese under two or more races are included, there are 2,879,636 Chinese Americans.

http://www.census.gov/prod/2002pubs/c2kbr01-16.pdf

http://www.census.gov/prod/cen2000/dp1/2kh00.pdf

Part 6. Text of the Chinese Exclusion Act (1882)

Preamble.

Whereas, in the opinion of the Government of the United States the coming of Chinese laborers to this country endangers the good order of certain localities within the territory thereof: Therefore,

Be it enacted by the Senate and House of Representatives of the United States of America in Congress assembled, That from and after the expiration of ninety days next after the passage of this act, and until the expiration of ten years next after the passage of this act, the coming of Chinese laborers to the United States be, and the same is hereby, suspended; and during such suspension it shall not be lawful for any Chinese laborer to come, or, having so come after the expiration of said ninety days, to remain within the United States.

SEC. 2. That the master of any vessel who shall knowingly bring within the United States on such vessel, and land or permit to be landed, and Chinese laborer, from any foreign port of place, shall be deemed guilty of a misdemeanor, and on conviction thereof shall be punished by a fine of not more than five hundred dollars for each and every such Chinese laborer so brought, and may be also imprisoned for a term not exceeding one year.

SEC. 3. That the two foregoing sections shall not apply to Chinese laborers who were in the United States on the seventeenth day of November, eighteen hundred and eighty, or who shall have come into the same before the expiration of ninety days next after the passage of this act, and who shall produce to such master before going on board such vessel, and shall produce to the collector of the port in the United States at which such vessel shall arrive, the evidence hereinafter in this act required of his being one of the laborers in this section mentioned; nor shall the two foregoing sections apply to the case of any master whose vessel, being bound to a port not within the United States by reason of being in distress or in stress of weather, or touching at any port of the United States on its voyage to any foreign port of place: Provided, That all Chinese laborers brought on such vessel shall depart with the vessel on leaving port.

SEC. 4. That for the purpose of properly identifying Chinese laborers who were in the United States on the seventeenth day of November, eighteen hundred and eighty, or who shall have come into the same before the expiration of ninety days next after the passage of this act, and in order to furnish them with the proper evidence of their right to go from and come to the United States of their free will and accord, as provided by the treaty between the United States and China dated November seventeenth, eighteen hundred and eighty, the collector of customs of the district from which any such Chinese laborer shall depart from the United States shall, in person or by deputy, go on board each vessel having on board any such Chinese laborer and cleared or about to sail from his district for a foreign port, and on such vessel make a list of all such Chinese laborers, which shall be entered in registry-books to be kept for that purpose, in which shall be stated the name, age, occupation, last place of residence, physical marks or peculiarities, and all facts necessary for the identification of each of such Chinese laborers, which books shall be safely kept in the custom-house; and every such Chinese laborer so departing from the United States shall be entitled to, and shall receive, free of any charge or cost upon application therefore, from the collector or his deputy, at the time such list is taken, a certificate, signed by the collector or his deputy and attested by his seal of office, in such form as the Secretary of the Treasury shall prescribe, which certificate shall contain a statement of the name, age, occupation, last place of residence, personal description, and fact of identification of the Chinese laborer to whom the certificate is issued, corresponding with the said list and registry in all particulars. In case any Chinese laborer after having received such certificate shall leave such vessel before her departure he shall deliver his certificate to the master of the vessel, and if such Chinese laborer shall fail to return to such vessel before her departure from port the certificate shall be delivered by the master to the collector of customs for cancellation. The certificate herein provided for shall entitle the Chinese laborer to whom the same is issued to return to and re-enter the United States upon producing and delivering the same to the collector of customs of the district at which such Chinese laborer shall seek to re-enter; and upon delivery of such certificate by such Chinese laborer to the collector of customs at the time of re-entry in the United States, said collector shall cause the same to be filed in the custom house and duly canceled.

SEC. 5. That any Chinese laborer mentioned in section four of this act being in the United States, and desiring to depart from the United States by land, shall have the right to demand and receive, free of charge or cost, a certificate of identification similar to that provided for in section four of this act to be issued to such Chinese laborers as may desire to leave the United States by water; and it is hereby made the duty of the collector of customs of the district next adjoining the foreign country to which said

Chinese laborer desires to go to issue such certificate, free of charge or cost, upon application by such Chinese laborer, and to enter the same upon registry-books to be kept by him for the purpose, as provided for in section four of this act.

SEC. 6. That in order to the faithful execution of articles one and two of the treaty in this act before mentioned, every Chinese person other than a laborer who may be entitled by said treaty and this act to come within the United States, and who shall be about to come to the United States, shall be identified as so entitled by the Chinese Government in each case, such identity to be evidenced by a certificate issued under the authority of said government, which certificate shall be in the English language or (if not in the English language) accompanied by a translation into English, stating such right to come, and which certificate shall state the name, title, or official rank, if any, the age, height, and all physical peculiarities, former and present occupation or profession, and place of residence in China of the person to whom the certificate is issued and that such person is entitled conformably to the treaty in this act mentioned to come within the United States. Such certificate shall be prima-facie evidence of the fact set forth therein, and shall be produced to the collector of customs, or his deputy, of the port in the district in the United States at which the person named therein shall arrive.

SEC. 7. That any person who shall knowingly and falsely alter or substitute any name for the name written in such certificate or forge any such certificate, or knowingly utter any forged or fraudulent certificate, or falsely personate any person named in any such certificate, shall be deemed guilty of a misdemeanor; and upon conviction thereof shall be fined in a sum not exceeding one thousand dollars, an imprisoned in a penitentiary for a term of not more than five years.

SEC. 8. That the master of any vessel arriving in the United States from any foreign port or place shall, at the same time he delivers a manifest of the cargo, and if there be no cargo, then at the time of making a report of the entry of vessel pursuant to the law, in addition to the other matter required to be reported, and before landing, or permitting to land, any Chinese passengers, deliver and report to the collector of customs of the district in which such vessels shall have arrived a separate list of all Chinese passengers taken on board his vessel at any foreign port or place, and all such passengers on board the vessel at that time. Such list shall show the names of such passengers (and if accredited officers of the Chinese Government traveling on the business of that government, or their servants, with a note of such facts), and the name and other particulars, as shown by their respective certificates; and such list shall be sworn to by the master in the manner required by law in relation to the manifest of the cargo. Any willful refusal or neglect of any such master to comply with the provisions of this section shall incur the same penalties and forfeiture as are provided for a refusal or neglect to report and deliver a manifest of cargo.

SEC. 9. That before any Chinese passengers are landed from any such vessel, the collector, or his deputy, shall proceed to examine such passengers, comparing the certificates with the list and with the passengers; and no passenger shall be allowed to land in the United States from such vessel in violation of law.

SEC. 10. That every vessel whose master shall knowingly violate any of the provisions of this act shall be deemed forfeited to the United States, and shall be liable to seizure and condemnation on any district of the United States into which such vessel may enter or in which she may be found.

SEC. 11. That any person who shall knowingly bring into or cause to be brought into the United States by land, or who shall knowingly aid or abet the same, or aid or abet the landing in the United States from any vessel of any Chinese person not lawfully entitled to enter the United States, shall be deemed guilty of a misdemeanor, and shall, on conviction thereof, be fined in a sum not exceeding one thousand dollars, and imprisoned for a term not exceeding one year.

SEC. 12. That no Chinese person shall be permitted to enter the United States by land without producing to the proper officer of customs the certificate in this act required of Chinese persons seeking to land from a vessel. And any Chinese person found unlawfully within the United States shall be caused to be removed therefrom to the country from whence he came, by direction of the United States, after being brought before some justice, judge, or commissioner of a court of the United States and found to be one not lawfully entitled to be or remain in the United States.

SEC. 13. That this act shall not apply to diplomatic and other officers of the Chinese Government traveling upon the business of that government, whose credentials shall be taken as equivalent to the certificate in this act mentioned, and shall exempt them and their body and household servants from the provisions of this act as to other Chinese persons.

SEC. 14. That hereafter no State court or court of the United States shall admit Chinese to citizenship; and all laws in conflict with this act are hereby repealed.

SEC. 15. That the words "Chinese laborers", whenever used in this act, shall be construed to mean both skilled and unskilled laborers and Chinese employed in mining.

Approved, May 6, 1882.
http://www.milestonedocuments.com/document_detail.php?id=38&more=fulltext

Part 7. Text of California Constitution, Article XIX (1879)

SECTION 1. The Legislature shall prescribe all necessary regulations for the protection of the State, and the counties, cities, and towns thereof, from the burdens and evils arising from the presence of aliens who are or may become vagrants, paupers, mendicants, criminals, or invalids afflicted with contagious or infectious diseases, and from aliens otherwise dangerous or detrimental to the well-being or peace of the State, and to impose conditions upon which persons may reside in the State, and to provide the means and mode of their removals from the State, upon failure ore refusal to comply with such conditions; provided, that nothing contained in this section shall be construed to impair or limit the power of the legislature to pass such police laws or other regulations as it may deem necessary.

SEC. 2. No corporation now existing or hereafter formed under the laws of this State, shall, after the adoption of this Constitution, employ directly or indirectly, in any capacity, any Chinese or Mongolian. The Legislature shall pass such laws as may be necessary to enforce this provision.

SEC. 3. No Chinese shall be employed on any State, county, municipal, or other public work, except in punishment for crime.

SEC. 4. The presence of foreigners ineligible to become citizens of the United States is declared to be dangerous to the well-being of the State, and the Legislature shall discourage their immigration by all the means within its power. Asiatic coolieism is a form of human slavery, and is forever prohibited in this State, and all contracts for coolie labor shall be void. All companies or corporations, whether formed in this country or any foreign country, for the importation of such labor, shall be subject to such penalties as the Legislature may prescribe. The Legislature shall delegate all necessary power to the incorporated cities and towns of this State for the removal of Chinese without the limits of such cities and towns, or for their location within prescribed portions of those limits, and it shall also provide the necessary legislation to prohibit the introduction into this State of Chinese after the adoption of this Constitution. This section shall be enforced by appropriate legislation.

INDEX